BUILDING AND PAINTING

Model Trucks

R H
TRANSPORT
R.H
RAY HAIGH
TEL.
0151499 8204
RAY HAIGH
№ 566
RAY HAIGH
95 380 ATi
DAF
R566 JGV

BUILDING AND PAINTING
Model Trucks

George Dent

THE CROWOOD PRESS

First published in 2021 by
The Crowood Press Ltd
Ramsbury, Marlborough
Wiltshire SN8 2HR

enquiries@crowood.com

www.crowood.com

British Library Cataloguing-in-Publication Data
A catalogue record for this book is available from the British Library.

ISBN 978 1 78500 918 1

Typeset by Simon and Sons

Cover design by Blue Sunflower Creative

Printed and bound in India by Parksons Graphics

CONTENTS

ACKNOWLEDGEMENTS

I would like to express my thanks to all the model and craft retailers who remained open during the Covid-19 lockdowns of 2020; their sterling efforts ensured that we could indulge our hobbies at a time of great stress and uncertainty. Particular thanks go to John at Scale Model Shop for speedily fulfilling my regular orders and maintaining stocks during a difficult period, ultimately allowing me to finish this book.

Alex Medwell, Lisa Munro and the staff at The Airbrush Company have also been a great help during this project. So too has John Bristow at Deluxe Materials and Peter Harvey at PH Designs.

Chris Gilson's encouragement via WhatsApp has been greatly appreciated; and I am indebted to the team at Crowood for their patience and support. Special thanks go to J-M and the Dent Collective.

This book is dedicated to Pep, who gave me the idea in the first place. Keep on truckin' babe!

Plastic truck kits offer an enjoyable challenge, especially in the larger scales. This 1:24-scale Mercedes-Benz Unimog snowplough/gritter has received a number of detail enhancements and makes for a very striking model.

CHAPTER ONE

AN INTRODUCTION TO PLASTIC KITS

I've been building plastic kits for as long as I can remember. Like many youngsters of my generation, if I wasn't outside kicking a ball around, I would be at the kitchen table sticking an Airfix kit together, wreathed in the odour of Humbrol polystyrene cement and enamel paint. I wouldn't really care what the kit portrayed, I was just obsessed by building and painting the parts as neatly as possible. Mostly they were 1:76- or 1:72-scale kits, bought at pocket-money prices from the local sweet shop. With birthday or Christmas money I might persuade my folks to take me to the Liverpool branch of Beatties to indulge in something a little more exotic, such as a 1:32-scale racing-car kit. But I would dream of the larger-scale truck kits on the upper shelves, stacked out of my reach and my budget, and for the time being, beyond my abilities.

Finally I got my hands on a 1:24-scale truck kit in my early twenties, and I remember being taken aback by the sheer volume of individual parts, as well as the time needed to put it all together. Looking back, those early efforts were a little rough and ready, but I was already heading towards pursuing model making as a profession, and had become determined to hone my skills across a wide range of genres. Trains eventually took over my life, after joining *Model Rail* magazine as the in-house model maker in 2004. Since then I've worked my way up to become editor, and over the years I've built countless railway locomotives and rolling stock, along with a wide variety of scenic items and dioramas, in a variety of scales – and what a great time I've had in the process!

However, everybody needs a distraction from the day job, and after a brief hiatus, I rediscovered my love of model cars and trucks a few years ago, especially those larger-scale kits that felt so elusive when I was a child. Building trucks has certainly taught me a great deal about assembly and finishing techniques, while customization and superdetailing still offer an exciting challenge. As some of the projects featured here attest, I relish getting my teeth into an upgrade job, especially when a degree of improvisation is involved. A facility for problem solving is essential for kit builders, as even the best kits can throw up something unexpected.

Trucks have also taught me the value of patience, a trait that modellers usually think they possess in abundance – but in reality, it's something most of us have to really work at. Who can resist the urge to get a model built sooner rather than later? And yet, with some of the more comprehensive kits, weeks might pass before the model starts to resemble anything like a truck.

I do not profess to any level of expertise regarding real trucks, aside from a general knowledge of models and makes, and a basic level of mechanical awareness. I do, however, have a love for them in a visual and visceral sense, as they have fascinated and terrified me in equal measure since I was a child. Just like my passion for diesel locomotives, the sight and sound of large, noisy machines inevitably grabs my imagination.

We didn't have a car when I was a child, so I didn't spend much time on the roads. Accordingly, heavy trucks became quite an exotic sight, and I do remember

Model truck kits are available in various scales, including 1:72, 1:48, 1:35, 1:32 and 1:24.

The difference between 1:72 and 1:24 scales is apparent. Both of these kits represent a Mercedes-Benz 2238.

an old DAF tractor unit that was regularly parked up on waste ground, which I would pass on my way to school. The risqué images in one of the side windows became a hot topic of the playground, but I was also drawn to the shabby nature of the paintwork, the rust patches and the oily stains on the chassis. It is memories such as these that have always fuelled my modelling passion: a mix of nostalgia and wonderment.

While I find the technical minutiae of heavy vehicle engineering interesting, the pure enjoyment of the building and finishing processes are a bigger motivation for me. Predominantly my trucks are built for myself, offering a vehicle for my creative expression (no pun intended!). That said, I always try to make them look as realistic as possible, and when suitable prototype information can be found, I will seek to replicate as much of the real thing as possible. But I'm rarely a slave to detail for detail's sake. After all, these models have been built as a way of escaping a demanding job, where detail is everything.

These two trucks may be made in the same scale, yet the Kenworth Aerodyne dwarfs the diminutive Mitsubishi Canter.

The purpose of this book, therefore, is not to educate the reader about engines and brake systems, but to showcase the possibilities afforded by the large range of truck models currently on the market. New models appear every year, from brands as renowned as Airfix, Revell, Tamiya, Heller, Fujimi and Italeri, along with ICM, Emhar, Hobby Boss, IBG and Mini Art. Kit subjects can be diverse, and the popular scales of 1:72, 1:35, 1:32 and 1:24 dominate, although there are also opportunities to be found in 1:48. Outside 1:24 and 1:32 scales, the majority of kits deal with trucks that have a military pedigree, but as we'll see, it is possible to 'de-mob' trucks into civilian life without too much fuss.

The following chapters have been arranged in ascending scale order, starting with 1:76/1:72 and working up to 1:24, which is by far the most popular scale for civilian truck modelling. The foibles and attractions of each scale will be discussed, while the projects have been chosen to help illustrate a wide variety of techniques and approaches. Assembly and finishing processes are covered throughout the book, but some of the basic tenets are outlined here to provide a solid foundation from which to work, especially if you are new to the hobby.

Military, or ex-military, trucks form the majority of kit subjects in the smaller scales.

The larger scale means that much more detail can be included, but the finished models invariably take up a lot of space, especially when pairing up a tractor unit and trailer.

ESSENTIAL TOOLS AND MATERIALS

Only a modest array of general modelling tools is needed to get started. Cutting tools such as knives and shears are essential, along with shaping implements such as files and sanding sticks, in order to extract the parts from the moulded sprue and prepare them for bonding. Handling tools, such as tweezers, pliers, clamps and a miniature vice, allow small parts to be retained and located safely and accurately, while a drill and bits, ruler and set-square are also vital aids for assembly. Other tools can be added to one's arsenal over time, such as a profile cutter, metal cutting shears, hold-and-fold units or punch-and-die sets, all of which are a great help when adding extra detailing components.

Sundries, including masking tapes, cotton swabs and paintbrushes, should also be on hand, while maintaining a supply of 'stock' material will allow for parts to be enhanced or replaced. Plastic, in sheet, strip and rod format, from the likes of Evergreen, Plastruct, Slaters or Maquett, can be invaluable. Brass and nickel-silver tube, strip, sheet and wire also have their uses, while real stripwood and veneer can also be harnessed to improve the realism of kit components.

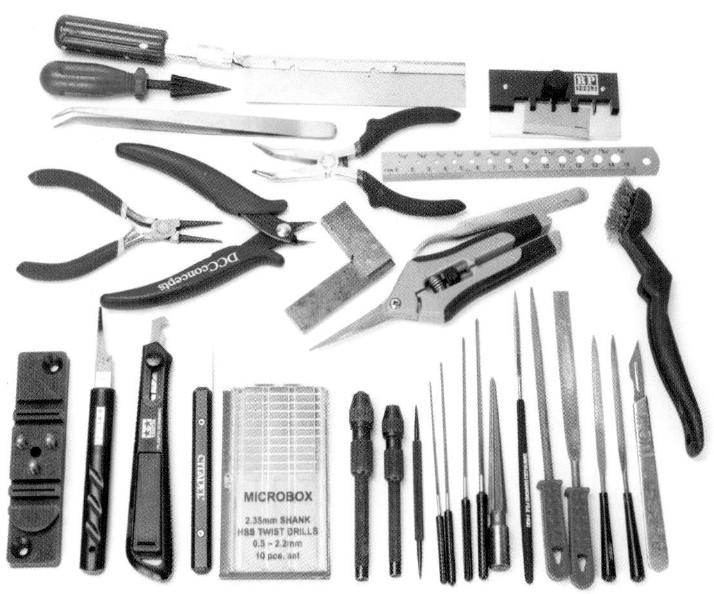

An essential truck modeller's toolkit: sprue cutters, knives, files and reamers help to prepare the parts, while a razor saw, profile cutter, pin vice and drill bits allow parts to be modified. Tweezers and pliers make small parts easier to handle, and folding tools and round-nose pliers are handy for shaping metal detailing parts and materials. A steel rule and set-square help to get the parts aligned correctly.

Abrasive sticks, sheets and pads, in a range of grits, are also essential. Components will need to be fettled and prepared for bonding and painting, especially if a good quality paint job is desired.

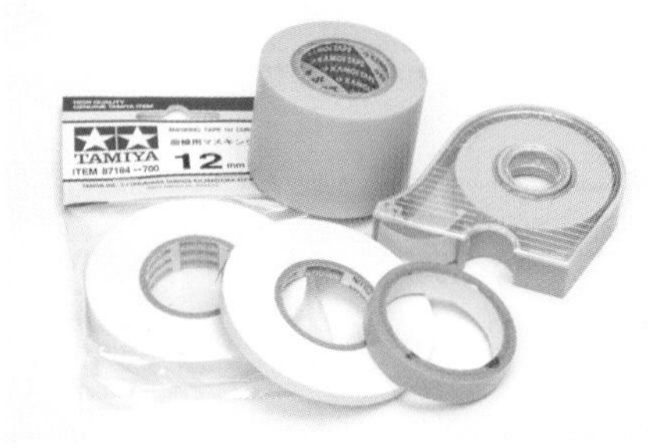

Masking tape comes in many forms. Flexible vinyl tapes are important for working on undulating surfaces, while cloth-backed tape is fine for more general use, especially clamping parts together while gluing.

Having a modest supply of stock materials to hand is highly recommended. With a variety of metal and styrene sheet, strip, angle and rod, along with brass, copper and nickel wire, we can take care of many detailing tasks.

Cotton swabs are vital to the weathering process, and cocktail sticks have many uses, particularly for applying small amounts of glue with precision. Micro-brushes are great for detail painting and weathering tasks.

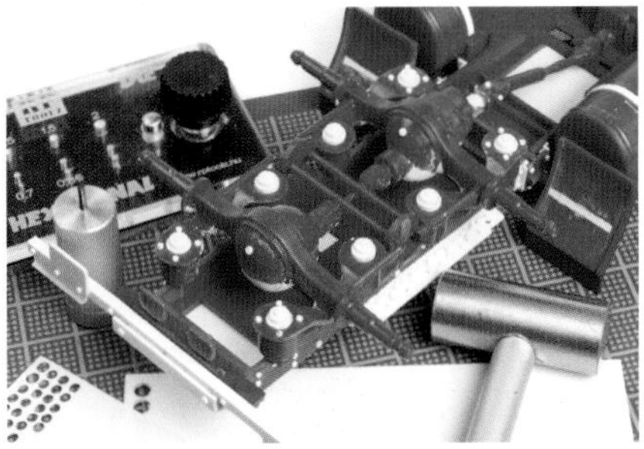

Punch-and-die sets are a loyal friend to those wanting to upgrade or modify kits, allowing individual hex bolt and disc washers to be created from styrene sheet.

Try not to throw away any offcuts of plastic, metal or wood, as they can be useful in the future. I keep a box full of scrap material, and it regularly provides me with the perfect raw materials for other projects.

Detailing components, designed to address shortcomings in specific kits or for more general use, are also available. Kit Form Services (KFS) offers an impressive array of 'kits and bits' for 1:24-scale trucks, including complete conversion kits to allow a broader range of prototypes to be reproduced, using existing kits as a base. Czech Truck Model (CTM) is another reliable source of 1:24-scale upgrade kits and components, including pre-painted logos, dashboard facia and realistic head- and tail-light lenses. Italeri also offers a handful of truck accessory kits to complement its range of 1:24 trucks, providing plenty of scope for customization, while Tamiya can provide packs of flexible cable that is perfect for replicating electrical cable or flexible hydraulic and air pipes.

Modellers have access to a range of detail upgrade kits and components, many of which are tailored to specific kits. Kit Form Services (KFS) and Czech Truck Model (CTM) are two of the best sources for a whole host of metal and resin parts.

There is also the option of creating your own detailing parts, and I recently commissioned this set of etched details from PH Designs for an ongoing conversion project.

My order from PH Designs included etched nickel-silver parts to create an impressive radiator cooling fan.

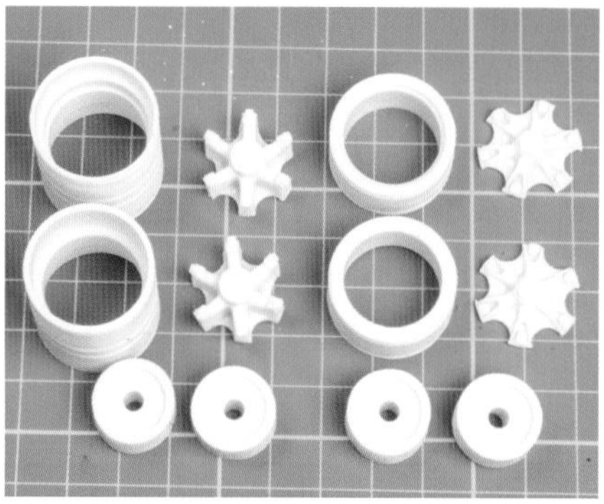

The wheels are a common area where 1:24-scale kits underperform, but resin replacements are available from KFS. Hubs and rims may need to be assembled from various layers.

Assembled and ready for painting, the KFS wheel range offers some welcome variety and a significant uplift in realism, compared to the kit's original wheel rim (right).

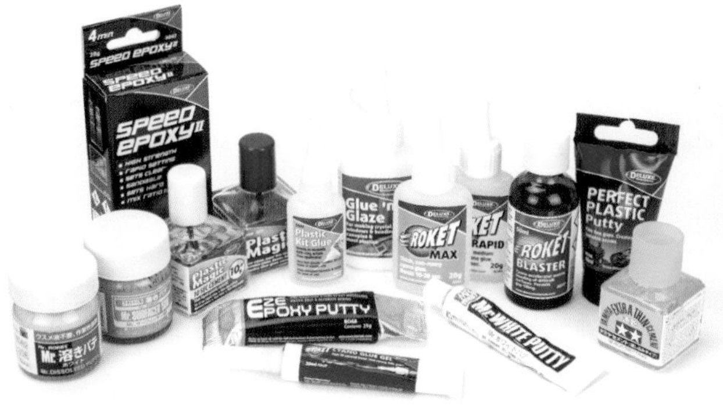

Glues are a modeller's best friend. Liquid poly-cement, cyano, epoxy and glazing adhesives are crucial. So, too, is a selection of model fillers, from regular putty to 'liquid fillers', such as Mr Surfacer and Mr Dissolved Putty, from the Mr Hobby range.

Different paint formulas lend themselves to specific tasks and application methods. Lifecolor and Darkstar acrylics are great for hand-brushing, while Tamiya, Mr Hobby and Alclad II lacquers perform best through an airbrush.

Good quality paintbrushes are a worthy investment. Flat and round, hard and soft, large and small – you'll need them all!

BASIC KIT ASSEMBLY

Each chapter offers plenty of assembly tips, but it's good to start with the basics. Mainstream plastic kits consist mostly of injection-moulded components, rendered in polystyrene (commonly known as styrene), a flexible material that is capable of taking very fine detail. Much depends on the quality of the moulds and the skill of the toolmaker, though as the moulds age, the level of finesse can diminish. Clear glazing parts are also moulded from polystyrene, but the lack of a colouring agent means that the material can be brittle and prone to scratching. Accordingly, clear parts need to be handled with care.

Kit makers often recommend that all parts be washed before assembly, in order to remove traces of mould-release chemicals that can interfere with glue and paint adhesion. As I usually abrade parts with files or sanding sticks before making any glue bonds, to remove imperfections and tidy up joint faces, there's little point in washing the parts beforehand. That said, completed sub-assemblies are always thoroughly cleaned before priming and painting, to remove any debris and other contaminants.

Parts can be cut from the sprue as and when needed, either with a stout knife or, preferably, a set of special sprue-cutting shears. This reduces the risk of damaging the parts – or yourself – with a knife. Cuts are made a few millimetres from the edges of the components, then the waste is removed with a file and the surface tidied with abrasives. Shears are not always suitable, however, especially when dealing with very small, delicate parts or where the jaws of the tool will struggle to reach within the tight confines of the sprue. In such instances, a miniature razor-saw blade can be used to cut through the material gradually.

It is rare for parts to be assembled straight from the sprue without some degree of intervention, as raised seams (from where the two halves of the mould meet) and ejector pin marks (caused by pins that force the parts from the moulds) inevitably require flattening and the surrounding surfaces tidying up. Needle files of various profiles, and multiple grades of sanding stick come to our aid here, and the amount of time spent on getting the parts perfect will be reflected in the appearance of the model at the end of a project. Imperfections, if not attended to, only serve to remind the viewer that the model was built from a mass-produced plastic kit, rather than portraying a convincing miniature replica.

The flip side of such a diligent approach to preparation is the ease with which excessive material can be unwittingly removed from plastic parts, leading to alignment issues during assembly – so take things steadily and test-fit the parts to their neighbours at regular intervals.

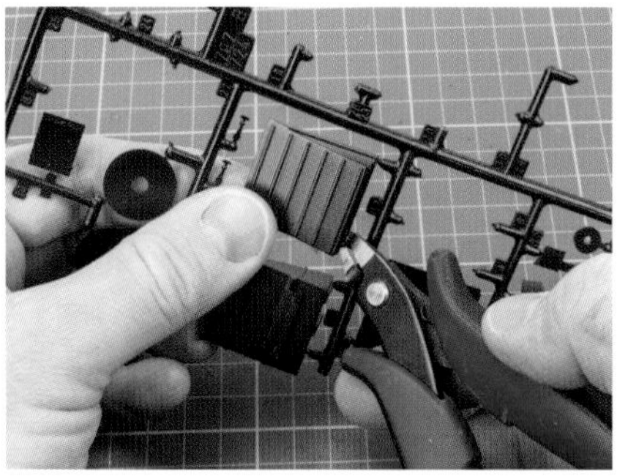

A set of sprue-cutting shears speeds up the process of trimming parts from the sprue, while also minimizing the risk of damaging the components and your fingers.

Fettling each and every part to remove imperfections and improve their fit is not always essential, but it will drastically improve the appearance of the finished model.

Glue is a vital modelling tool in its own right, and choosing the right adhesive to suit specific materials and situations is important. Liquid poly-cements are generally the core adhesive for the majority of plastic kit assembly. This thin liquid acts by chemically fusing the two parts together, but it relies on the parts meeting snugly in order to effect a reliable bond. The parts should be held in contact before applying the cement directly into the joint with a fine brush. If the parts can't be held together before the glue is applied, a slower-drying poly-cement is required, which can be applied to one of the joint faces before the parts are brought together. The thicker formulas of cement can be a little difficult to use neatly, but they do have their uses from time to time.

Poly-cement's major drawback is the fact that it needs to work on bare, unpainted plastic surfaces. Paint will have to be scraped away to effect a joint, and the solvent may cause any surrounding paintwork to blister if applied excessively. Furthermore, poly-cement is not recommended for use on clear styrene components, as the solvent will eat into the plastic and cause it to cloud over. Instead, non-solvent glues such as PVA or a dedicated glazing adhesive such as Glue 'n' Glaze are better suited, as they produce a flexible, resilient bond, and dry crystal clear. Such glues can also be employed on painted plastic parts or other detail fittings that may be sensitive to the use of strong solvents, or where a degree of flexibility is required: this will be illustrated in the following chapters.

The styrene parts need to marry up snugly in order that the liquid poly-cement can work effectively.

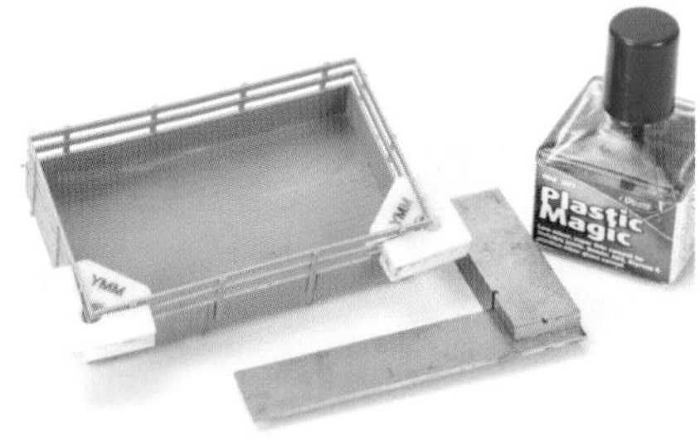

A set-square will help to check the angle of corner joints. These miniature magnetic clamps, from York Modelmaking, can be used to orient the parts accurately before the cement is applied.

Sprung clothes-pegs make perfect clamps for holding parts together whilst gluing. Allow the parts to cure fully overnight.

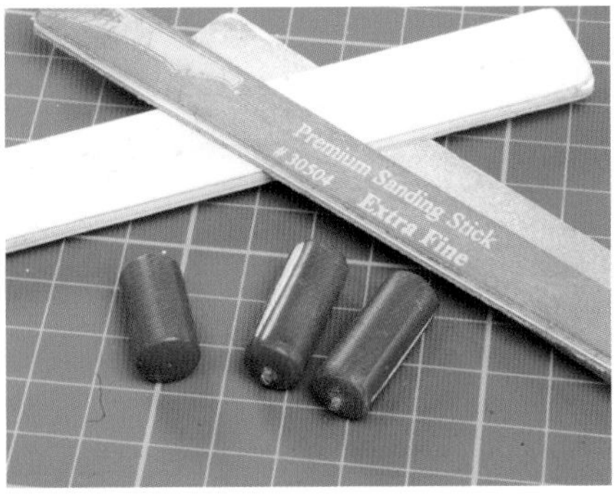

Any seams between parts can be rendered invisible by abrading the surfaces, then adding filler where needed to create a seamless joint.

As each part and sub-assembly is laboriously prepared, they can be stored safely until required.

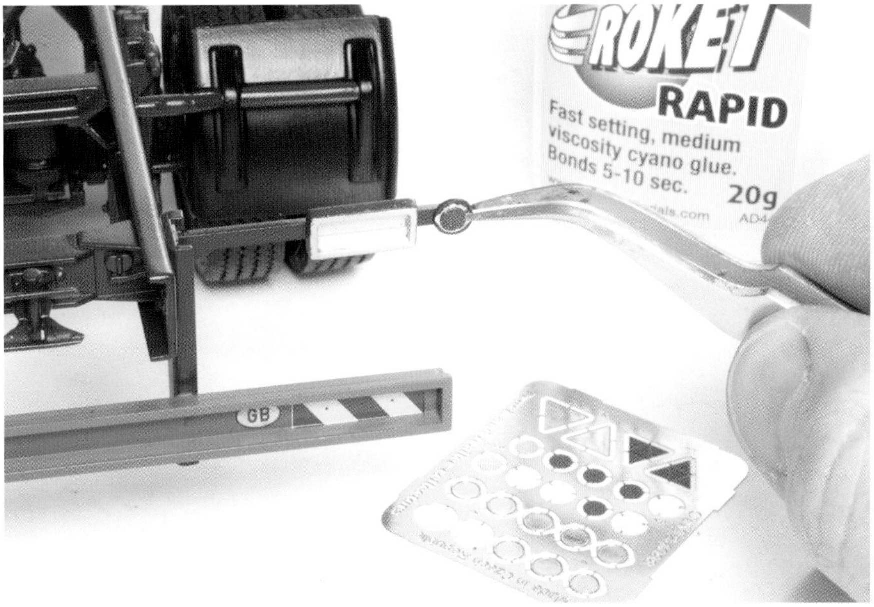

Cyano glue is ideal for bonding smaller detail parts and painted sub-assemblies to the main chassis or bodyshell. Different formulas exist, so different glues are suitable for general use or for more specific tasks.

Not every element of a model truck is rendered in styrene, and when fixing plastic to other materials, a different type of glue is required. Whereas liquid poly-cements create bonds chemically before evaporating away, epoxy and cyanoacrylate glues produce mechanical joints, where the parts are physically held together by the hardened glue. Two-part epoxy glues come in various formats, with fast (5min) and slow (30min) working times, and they all require mixing before use. They often smell like blocked drains and can be a little messy, but the bonds are strong and flexible.

Cyanoacrylate, sometimes referred to as superglue, also comes in a range of drying times of between 1 to 30sec. Different viscosities are also available, with the thicker versions being ideal for bonding parts that may not fit perfectly, with the glue acting as a filling medium as well as an adhesive. Bonds can be very strong, but some cyano formulas can damage clear glazing if used in close proximity. Only a small amount of adhesive is required to make a good joint, and accordingly it is an ideal glue for fixing small detail fittings of any material, as well as installing painted sub-assemblies together.

Where gaps between parts arise, or where other remedial work is required, we need to employ model filler and putty. Again, there are plenty of suitable products from the major model kit manufacturers. Solvent-based versions offer superior adhesion to bare plastic surfaces, although deeper holes will have to be treated over several sittings, with each layer allowed to dry in-between. Acrylic-based putties, as offered by Vallejo and Deluxe Materials, have little or no smell and can be cleaned up with water, but otherwise they behave in similar ways to solvent-based putties. However, neither are very good at filling holes larger than a few millimetres wide. Epoxy putties are much better suited to filling larger apertures and are rock hard when fully cured, although they do require mixing before use.

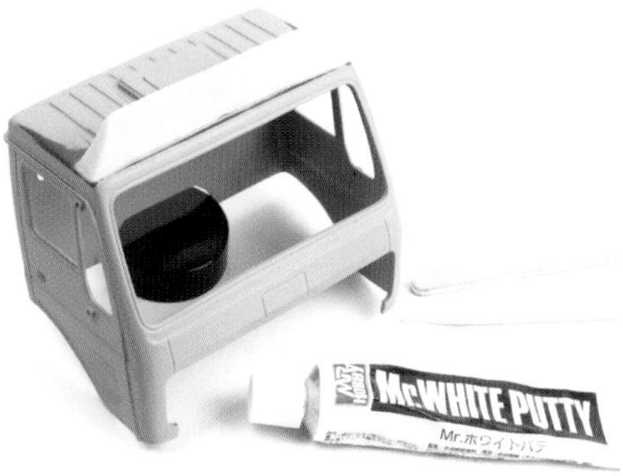

Fixing metal or resin detail parts demands the use of epoxy or cyano adhesives. Be prepared to fill any gaps between the new and original parts with putty, which can be tidied and smoothed with abrasives once it has cured fully.

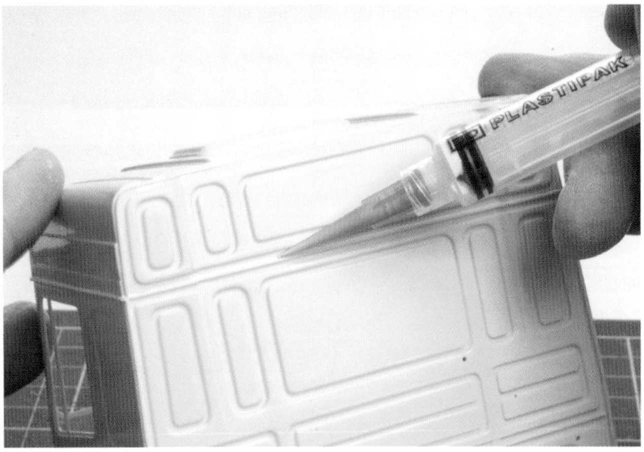

Take your time to get the bodywork correctly prepared before and during the finishing stages. Decanting Deluxe Materials' Perfect Plastic Putty through a syringe allows it to reach into hairline gaps without clogging up the relief. A damp swab will clean away the excess and smooth the surface, with little need for abrasives.

The first primer coat usually reveals surface imperfections hitherto invisible, so wet sanding with fine-grade abrasive sheets and a thorough clean will prepare the model for the next layers of primer.

Aerosol-based paints and primers offer convenience with the potential for a high-quality finish.

Spraying paint must be done responsibly. Always wear a facemask and work in a well-ventilated space. An extraction booth helps.

We'll discuss a variety of painting and weathering techniques in detail during each of the book's chapters, and I have presented a range of approaches that suited the needs of each particular truck. There is no shortage of good quality painting and weathering products these days – indeed, we've never had it so good in terms of kits and ancillary items to keep us all busy and out of mischief.

Now that we've covered the basic principles of plastic kit assembly, it's time to get started on the practical work...

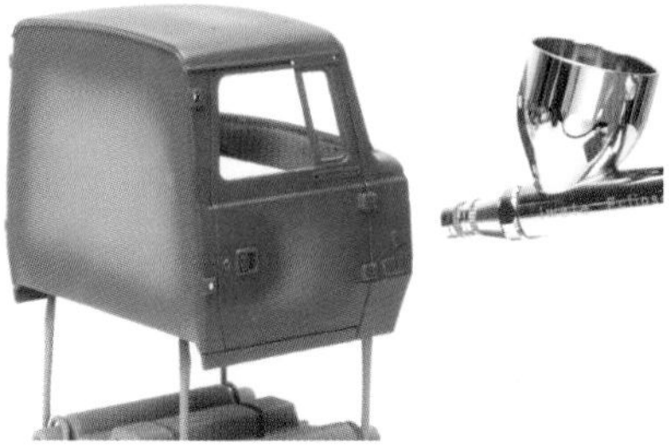

An airbrush offers greater precision and control over the paint flow, allowing the colour to be built up gradually.

Improvisation is a key modeller's attribute. These Victorian-era railway decals were chopped up to create a fictional haulier's logos.

Weathering washes are a highly versatile medium. Enamel-based washes can be particularly effective.

Enamel washes can be brushed liberally over the surface, before wiping most of the pigment away with tissue or cotton swabs, preferably in downward strokes to mimic gravity-led staining.

As will be seen throughout this book, there is plenty of work for dry weathering pigments.

CHAPTER TWO

STARTING SMALL: MERCEDES-BENZ 2238 AND VOLVO F12 IN 1:72 SCALE

There is no doubt that truck modelling enthusiasts tend to prefer working in the larger scales, such as 1:24 or 1:35, but there are also those who enjoy the challenge of producing something smaller. Whether it's about the joys of greater miniaturization, or dictated by a limited display space, 1:72- and 1:76-scale kits offer plenty of opportunities. Furthermore, they may allow us to enjoy parallel interests in building dioramas or model railways, where the trucks will form a small part of a scenic whole.

1:72 scale, where 1in = 6ft, has been a popular scale for model aircraft enthusiasts since the 1930s, allowing the fighter and bomber aircraft of the day to be reproduced in miniature to a practical size. Figures, trucks and ground-support vehicles soon followed from leading model and toy brands, allowing modellers to create believable air-base dioramas.

Many landmark kits have appeared in this scale over the years, from the likes of Airfix, Revell, Italeri, Tamiya, Heller and Matchbox. These have proven especially popular with junior modellers, thanks to their pocket-money price tags, modest number of parts and relative ease of construction. Indeed, there are plenty of kits still around today that date back several decades, such is their enduring popularity.

Confusingly, some kits are offered in the slightly smaller 1:76 scale (4mm = 1ft), which is perfect for model railway enthusiasts who work in OO, EM or P4 gauges. At first glance there might not appear to be too much difference between 1:72 and 1:76, but when two similar vehicle types of each scale are placed side by side, there will be a discernible difference.

These days there are plenty of high-quality die-cast cars and trucks to choose from, to suit OO-, O-gauge (1:43.5) and even N-gauge (1:148) model railways and dioramas, thanks to the likes of Oxford Diecast. However, in my youth there was a real dearth of 1:76 civilian road vehicles in either die-cast or kit form, to complement my OO-gauge railway. Matchbox 1:72 die-cast cars from the local toy shop had to suffice, but they seldom looked at home in their surroundings.

Certain military truck kits from Airfix and others were an option, although they needed converting to civilian use, which wasn't always easy. A number of 'cottage industry' resin and white-metal kits could also be found in the 1980s, if you knew where to look, but the main source of HGV subjects was the Kiel Kraft range of plastic kits.

FROM KIEL KRAFT TO KNIGHTWING

Also sold under the Scan Kit moniker, Kiel Kraft offered a wide range of plastic 1:72-scale truck kits during the 1970s and 1980s. Sold at bargain prices and available from toy or convenience stores, kit subjects included post-1960s European designs from Ford, DAF, Mercedes-Benz, Foden and Volvo, plus a couple of US examples such as the iconic Kenworth Aerodyne and Peterbilt 359. Virtually all came in the form of tractor units (with or without trailers), save for a fetching Foden Haulmaster eight-wheel tipper.

Kiel Kraft also produced a few kits of vintage prototypes, ranging from Atkinson or Foden steam wagons to an elegant Edwardian fire engine. Of particular interest to railway modellers was a Thorneycroft 1½ ton parcels delivery truck (originally a Davric kit from the 1970s), a version of which was offered with interwar period Great Western Railway livery decals.

All the Kiel Kraft kits were fairly basic (especially the Thorneycroft), but most of the trucks can make very convincing models if some extra time is invested in adding and refining certain details. Furthermore, they're still available today, thanks to the Knightwing brand.

Despite the age of the original moulds, the current Knightwing versions are crisply moulded and the parts fit together well. The frames are sparse, and most tractor units share the same one-piece chassis with a 6×4 axle configuration. The cab mouldings have a surprising degree of finesse in the most part, and left-/right-hand drive conversion is as simple as it gets: simply fix the steering wheel on your side of choice!

Despite being previously marketed as 1:72-scale kits, Knightwing now brand them as OO-gauge models (1:76), so things can get a little confusing. That said, the assembled vehicles look very much at home on OO-gauge layouts, especially when placed judiciously within a scene. Forcing the perspective is a useful tool for scenic modellers, placing slightly under-scale models in the background and over-scale models nearer the viewer.

Of course, if you are not a railway enthusiast or diorama builder, the issue is irrelevant. More importantly, the kits tend to capture the basic character of the prototypes, and they still offer decent value. There's no end of possible

Kiel Kraft was once a great source of 1:72-scale plastic truck kits, with a small number still available under the Knightwing brand. Dating mostly from the early 1980s, they're a little basic, but fun to build and readily detailed.

Despite their heritage, the parts only need a cursory amount of fettling with needle files to remove excess material and tidy up any moulding seams.

detail improvements that can be visited upon these kits, with existing fittings enhanced or replacements fashioned from stock materials. Suitable figures in HO or OO gauge are freely available, to incorporate a driver or to populate a diorama. Furthermore there is also the option of converting a tractor unit into a rigid flatbed or dropside body, including the fabrication of realistic payloads.

BUILDING A 1:72 MERCEDES-BENZ 2238S

The Mercedes-Benz 'New Generation' SK series of trucks was first introduced in 1974, and remained in production well into the 1980s. I've long been a fan of these trucks, and kit makers have also been drawn to the SK series, with a variety of offerings available in different scales since the 1980s. The Kiel Kraft kit that features here had been in my collection for decades and portrays a heavy-duty, long-range 2238 6×4 model; this kit is still available from Knightwing. Incidentally, a 1:24-scale kit of this prototype is available from Italeri, and features in Chapter 11.

The original kit's illustrated instructions contain a number of errors, the most obvious involving the engine block, which is shown back to front: the sump needs to be placed at the front. Be aware also that the rear spring/axle mounts are handed, so check the orientation of the parts carefully before gluing them in position, temporarily adding the wheels and axles to ensure that the fenders will fit.

The engine block is rudimentary, to say the least, but it's nice to have something there rather than a just a void. However, I did replace the driveshafts with plastic rod, and added extra cross-members to enhance the overall appearance of the chassis. A number of scratch-built fittings were also installed, including replacement mirrors, a chequer-plate flooring panel and a set of coiled susie cables. The original exhaust pipe was also replaced, with a scrap of thick wire rod employed for the front section and fine brass tube for the outlet pipe.

A choice of front bumper is supplied: either a regular pattern fitting, or one with a huge bullbar attached, which looks grossly over-scale. Replacing the bars with brass wire, shaped and slotted into holes drilled into the uprights, would look far superior. However, for my model I wanted to keep it simple, and fitted the plain bumper.

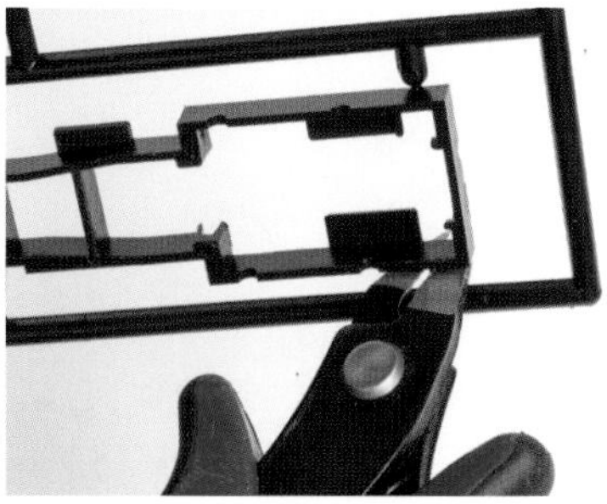

Most kits from Kiel Kraft feature a generic open-framed chassis, moulded as a single unit. Cut small parts from the sprue carefully, preferably with a sharp set of sprue-cutting snips.

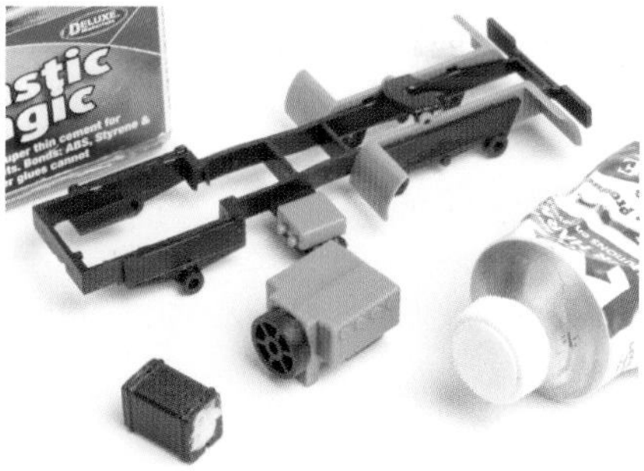

Pay attention when fitting the rear mudguard and suspension assemblies, as they are handed and will only provide sufficient clearance for the wheels if fitted correctly. The rudimentary engine and fuel tanks are made up of several elements, and any gaps need filling and dressing before they are fitted to the frames.

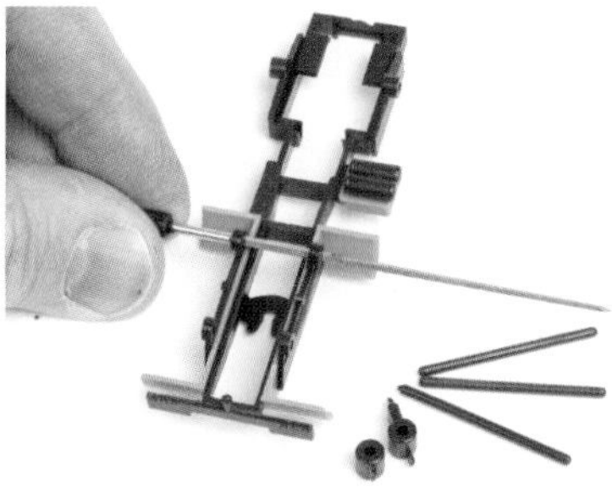

The axle holes need rifling with a reamer to allow the axles to fit snugly, once they, too, have been fettled to remove the pronounced mould seams along their length.

As well as upgrading the exterior, I also added some extra detail to the interior of the cab. The Ten Commandments range of modelling accessories includes packs of printed truck-interior details, including licence plates, road atlases, newspapers, magazines, flags and even high-visibility tabards. Simply cut them out, fold where necessary, and fix in place, to instantly bring life to the cab. Red/yellow warning panels were also provided in these packs, so a set of

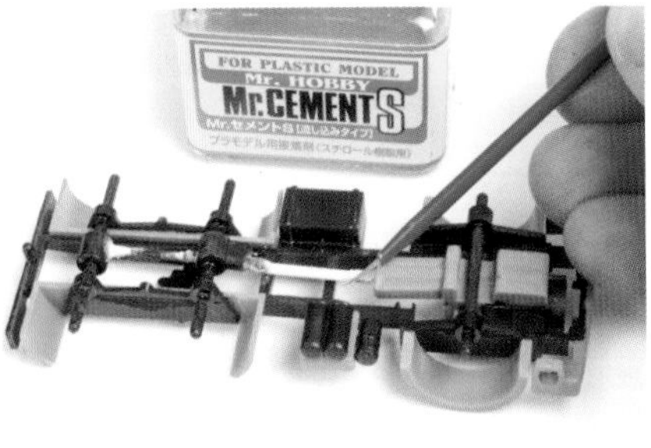

The main driveshaft was replaced with a length of plastic rod.

The wheels and tyres are produced as single units, but their tread faces featured unsightly raised seams, so these were sanded away.

The ends of the steering axle were bent slightly to allow the truck to be posed with the front wheels at a very slight angle, which always improves the look of any model road vehicle.

The wheels were test-fitted to the axles while the model was sat on a small sheet of glass, to check that everything was concentric. The axles were then glued to the frames, although the wheels were removed and painted separately.

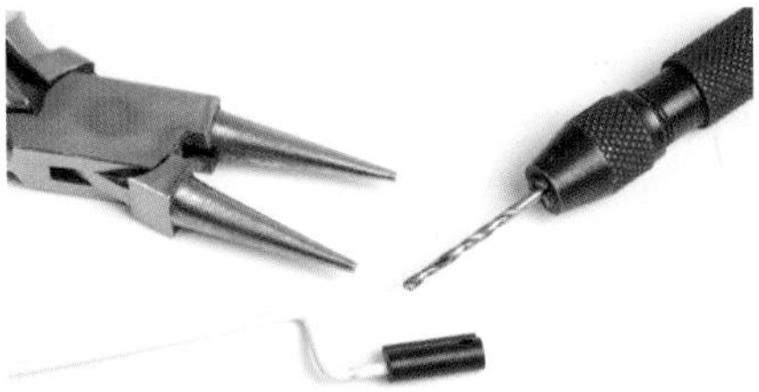

Apart from the silencer, the rest of the kit's exhaust was discarded. The primary section of pipe was created with a scrap of thick metal wire, fixed into a hole drilled into the silencer.

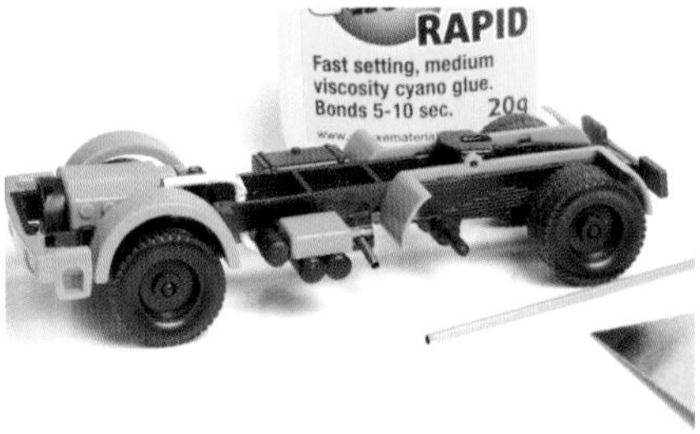

The outlet section of pipe was cut from fine brass tube, using a razor saw to avoid damaging the soft, hollow material.

The cab was test-fitted to ensure that the exhaust system didn't interfere with the mounting brackets. I also crafted some extra cross-members from plastic strip and fixed them between the frames at the rear end.

As well as a mounting plate for the fifth wheel, I also added a tread panel from etched brass (from PH Designs), cut and filed to shape. This helps to disguise the basic nature of the frames.

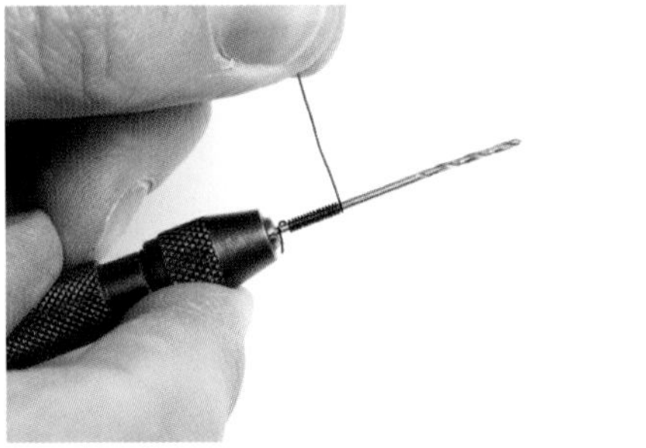

Black-coated 28-gauge copper jewellery wire was wound around a 1.5mm drill bit to create a set of susie cables. Leave a short length of straight wire at each end, and cut the wire with snips.

these was cut out and fixed to the rear fenders. The UK licence plates were too modern for a 2238, so I obtained some waterslide decals from Fox Transfers to create my own numberplates. Fox also supplied the corporate logos, although it must be stated that this isn't a rendition of a real truck: rather, I needed some ready-made logos for a haulage firm based near Liverpool for one of my model railway projects, set in the early 1980s.

The cab requires little in the way of assembly, although the front grille needs to be secured carefully so as not to damage the delicately moulded detail. Tamiya's Extra Thin poly-cement is ideal for jobs like this. Use the precision brush provided to run a small amount of cement into the gap around the edge. The fluid will find its own way into the joint.

A simple bracket was created from more scrap plastic, with holes drilled to accept the cables, which won't be fixed in place until after the truck has been painted.

Another small detail addition to the chassis was a pair of mud-flaps, cut from paper and secured with cyano glue.

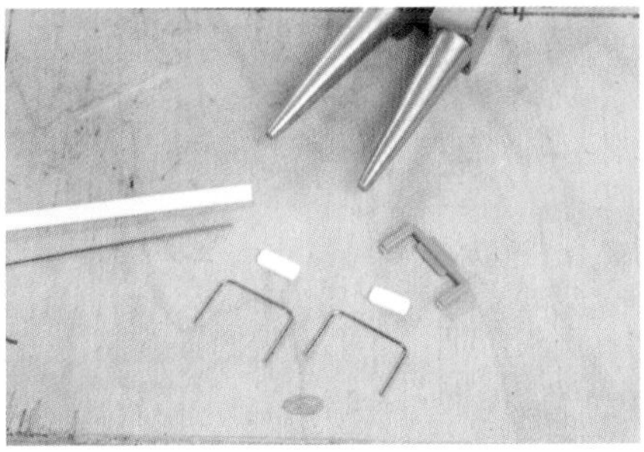

The chunky mirrors were replaced with 0.4mm brass wire, shaped with round-nose pliers to get a nice curve at the corners. The mirrors were cut from plastic strip, and a groove filed into the rear to help them sit on the wire more securely.

Mounting holes were drilled into the cab, and the new mirrors secured with cyano glue. The wire shouldn't protrude into the cab, or it will interfere with the glazing unit.

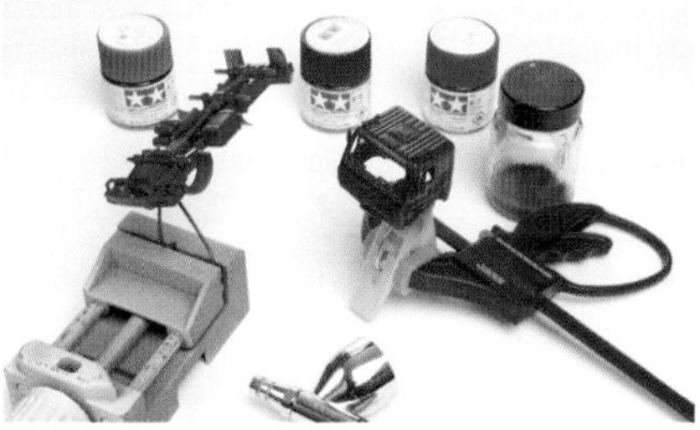

After a coat of grey primer (from an aerosol), the cab and frames were painted separately, using Tamiya acrylics and an airbrush. The cab's colour was created by mixing red and brown, plus a drop of green. After hand-painting the smaller details, the cab and chassis were sprayed with a clear gloss coat.

The clear gloss provides the perfect surface on which to apply waterslide decals; these logos were taken from a Fox Transfers pack for 1:76-scale/ OO-gauge trucks.

The cab interior was adorned with designs, courtesy of a pair of printed detailing packs from the Ten Commandments range.

The Ten Commandments packs also provide warning panels for the rear flaps, while the numberplates had to be created from individual waterslide decals, from Fox Transfers.

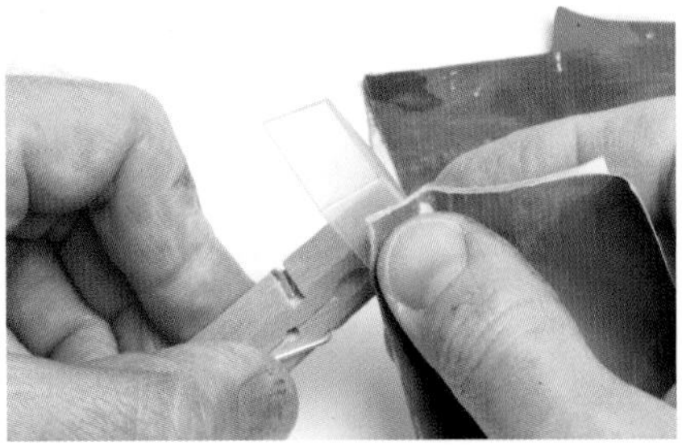

The one-piece glazing unit was very cloudy, so I tried to salvage it by polishing with fine abrasives, starting with 4,000 grit and working up to 18,000, using plenty of soapy water as a lubricant.

The finished truck certainly looks like a Mercedes-Benz 2238, although I'd venture to say that the windows appear to be too small. It remains fairly basic in terms of detail, especially when compared to the Diamond T dumper in Chapter 3, confirming that this kit hails from another age. But its relative cheapness and ease of assembly, plus the nostalgia factor – I can remember buying this kit from a musty old hardware store with my pocket money – made for a fun project.

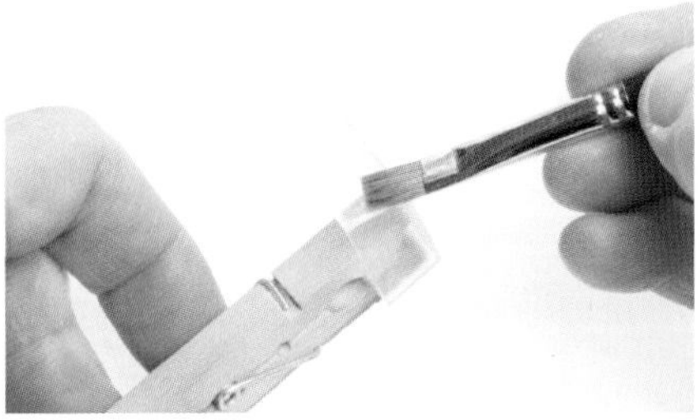

After rinsing and drying, Johnsons Klear acrylic floor polish was brushed on to the glazing unit to restore the transparency and shine. Allow to dry for a few hours before handling.

MODIFYING A VOLVO F12

The Volvo F10 and F12 series of trucks were introduced in 1977 and featured a range of ground-breaking elements, especially in terms of cab ergonomics. The number following the 'F' prefix denoted the size of engine in litres, and the mechanical aspects were a development of the earlier N series of rigid and articulated trucks.

Utilizing another kit from the erstwhile Kiel Kraft range (although this time a more recently manufactured Knightwing version), I initially envisaged keeping this truck as a tractor unit to complement the Mercedes 2238. However, after a change of heart I decided to extend the chassis to form an 8.5m (27.9ft) rigid dropside version, harnessing a Knightwing trailer kit to provide some of the necessary materials.

Enlarging the chassis was simple enough, with lengths of styrene strip inserted just behind the cab. A little arithmetic revealed that, to create an 8.5m-long chassis in 1:72 scale, the existing 92mm (3.6in) frames required an additional 26mm (1in) in length. Looking at the kit's chassis, the area immediately behind the cab seemed like the best place to insert the extra material, so plastic strip was sourced, as close to the dimensions of the existing frames as possible. Evergreen's 1.0 × 3.2mm (0.040 x 0.125in) was the closest I could find, leaving the Knightwing frames needing a degree of tapering on the lower edges of the frames.

The assembled cab simply clips on to the chassis. The Kiel Kraft kit might be basic, but it can provide a fun project that isn't overly challenging.

The kit's instructions include a few errors, most of which I spotted early. Alas, I was too late to realize that the rear light boom should be fitted the other way around, so mine is upside down! The extra details added to the chassis have made a big improvement.

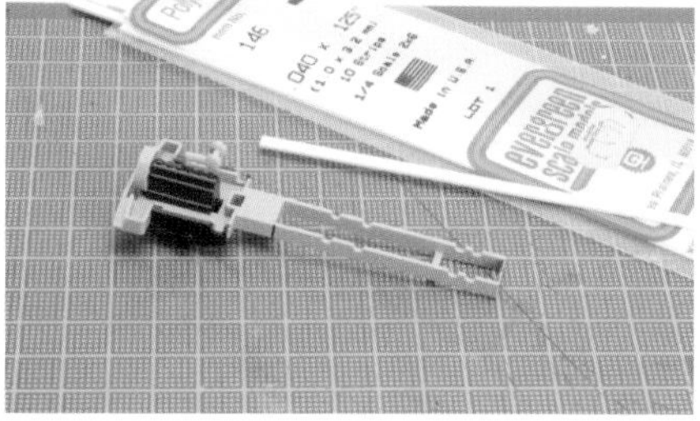

This Knightwing Volvo F12 kit is another ex-Kiel Kraft product, which I'd decided to convert from a tractor unit to a rigid dropside truck. The chassis comes as a single unit and its rudimentary nature makes it easy to modify. Evergreen 1.0 × 3.2mm styrene strip is a close match for the dimensions of the side frames.

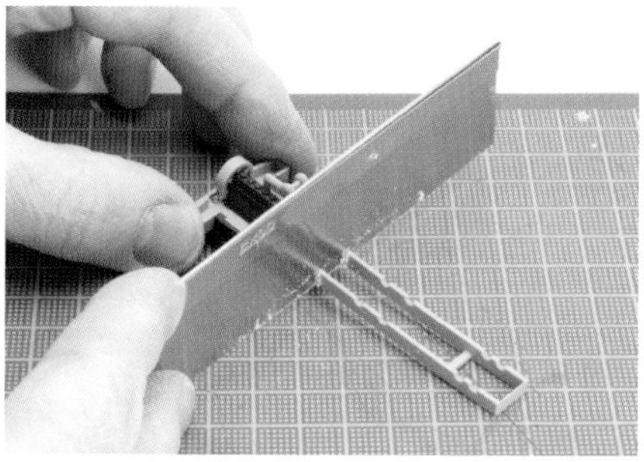

It made sense to cut the frames at the end of the solid area beneath the cab, leaving the rearmost section untouched, thus preserving the locating slots of the axles and suspension. A fine-toothed razor saw was employed, and the cut was made gently, aiming for a nice square edge.

A set-square revealed how square and even the cut faces were, and a flat needle file made any necessary adjustments.

Lengths of the 1.0 × 3.2mm strip were cut and fixed to the rear section of the frames, one at a time, using a straightedge to ensure correct alignment. A pair of cross-members was also cut and inserted between the frames.

With the axles and wheels temporarily fitted, the two elements of the chassis were brought together on a flat surface. After checking that everything appeared square and true, the bond was made behind the cab. Small reinforcing brackets were formed from plastic angle.

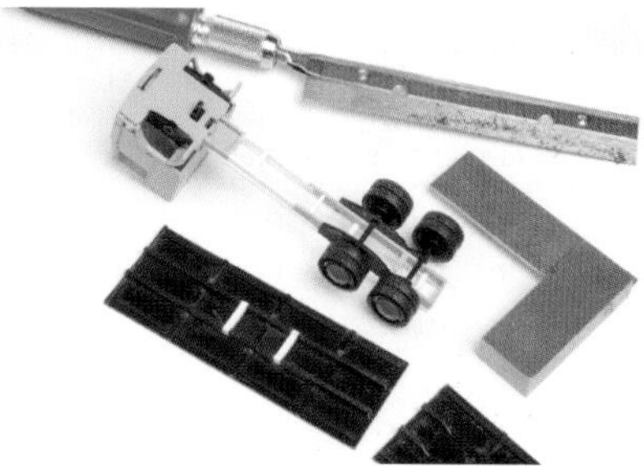

The extended chassis will be fragile until the load bed is installed, so it needs to be handled carefully. The floor from a Knightwing trailer kit was marked out and cut, again making sure that the edges were square.

After fixing the load bed in position, the chassis instantly gained strength and rigidity. The various underframe fittings could now be added.

The sides from the trailer were also cut down and installed, with new upright strengthening brackets added from styrene strip and angle.

The vital element to this process was accuracy of marking and cutting, ensuring that the edges were square and true, with the new material carefully aligned and bonded securely. Extra bits of styrene strip and section served to reinforce the joints, and the decision to maintain the twin rear axles meant that the kit didn't need many other modifications. The trailer kit parts were trimmed to fit the elongated chassis, and once the load bed was fixed in position, the chassis became very rigid and resilient.

The Volvo then received similar detail upgrades to those employed on the Mercedes truck, while the load deck was enhanced with thin hardwood veneer, which replicates the real material far more effectively than painted plastic. Indeed, Ribbon Sapele, a type of mahogany, features a very straight and fine grain that mimics the appearance of individual planks.

An extended driveshaft was formed from plastic rod, and the underrun barriers fabricated from plastic strip.

A Tamiya aerosol (TS-44) provided the main colour for the cab and bodywork. Once this had dried, the chassis was hand-painted and smaller details picked out before everything was coated with clear gloss.

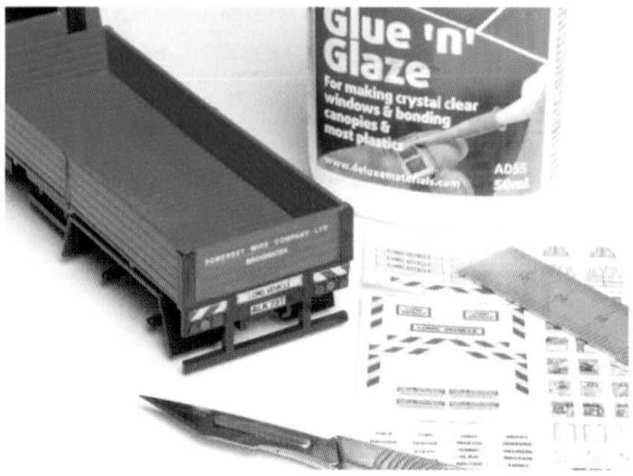

This detail pack, from Ten Commandments, provided 'Long Vehicle' legends and warning panels. As with the Mercedes truck, the licence plates were created from individual decals.

To give this truck a work-stained look, the bodywork and chassis were treated to a brush-on, wipe-off acrylic wash. Working on a small section at a time, a grimy mix of regular acrylic paints was brushed on to the surface. Immediately, most of the paint was wiped away with cotton swabs, working in vertical strokes and leaving behind deposits of pigment within recessed panels and seams.

The acrylic wash stage can be effective on its own, but it is liable to create hard 'edges' to the dirt deposits. A fine misting of similar paint shades from an airbrush will soften the effect, with Tamiya's acrylics being perfectly suited for this task. Restraint is important, as it's easy to apply too much paint, especially on smaller models. Free-flowing paint and a low air pressure (maximum 15psi) are crucial.

The floor of the load bed can be greatly enhanced by laying a piece of wood veneer. I used Ribbon Sapele, which has a fine, straight grain. The veneer was fixed to a strip of double-sided tape before cutting to size, to reduce the risk of its splitting. A little trimming was needed to achieve a perfect fit. It wasn't installed just yet, though.

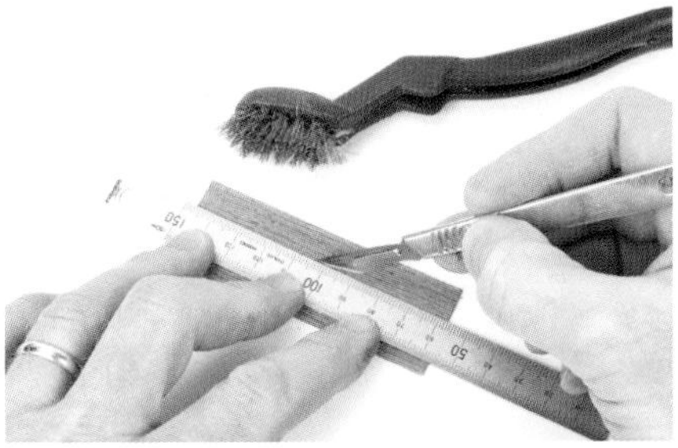

Individual planks were created by scoring the veneer carefully with a sharp scalpel against a straightedge. The double-sided tape will hold everything together, but don't cut all the way through the material.

The surface of the veneer was distressed with a brass wire brush. Both the scoring and brushing will improve the wood's appearance and help it respond to the weathering process.

The veneer has to be cut with care, using a fresh blade against a straightedge and by exerting gentle pressure, taking several passes to cut through the material. The grain will splinter freely if the knife is forced through the wood, especially when cutting in parallel to the grain's direction. A handy – and convenient – tip is to lay the veneer on to a strip of strong double-sided tape, which will help hold the grain together as you cut. The other side of the tape then provides a means of fixing the veneer to the model. Furthermore, avoiding the use of glue reduces the risk of sealing areas of the grain, which will impede the penetration of the weathering washes, which are an effective way of ageing the appearance of the timber decking.

Incidentally, I prefer to use enamel washes on bare timber, as it soaks readily into the wood without raising the grain or causing distortion, as some water-based washes can do.

The timber decking and the surrounding bodywork can be finished off with a light misting of general grime-coloured paints from the airbrush before a load is created. To suit the truck's branding, various coils and lengths of steel wire were created and installed. The straight lengths were simple enough to fabricate from stiff nickel wire, but the coils took a little longer to wrap around the shaft of a drill bit, using much finer nickel wire.

After fixing the veneer in place, enamel washes and filters were brushed on to the wood. The pigments will settle into the scored plank seams, and the distressed surface adds some welcome texture, avoiding too pristine an appearance.

More staining and shading effects can be achieved with the airbrush or dry pigments (or both), concentrating the darker shades around the corners of the load bed.

Once assembly and weathering were complete, a set of etched brass mirrors was installed, from a pack of lorry detailing parts in the excellent Langley Models range. The brass parts had been painted beforehand, with Mr Surfacer black aerosol primer, followed by a dry-brushed coating of acrylic dark grey and earth brown tones.

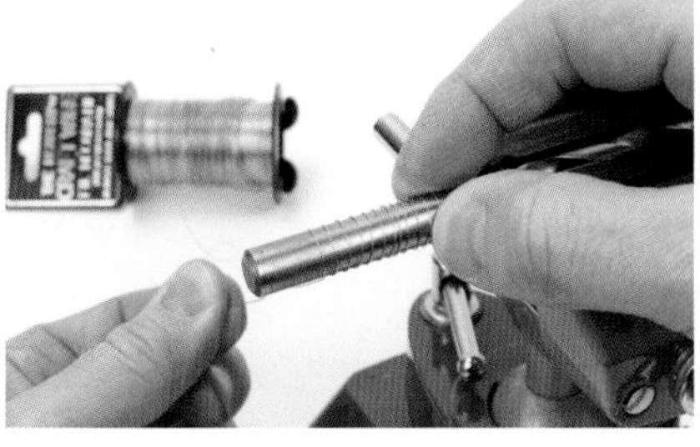

To suit the wagon's corporate identity, I decided to create a suitable load. Lengths of 28-gauge nickel wire were wrapped around the shank of a 10mm-diameter drill bit.

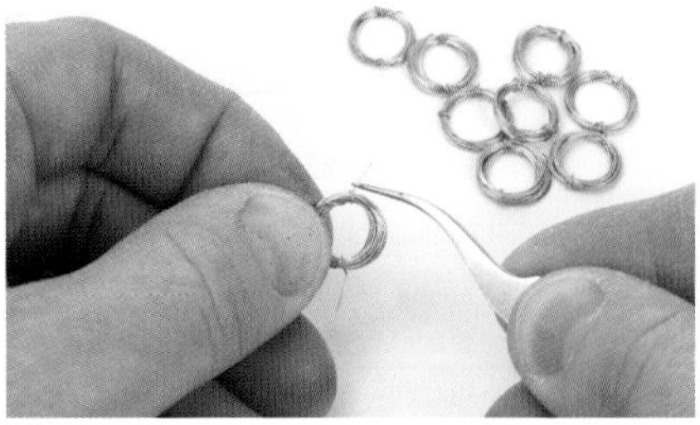

After compressing the coils, the ends were shaped to act as retaining straps, holding the wire into tight coils. The process was repeated until a stash of coils was created.

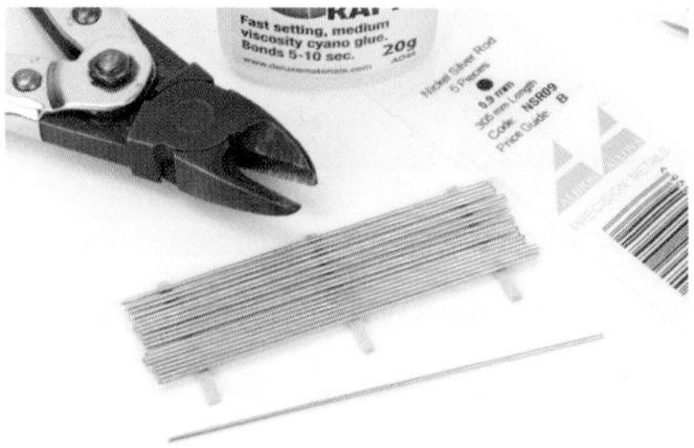

I couldn't motivate myself to craft enough coils to fill the entire truck, so a number of straight lengths of 0.9mm nickel wire were cut to a uniform length and secured to scraps of wood.

After dry-brushing with brown and rusty-coloured paints, the loads were installed in the truck.

NOT BAD FOR THEIR AGE

Both trucks do look a little basic, especially compared to contemporary kits in similar scales. However, they provide a good value source of kits featuring prototypes unavailable elsewhere, in the same scale. My renditions were built for fun, but there is potential here for adding a lot more detail and refining some of the coarser elements of these kits, which are, after all, around forty years old.

Providing an interesting and fun conversion project, this Knightwing Volvo F12 has provided a useful vehicle for my OO-gauge model railway.

The kits might be basic in some ways, belying their age and pocket-money nature, but these ex-Kiel Kraft truck kits offer great potential for detailing and conversion projects.

CHAPTER THREE

FURTHER ADVENTURES IN 1:72 SCALE: ZIL-131 AND DIAMOND T 972 DUMPER

As mentioned in the Introduction, the focus of this book lies firmly on civilian trucks. However, following both World Wars, the civilian market was flooded with ex-military vehicles, many of which remained in service for long periods. Military modelling accounts for a huge portion of the plastic kit market, so it's no surprise that there is an endless supply of vehicles from brands such as Tamiya, Airfix, IBG, ICM, Italeri and Trumpeter. We'll come to the military-dominated 1:35 scale in Chapter 5, but there are also many fantastic military truck kits available in 1:76, 1:72 and 1:48 scales. If you're a fan of post-war Soviet, European or US prototypes in particular, then you'll have plenty of examples to choose from, many of which are ideal for a demilitarizing project.

ZIL-131

Soviet trucks of the post-1960s era provide modellers with a source of interesting prototypes, especially as examples were built for both military and civilian use, with few discernible alterations other than colour schemes. Featured here is ICM's 1:72 scale ZiL-131 kit, representing a landmark prototype from behind the Iron Curtain. Making its first appearance in prototype form in 1956, the ZiL-131 eventually entered full-scale production in 1966.

The truck's specification was dictated in part by the Soviet military, who preferred angular (rather than curved) front wings, a split windscreen, and a roomy cab that was large enough to accommodate three fully kitted-out soldiers. The six-wheel-drive transmission, high ground clearance and flexible suspension allowed the truck to cope with extreme terrain, and a wading depth of up to 1.4m (4.6ft) was possible. Power steering was fitted as standard, as was a potent petrol engine, and a payload of up to 5 tons could be carried on regular road surfaces.

The ZiL-131 proved popular with civilian owners and operators, as well as the Soviet Army and Air Force. Such was the truck's versatility that it was offered in a wide range of cargo, tanker, fire engine, crane and tractor unit configurations. Some army examples were also employed as command vehicles, or fitted with rocket-launching gear on the rear. Production numbers were impressive, with over 150,000 being built in 1969 alone; they were employed throughout Soviet Bloc countries in Europe, as well as various parts of Africa, the Middle East, Cuba and Finland.

ICM – a Ukranian company – produce a vast range of high-quality, great value plastic kits in 1:72 and 1:35 scales. Having built a number of ICM's 1:35 kits, I was keen to try this smaller-scale offering, although the kit apparently dates back to the 1990s and was originally released under the Omega-K brand. Several versions of the ZiL-131 are available, from a drop-side cargo variant (as built here) to a command vehicle and a fuel bowser. All are pitched at the military enthusiast, with suggested colour schemes and decals to match, but the cargo version in particular is equally suited to civilian use.

This kit serves as an indication of how smaller-scale kit design and manufacture improved during the 1990s, especially compared to the Kiel Kraft kits featured in the previous chapter. The ladder frame chassis is produced as a single moulding, but there are plenty

I'm a big fan of ICM's 1:35-scale kits, so I was keen to try one of the same brand's 1:72 offerings. This ZiL-131 kit dates back to the 1990s, but it's still a great package.

of other separate fittings that combine to form the suspension, axles and transmission. Only the base of the engine and gearbox is rendered, but there's plenty of fine detail relief, nonetheless. The cab and bonnet come as a single unit but, again, the detail is crisp and impressive, with open slats that allow the radiator to be glimpsed behind.

The generous provision of small parts is great in many respects, but the need to clean them of excess plastic and moulding imperfections before assembly can be a fiddly and tiresome task. Luckily, the parts in this ICM kit weren't too bad, although I found the exhaust pipes impossible to fettle without breakage. In fact, one of the sections broke before I'd even removed it from the sprue, despite my best efforts at working gently. This is a common problem with kits in the smaller scales, especially modern high-specification kits with ultra-fine components. There's a limit to how finely plastic parts can be rendered before they become unusable.

Breaking the exhaust pipes wasn't a big deal, as substituting such components with brass or copper wire provides greater resilience and improves their appearance. Having drilled mounting holes in the silencer, 0.7mm-diameter wire was shaped with round-nose pliers, using the kit's original pipes as a guide. I used brass wire for the twin front sections of pipe, as these were predominantly straight. The outlet pipe, in contrast, had to be shaped to a more complex profile, so copper wire was chosen, as it is much more pliable.

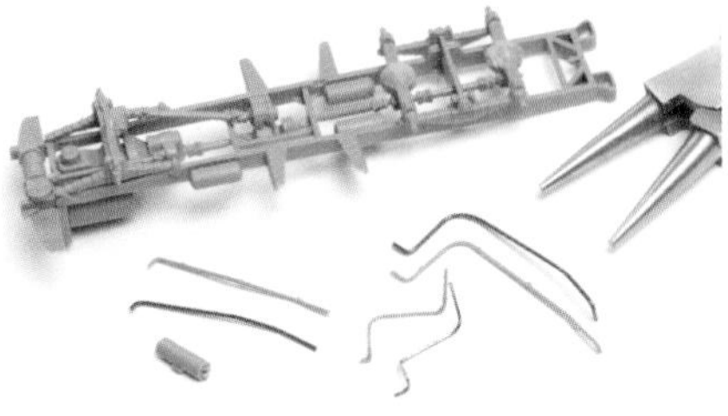

Like many 1:72 kits from the same period, chassis construction is straightforward, with a one-piece ladder frame and separate suspension and transmission components. The plastic exhaust pipes were full of flash but too delicate to fettle effectively, so I replaced them with 0.7mm-diameter wire.

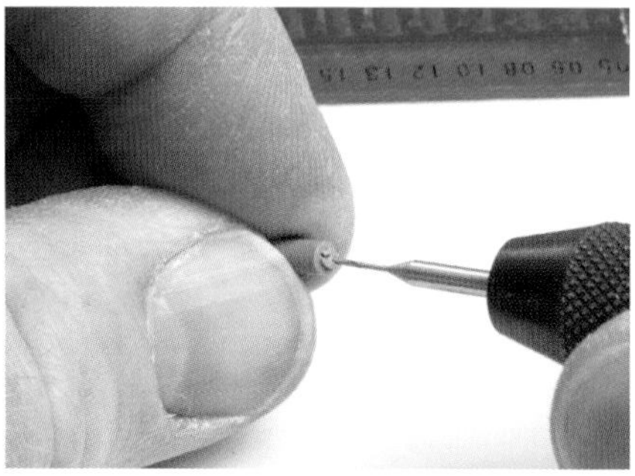

Mounting holes for the exhaust pipes were drilled into the silencer to a depth of about 2mm, which is just enough to provide a reliable glue bond.

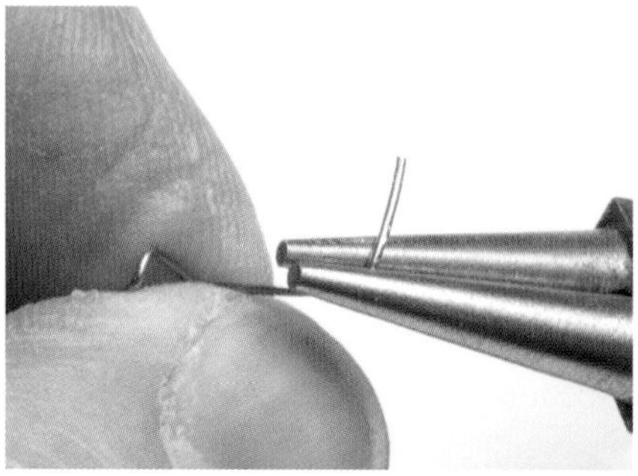

The wire sections were shaped with round-nose pliers, using the plastic originals as a guide. The outlet pipe's shape was more complex, so copper wire was employed, which is easier to manipulate.

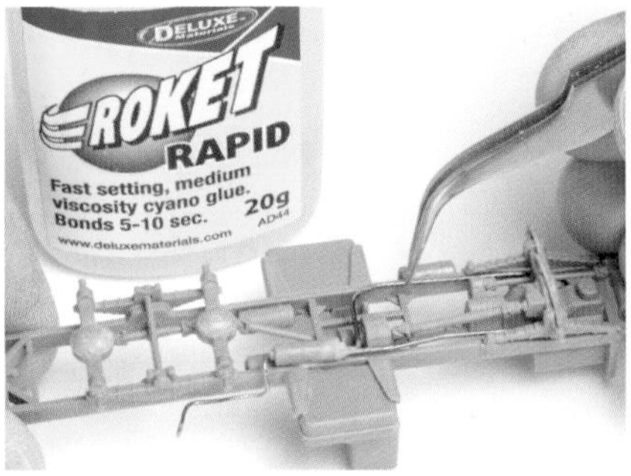

As the front pipes consisted of long straight sections they were formed from brass wire, which is stiffer and holds its shape better than copper. The wire was secured with small drops of cyano glue.

The design of the kit allows distinct sub-assemblies to be created, which makes the painting and weathering stages much easier, especially as the bodywork and chassis are to be rendered in contrasting colours.

After painting and weathering, the chassis was wheeled up, using a small offcut of mirror glass to ensure that the wheels were correctly aligned. The wheels were fixed with a tiny amount of cyano.

ICM's instructions suggest a pair of colour schemes: Soviet Army Field Green or United Nations White, with suitable decals supplied for both. Instead, and in keeping with my mission to build only civilian vehicles, I took inspiration from Andy Thompson's excellent reference book, *Trucks of the Soviet Union – the Definitive History*, which includes a number of images of ZiL-131s built for non-military use. I was particularly taken with the sand and blue-grey colour combination.

The most challenging aspect was encountered at the end of proceedings, with the individual glazing panels requiring very careful fettling with a needle file in order to slot snugly in place. The windows fit from the outside, sitting into tiny moulded recesses, so there are very fine tolerances involved. Therefore, it was a case of regular test-fitting and dressing until a perfect fit was achieved for each element. Filing the edges of clear plastic glazing always raises the risk of damage to the faces of the component, but following the file with fine abrasive pads will help to polish the surfaces smooth and reduce the prismatic effect of light reflecting off the edges of the clear plastic.

Once all the individual glazing elements were treated and ready to fit, they were cleaned of debris and fixed in place with a thin clear acrylic gloss, applied with a fine brush so that it ran into the frame surround. As the varnish dries, it will form a surprisingly strong bond between the glazing and the cab, provided that the parts fit together snugly. Covering the glazing, both inside and outside, with the same gloss clear coat avoids the chance of any unsightly tide-marks around the edges of the windows, and presents a uniform finish. It also adds a more resilient coating to the glazing, and can improve transparency. Avoiding brush marks is important, though, so use a good quality brush and don't over-brush the medium once it has been applied, especially when using faster-drying formulas. Remember that only acrylic varnishes are suitable for this task – solvent or lacquer-based formulas may damage the glazing.

This proved to be a very enjoyable building project, recreating an interesting and stylish truck. A rendition of the ZiL-131's predecessor, the ZiL-130, would make a great companion for this model. Being more of a civilian-focused design, the styling of the '130' was influenced by contemporary American styles. The ZiL-130 has been portrayed in kit form by AVD Models, in both 1:72 and 1:43 scales, so I really ought to try to track one down and have a go.

To avoid damaging the paintwork, final assembly was achieved with Glue 'n' Glaze adhesive, applied through a precision tip and left to turn tacky for a few minutes before the parts were brought together. Any excess glue was wiped away with a damp swab.

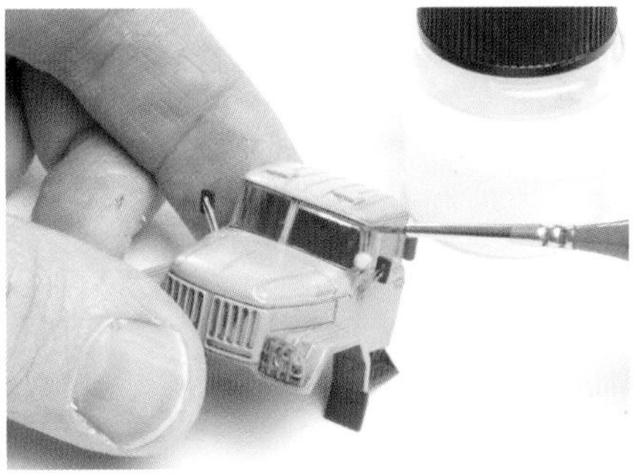

The glazing stage is always crucial. In this case, the kit's parts were well executed and needed only minimal fettling before installation, from the outside rather than the inside, as is more common. I used Johnson's Klear floor polish as an adhesive and as a high gloss, protective coating, applied with a soft brush. Other gloss acrylic clear coats will do a similar job.

Although this kit has been around for a while, it builds into a handsome model and features plenty of fine detail.

DIAMOND T 972 DUMP TRUCK

This heavy-duty tactical truck was built for the US Army by the Diamond T manufacturing company of Chicago, between 1940 and 1945. Several configurations were produced, based around a 6×6 chassis, including a tanker, wrecker, dropside and dumper. Powered by a Hercules 6-cylinder inline petrol engine and designed to operate over rough terrain, the trucks were also supplied to other Allied forces, including Canada, the UK and France.

IBG Models offers a choice of four different Diamond T truck kits in 1:72 scale, covering each of the aforementioned prototype variants. First appearing in the mid-2010s, the kits offer a high parts count and an impressive level of detail for a very reasonable price. Like the real thing, each of the kits shares the same chassis and cab components, and such was their reliability and versatility, a large number of vehicles made it into civilian and industrial employment once their military careers were over.

For a smaller-scale kit, IBG Models' package provides an astonishing amount of plastic, with an array of separate chassis frame members, a fully rendered powerplant and transmission, detailed brake drums, plus a choice of tipping gear, allowing the dumper body to be accurately modelled in the raised or

IBG Models offers a variety of Diamond T trucks in 1:72, but I chose the dump-truck variant, which can be readily converted to post-war civilian condition.

The IBG kit boasts some truly impressive detail and a high parts count for such a diminutive model.

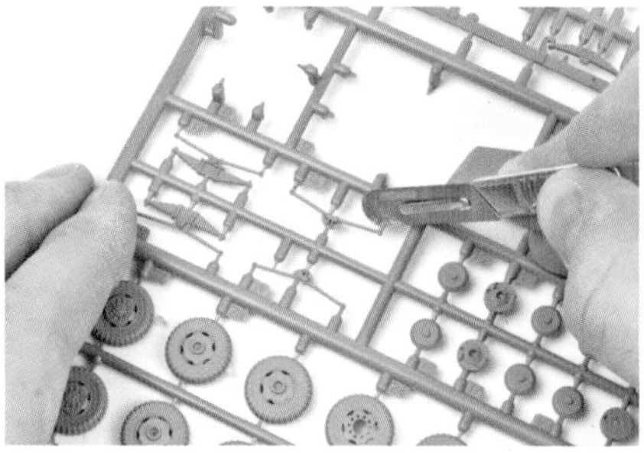

Some of the parts are tiny and need to be cut from the sprue with care. In some cases, a razor-saw knife blade is preferable to a knife or sprue cutters. Work gently through the plastic, leaving a little material on the waste side.

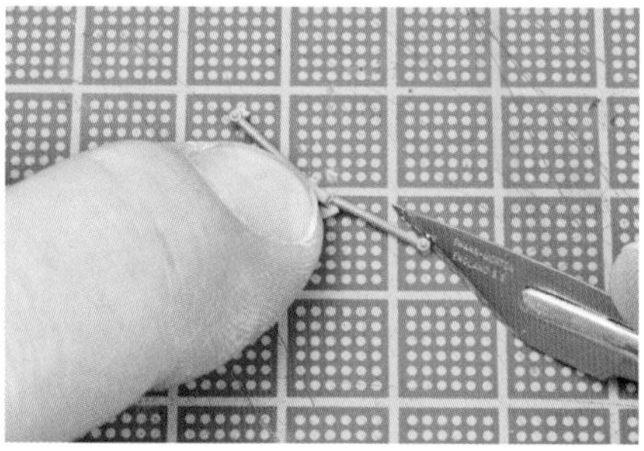

Once the part has been freed, any remaining waste can be pared away with a fresh scalpel blade. Support the component firmly with your finger while cutting.

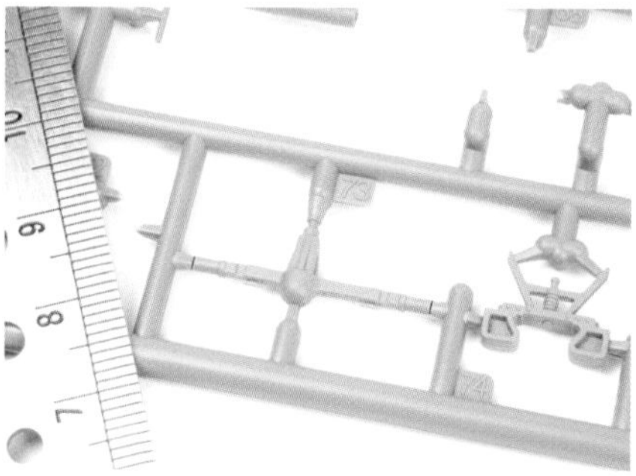

Due to the size of the sprue gates, it was difficult to discern where they ended and the component began. A magnifier proved useful, and the ends of the part were marked with a fine red marker pen before cutting.

lowered position. There must be nearly seventy individual components that make up the underframe alone, so this is by no means a quick kit to assemble.

Some of the parts are very delicate, especially elements of the suspension and the exhaust pipes, and a gentle approach is needed when cutting the parts from the sprue. A set of fine, sharp sprue cutters will be useful for most components, but the finest parts may benefit from being freed with a precision razor-saw blade. Wherever possible, support the plastic parts with the fingers of one hand while sawing gently through the sprue gate with the other. The remaining excess plastic can then be gradually pared away with a fresh scalpel blade, again supporting the rest of the components as much as possible.

Patience really is the key to success in such instances: rush the job and you're bound to break a few bits – I'm talking from experience here! If breakages do happen, the parts can be fixed back together with liquid poly-cement and set aside to cure fully. If there will be difficulty in ensuring the correct alignment of the broken components, sometimes it's better to repair them at the same time as bonding them in position, using adjacent parts to help with the positioning.

What is more frustrating is when parts do not break cleanly, leading to their overall dimensions being compromised, and thus their ability to fit properly. A few such instances occurred during the erection of the Diamond T's chassis, most notably with the curved cross-member, which is extremely delicate. Having broken and repaired it twice, it ended up about a millimetre too short, although scraps of thin plastic strip were fixed to the inside of the frames to act as fillets. Not a serious problem, therefore, but a fiddly and tiresome one to correct, nonetheless. But then I should have been more careful!

Overall, IBG Models has done an excellent job of rendering the parts crisply, with very little flash to trim away before assembly can begin. On the other hand, the size of the sprue gates is rather large in some instances, especially in relation to some of the tiniest parts. As a result it can be difficult to discern where the component ends and the sprue begins, leading to the risk of parts being trimmed too short. I would recommend studying the parts carefully, perhaps with the help of a magnifier, and marking the ends of the parts with a fine marker pen before cutting through the sprue gates.

In order to ensure squareness, the frames and cross-members are best assembled on as flat a surface as possible. A small mirror or piece of sheet glass is a useful modelling aid for such purposes (ask your local glazier for any small offcuts), or the handle of a steel set-square can also suffice for smaller assemblies. Any twisting in the frames will be magnified once the axles and wheels are installed, while it can also hinder the fitting of the bodywork, leading to the need for frustrating remedial work further down the line.

A sign of a well-designed kit is the presence of locating aids to help the parts slot together neatly and accurately, although these tabs and slots can be less effective on smaller parts. This IBG kit does sport a number of assembly aids designed into the moulds, but vigilance was needed when fitting the chassis cross-members and suspension units, to ensure that everything was correctly aligned.

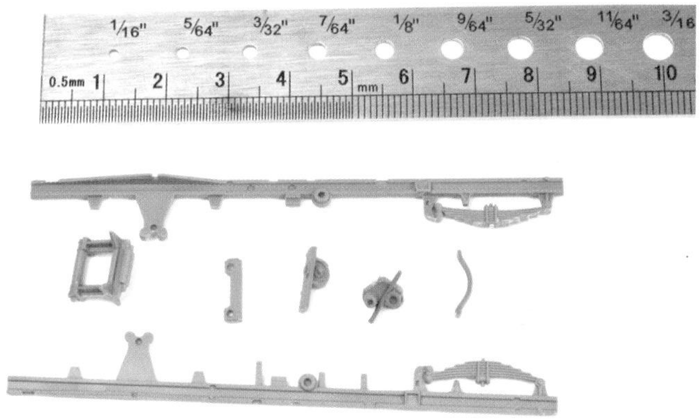

In common with larger-scale truck kits, IBG Models provided separate chassis frames and cross-members. Each element required careful fettling before assembly.

Working on a flat surface, the cross-members were installed to one of the side frames, ensuring that they were aligned squarely.

The other side frame was then installed, again checking that the whole assembly was square and true.

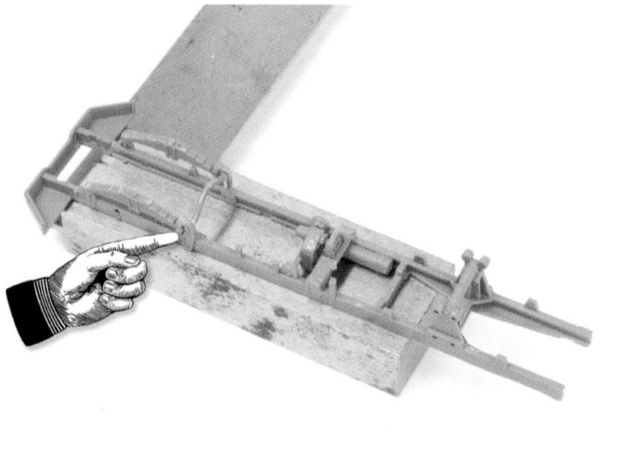

I managed to break the curved cross-member, and despite fixing it back together, it was now about 1mm too short. With the front bumper temporarily fitted, in order to maintain the correct spacing between the frames, small fillets of 10 thou' plastic strip were inserted to fill the gap between the cross-member and the frames.

Parts are provided to build a full – and impressive – rendition of the Hercules 6-cylinder petrol engine. To put it in context, here it is beside the engine from a 1:24-scale DAF 95 (see Chapter 9).

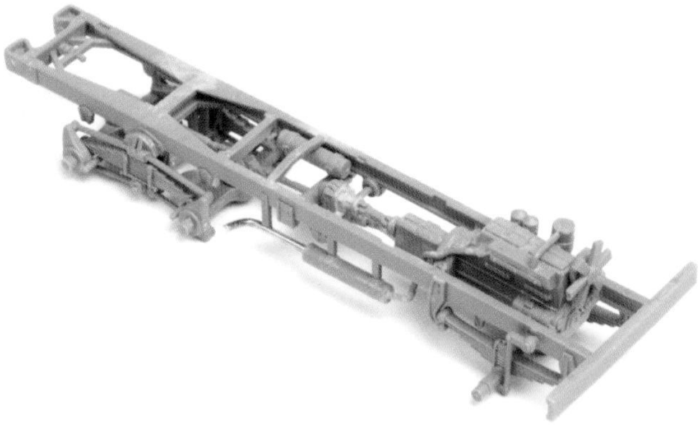

After installing the engine and transmission, the exhaust system was added. Again, I omitted a section of fiddly – and fragile – plastic in favour of brass wire.

Like the ZiL-131, I found the plastic exhaust pipes a little too delicate, although this time I only replaced the short outlet section with brass wire, checking that there would be adequate clearance for the wheels before fixing it into place. Most of the plastic components fitted together neatly, with only a small amount of filler required to tidy up a few joints. Abrading the chassis once the filler was dry would risk damage, so solvent-based plastic putty was applied with a cocktail stick, and manipulated immediately with a small brush dipped in liquid poly-cement. This helps work the putty into awkward areas, while also smoothing the surface and minimizing the need for sanding sticks or files later.

This is a useful trick to learn, as it can save a lot of tedious and messy remedial work, but a degree of practice is required. Applying too much liquid poly can have a deleterious effect on the plastic, so a little restraint is needed. Perfecting the technique on scraps of plastic is recommended.

Another useful tip is to create a paste of plastic filler and liquid poly by mixing a small quantity of each on a scrap surface. The thickness of the paste can be tailored by altering the ratio of filler to liquid poly, and the resulting medium can be applied by brush in a more controlled fashion. This is especially effective for filling hairline gaps or minor surface imperfections, rather than holes or gaps. The two components have to be compatible, of course, but most solvent-based plastic putties, such as Tamiya, Mr Hobby, Humbrol and Revell fillers, work well with most liquid poly-cements.

Mr Hobby's Mr Surfacer, supplied in jars, is a liquid medium that can be employed in a similar way. Indeed, I like to employ Mr Surfacer as a means of creating texture to smooth plastic surfaces, prior to painting. Cast metal components, such as engine blocks, transmission casings and axles, all benefit from a subtle coarseness, which can be enhanced during the weathering stages, taking away the inevitable uniformness of moulded plastic components. A small amount of cellulose thinners will thin the Mr Surfacer if required, helping it to be brushed more evenly, while a stippling action with the brush will increase the level of texture and produce a more random pattern.

Mr Surfacer dries very quickly, and excessive use of cellulose thinners can be damaging to the plastic, so again, a rehearsal on scrap components may be a good idea. Also the cellulose thinners will serve to clean your brushes afterwards.

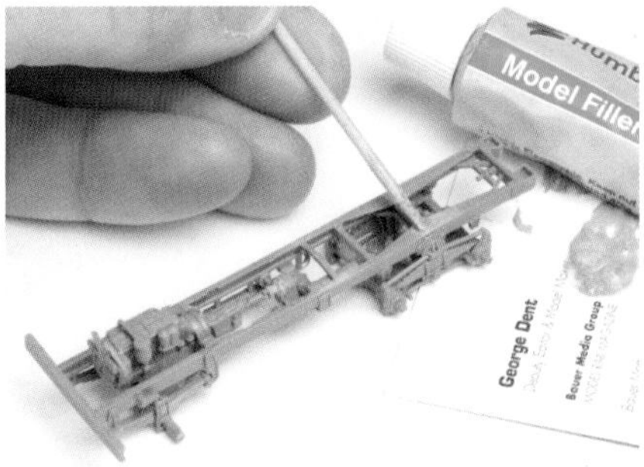

Any visible gaps between the components were filled with a solvent-based plastic filler, applied with the tip of a wooden cocktail stick.

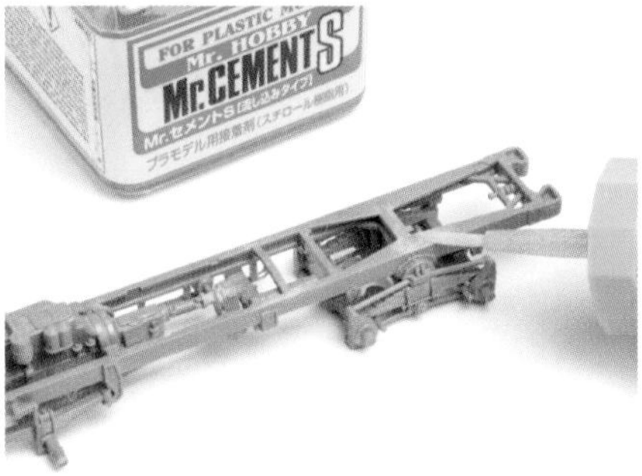

Before the filler had cured, liquid poly was applied, which reactivates the putty and allows it to be manipulated and smoothed, removing most of the need for abrading later.

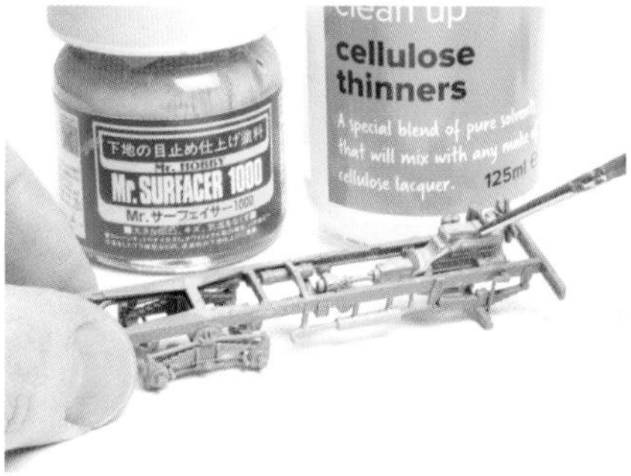

The engine block, transmission and exhaust system were treated to a textured coating, courtesy of Mr Surfacer 1000, thinned slightly with cellulose thinners and applied by brush. As well as adding an authentic texture, this medium also fills any other small gaps and imperfections.

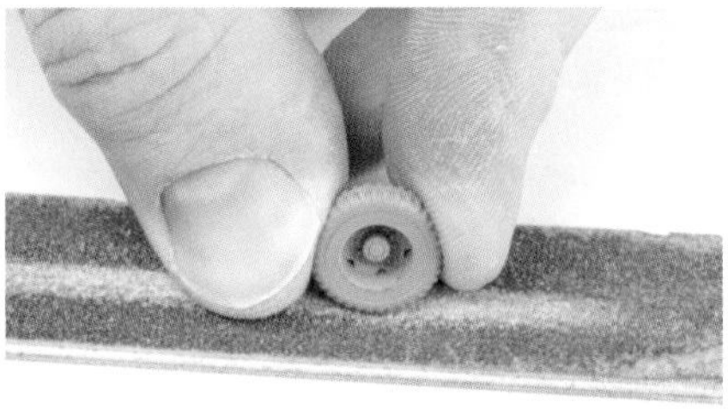

In an attempt to capture the bulky nature of the prototype, I decided to 'weight' the tyres slightly, by creating flat spots. Holding the wheel perpendicular to the surface of a file or sanding stick, it was moved back and forth.

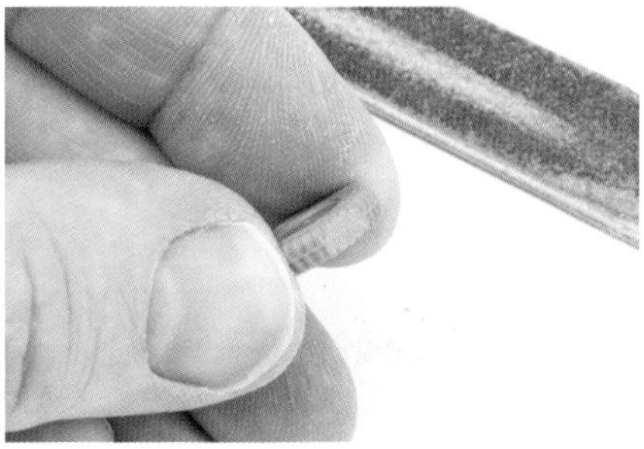

Just a small flat spot is sufficient, and each tyre needs to be treated consistently to avoid unsightly gaps when the truck is posed on a flat surface.

Having test-fitted the weighted tyres, the dumper support mechanism was installed. I opted for the raised version, so that the detailed chassis could be displayed.

After painting and weathering, the wheels could be installed permanently, using a set-square on a flat surface to check that they stood squarely.

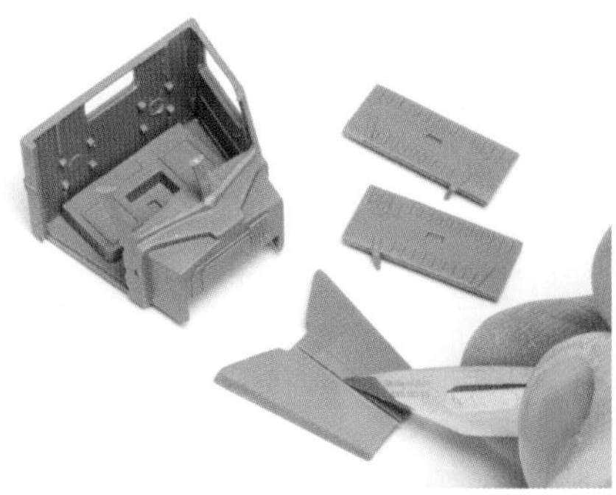

I also wanted to ensure that the detailed engine could be seen, so I opened up one side of the bonnet. The top section was cut carefully along the seam, over several passes until the plastic broke apart.

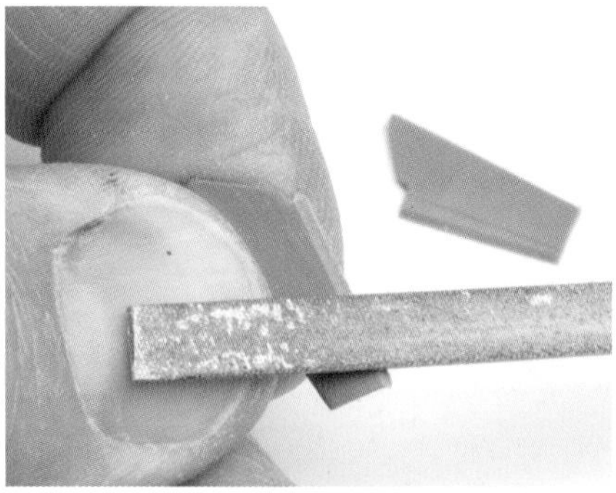

The mating faces of the bonnet were then chamfered with a flat file, checking intermittently until the correct fit was achieved.

The folded bonnet sections were then fixed in position, and the front wings and radiator grille installed. A small bracket linking the grille and the right-hand wing was fabricated from plastic angle, compensating for the lack of support from the open bonnet side. The cab roof and one door were left off, to allow access to the interior for painting.

Having made the decision to model the dumper body in the raised position, the extended hydraulic ram and associated equipment was assembled and installed on the chassis frames. An alternative set of components is also provided for those preferring a lowered dumper. My choice was partly down to a desire to pose the finished truck in a miniature quarry setting, but also as a way of displaying all of that lovely chassis detail. It was while pondering the choice that I also wondered about displaying the engine, which would ultimately be hidden beneath the fixed bonnet. This seemed a shame, so I carved up the bonnet components to allow one side to be fixed in the open position.

This took a little work, filing a camber on the side and top panels so they could be joined in a way that suggested they were hinged as per the prototype. However, as pleased as I was with the finished results, I did make the error of treating the wrong side of the bonnet. As it was, the right-hand side of the engine is less interesting, with the exhaust manifold being visible, whereas the opposite side features the various filters, offering more tonal variety. That aside, it proved a worthwhile endeavour, as did posing one of the cab doors ajar, displaying the detailed interior.

Once the painting and weathering stages were complete, the last job before final assembly was to install the cab's glazing. Surprisingly, given the immense detail provided in this kit, there were no clear moulded glazing parts. Instead, a sheet of clear film was supplied, printed with the outlines of each component, leaving the modeller to cut them out with scissors and fix them in place. Small moulded rebates are incorporated into the inner faces of the window apertures, and it took time to get the individual windows to fit neatly. Once happy with the fit, they were secured with a tiny bead of Glue 'n' Glaze adhesive, applied with a needle-point tip. The provision of the thin film came initially as a surprise, but the thinness of the material looks very effective, avoiding the inevitable prismatic effect of clear moulded styrene components.

PAINTING AND WEATHERING SCALE MODELS

We rather glossed over the painting stage in the previous chapter, primarily due to the relatively simple nature of the kits involved. As we'll see throughout the rest of this book, painting chassis and bodywork separately is nearly always the best practice. With more complex kits, in any scale, we often have to plan the painting stages carefully from the outset, to ensure that we can get the paint safely and effectively into all visible areas of a model, without damaging delicate parts. Our goal is always to create a high-quality finish, and in order to achieve that, we're likely to have to create many separate sub-assemblies. Such was the case with each of the models featured thus far, with the main cab and bodywork sections being assembled and treated separately to the chassis and wheels.

The design of the kit can be a help to the modeller at the painting stage, with sections logically and clearly divided. The smallest detail fittings can even be painted while still attached to the sprue, and only released and installed at the very end of proceedings. Each of these separate entities can be primed, painted and enhanced remotely, allowing easy access for paintbrushes to do their work.

That's the ideal scenario, yet life is seldom so straightforward, and we often have to improvise in order to achieve the best results. This is another instance where careful planning pays dividends, as we can make considered decisions about which parts to bond before or after painting. The models illustrated here show some of the most common approaches, tailored to accommodate the nature of each kit. For instance, the single-piece cab and bonnet of the ZiL-131 was easy to treat, with the interior unit rendered separately. In contrast, the roof of the Diamond T dumper had to be left off in order to allow the interior to be treated.

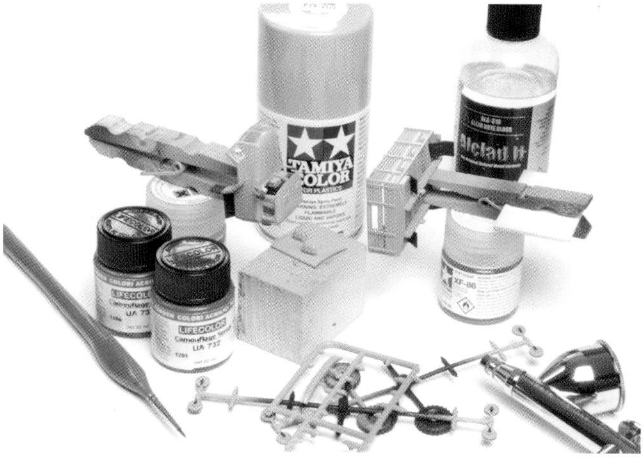

Often, kits can be built up into logical sub-assemblies to simplify the painting stage.

AIRBRUSHING versus AEROSOLS

With smaller models, it's easy to obliterate the subtle details by adding over-thick layers of paint – which is where an airbrush comes into its own. Provided that the user has a certain level of proficiency, the amount of paint can be safely regulated and applied accurately in order to build up several thin, even coats until full opacity is achieved. However, attaining that level of proficiency does take time, practice, and an understanding of how to thin the paint correctly and choose the correct air pressure.

Airbrushing is a weighty subject and readers may want to consult my book *Airbrushing for Railway Modellers* (The Crowood Press) for an in-depth look at the subject. In brief, though, the airbrush must be clean and in good order, and a reliable air supply should be on hand with the facility to control the output pressure. For the majority of tasks, a pressure of between 12 and 18psi is sufficient. Higher pressures cause the paint to dry in mid-air and to land on the surface uncontrollably. Lower pressures are possible, but the paint must be thinned even further, to a water-like consistency. The optimum paint thickness is usually similar to milk: just thicker than water, but not by much.

Good quality aerosol-based paints are a boon in many respects, as they remove the need to invest in an airbrush and the associated equipment. However, they can be very expensive in the longer term, and control of the paint flow is difficult – it's either on or off, and when on, the pressure can be high and the flow excessive. This is a particular issue when working on smaller models and components, as it's easy to apply too much paint and thereby create puddles or bury delicate detail features.

The kits featured here were all treated with a mix of aerosols, airbrushed paints and hand-applied finishes, with each approach chosen for matters of convenience and expedience. Whether using an airbrush or aerosols, it's imperative that you follow safety precautions to avoid the inhalation of paint vapours. A facemask with the requisite filters is essential, and a fume-extraction booth is recommended. Failing that, working outside or in a well-ventilated space is vital. Many paints contain highly toxic ingredients, so your personal safety (and the safety of those around you) should be a priority.

PAINTING BY HAND

Models don't have to be spray painted, but working with hand brushes can be labour intensive and disguising brush marks demands a certain level of skill. Building up colours often requires multiple coats, with each layer being rubbed down with fine abrasives when fully dry. This precludes the fitting of delicate details until painting is complete, while multiple layers of paint – inevitably leading to a thicker overall coating – runs the risk of spoiling any subtle surface relief. Some paint brands are better matched to hand-brushing than others, with slower-drying formulas being preferred. Vallejo and Lifecolor acrylics and Humbrol and Revell enamels are good examples of hand-brush-friendly paints, and good quality, well-maintained brushes are essential.

SCALE COLOUR AND SHEEN

There's a school of thought that colours should be modified when dealing with smaller models – or rather, that the shade of the colours should be tweaked, with an increase in miniaturization being followed by an increase in paleness of 'standard' colours. This has been occupying groups of modellers for some time, with some even drawing up specifications for the amount of white that should be added to a colour, depending on the model's scale.

I can see the relevance of this approach, as colours rarely look the same when viewed from varying distances, especially outdoors. The deep red of a full-size truck, for instance, will look different at close quarters compared to 100 feet away. Add to the mix the variables of lighting (the time of day and weather conditions) and the age of the paint, and things can get very complicated.

Colour will always be a subjective issue and many of us interpret shades differently anyway, so I've always kept to the mantra of 'if it looks right to me, it'll do'. Trying to paint models so that they look good for other people will seldom prove rewarding. That said, I do tend to modulate certain colours when working on models in smaller scales, avoiding darker, uniform shades wherever possible. Black is a prime example: there's seldom a time when an object can be described as being wholly black. Even at full size, it's likely to appear as a dark grey, due to the reflection of light. Therefore, painting elements of a smaller model in 'regular' black rarely looks correct, even when a showroom finish is envisaged. Numerous model paint manufacturers have acknowledged this, and offer a variety of black shades, branded under terms including 'burned black', 'weathered black', 'dirty black' or 'worn black'. I also try to avoid applying pure white on smaller models, preferring a very pale grey or cream instead.

Again, it's all a matter of choosing what looks right to your own eye. If you are replicating a specific truck livery on a 1:72-scale truck and have managed to get hold of the correct specification paint, try adding a drop of a compatible pale grey and apply the paint to a scrap of plastic. Make a note of the mixing ratio, and experiment until you find a tone that you're happy with.

A paint's sheen also has a dramatic effect on our perception of colour. Gloss coats often appear darker, while flat matt paints may present a dull, greyish hue. It's all to do with how the light is reflected off the painted surface. High gloss finishes often produce a toy-like impression on smaller objects, so I tend to prefer semi-gloss and satin finishes on anything other than 1:24-scale trucks.

WEATHERING

Most of the weathering process can also be undertaken before all the sub-assemblies are united. This patient approach can make a project feel like a drawn-out affair, but it certainly makes the job easier and produces superior results. The complex nature of the chassis and bodywork would make the weathering process, in particular, very difficult if the model were treated as a whole. Treating the sections separately allows for greater nuance to be added to the surfaces, helping to bring out the best of the moulded detail. It also prevents the more delicate fittings from being damaged.

A range of weathering techniques are showcased throughout the book, each of which can be transferred to any scale or subject. Weathering washes are highly diluted paints, and provide a means of highlighting the surface relief without necessarily making a truck look filthy. Choosing appropriate wash shades to suit the colour of the truck's paintwork will also dictate how grubby the results will be. For lighter colours, such as white, yellow or grey, a neutral wash shade will produce very subtle shading effects as it nestles into recesses, seam lines and around raised projections. Deeper livery colours, such as red, blue and green, may benefit from a darker wash, which will produce similar shading effects. Where a suggestion of dirt is required, we can choose brown washes, again tailoring the shade to suit the underlying colour, to determine how noticeable the effects will be.

Washes can be applied in a variety of ways, depending on the desired outcome. A fine brush can be used to deposit small amounts of wash into key areas, such as panel seams. Alternatively, a larger brush can treat the whole surface, with cotton swabs used to remove the excess fluid and produce streaking effects.

The weathering process is also made easier when the chassis and bodywork can be treated separately.

A neutral weathering wash shade can be effective when brushed into panel seams or around raised details, enhancing the sense of relief without making the truck appear too dirty.

Washes are effective for a variety of tasks, but they seldom alter the sheen of a surface, unless applied in very heavy layers. Powdered dry pigments, however, create a matt finish, providing a welcome contrast to shiny bodywork. Great for recreating a dusty, grubby look, the pigments can also be mixed with paint to create textured finishes, making them a very versatile medium. Regular paints are also an essential resource for the weathering process, and a wide range of techniques featuring paints, washes and dry pigments will be featured and explained throughout the following chapters.

Weathering separate sections of a truck individually does, however, mean that there's a risk of creating contrasting effects, rather than a unified, overall finish. By being aware of this possibility, we can take a considered, restrained approach and check repeatedly that each section sits well beside its neighbour. Furthermore, once assembly is complete, we can add some final touches to help bring everything together.

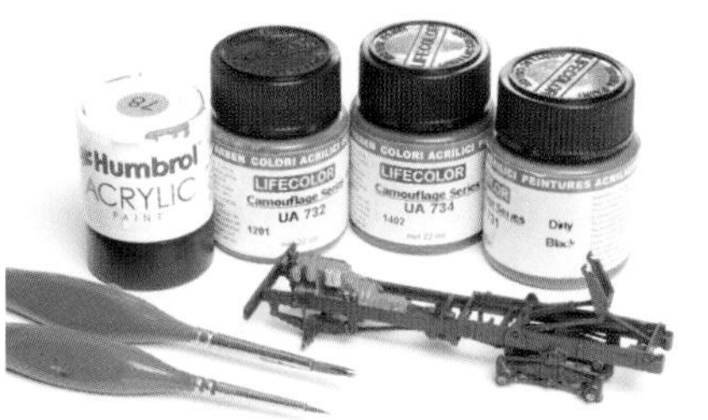

On smaller models in particular, I try to avoid applying regular black paint. Instead, a variety of 'shaded black' paints can be more effective. The Diamond T chassis has been hand-painted, using three different versions of black: Dirty Black, Worn Black and Vulcanized Rubber, all from the Lifecolor range.

The tyres were painted with Lifecolor's Tire Black, with the wheel hubs treated with Dirty Black.

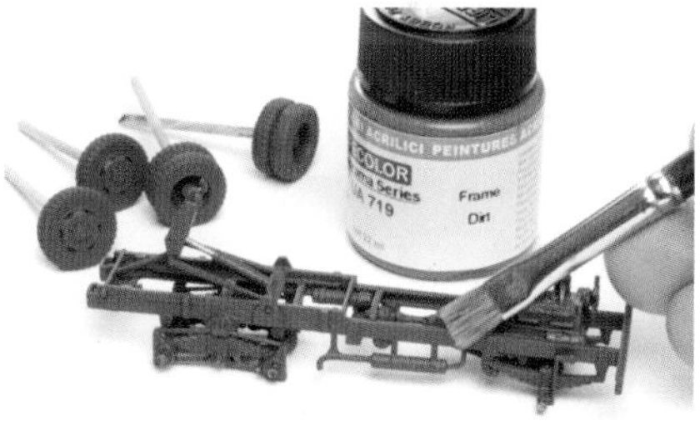

To add more tonal variety, the frames and wheels were dry-brushed with Lifecolor Frame Dirt, a generic dirty brown. Dry-brushing consists of wiping virtually all the paint off the brush on to tissue, then lightly rubbing the bristles over the model, depositing just the faintest hint of colour, usually on the edges and raised surfaces only. A soft flat brush is best suited for this work.

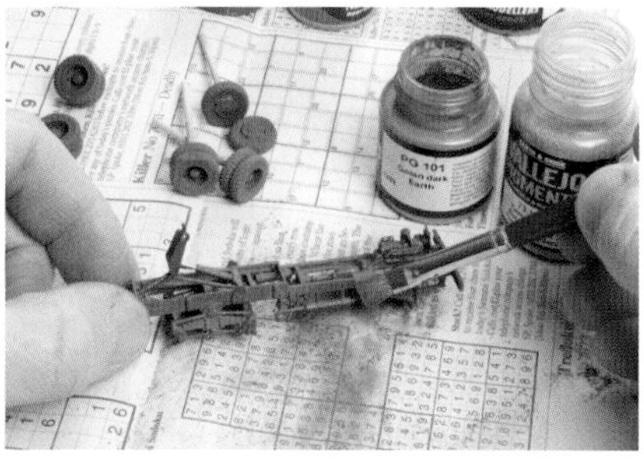

Once the paints had dried, a different range of effects was created with dry pigments. Various brown and dark grey shades were gently brushed over the frames, depositing a dusty, matt effect. This can get messy, so protect your work surface with newspaper. Dry pigments adhere best to matt surfaces.

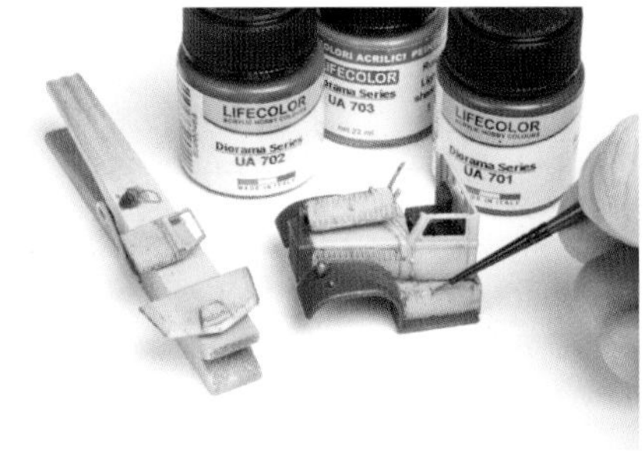

The dumper's pale blue bodywork was painted with a Tamiya aerosol, with the wings, grille, interior and small details painted by hand. After a coat of satin varnish, the weathering began. Following treatment with washes and dry pigments, corrosion effects were created with rust-coloured acrylic paints, applied with a super-fine brush.

The rust deposits were then manipulated slightly with a clean brush dipped in Tamiya acrylic thinners, creating fine streaking effects.

Slightly different streaking effects can be created by manipulating the rust marks with a flat brush dipped in the acrylic thinners.

Lifecolor's Tensocrom paints are essentially weathering washes in acrylic form. They dry slightly translucent and are great for portraying spills and stains, such as around the fuel-tank filler caps. This Oil shade dries to a slightly greasy-looking sheen.

A light application of dry pigments gave the running boards and fenders a suitably dusty sheen.

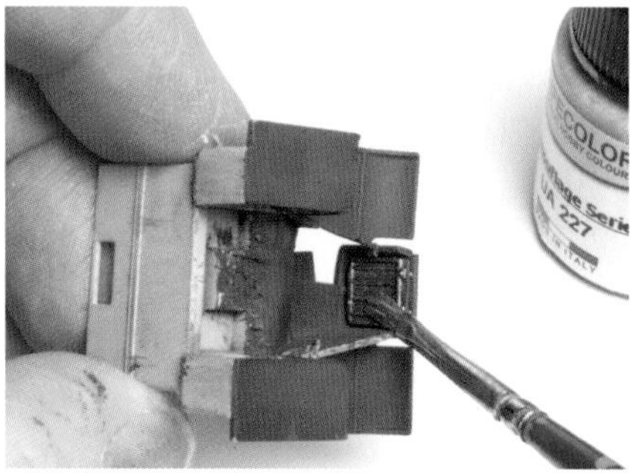

Dry pigments were used extensively on the bonnet interior and the underside of the cab and dumper body. The radiator grille was dry-brushed with grey paint to highlight the relief in the moulding.

The dumper body was treated in much the same way as the cab, with general washes applied prior to the rust effects, although I made sure that a greater amount of grime was retained on the bodywork, both inside and out. The interior floor was painted by hand, using a variety of rusty red and brown shades, layered gradually with a flat brush. All of the strokes followed the line of gravity on the raised body. Following the use of dry pigments to give a dusty aspect, the surface was dry-brushed with just a trace of a metallic silver shade, which imparted a burnished metallic sheen.

SMALL-SCALE FUN

Both of these 1:72-scale projects proved to be enjoyable, each offering a variety of challenges and rewards. The differing design approaches of the two manufacturers – and the different eras that the moulds derive from – was fascinating. The different instruction formats were also revealing, with ICM's 1990s-era ZiL-131 supplied with a single sheet of folded A4 paper, adorned with a handful of exploded diagrams. Meanwhile the twenty-first-century heritage of IBG Models' Diamond T was confirmed by the twelve-page instruction booklet, with clear, computer-rendered step-by-step diagrams.

Opening up the bonnet of the Diamond T dumper proved to be great fun, and I now wish that I'd added some extra details, such as pipes and cables. There's no reason why I can't do that in future, mind you, and I'm certainly looking forward to building a quarry diorama on which to pose the finished truck.

IBG's kit proved to be one of the most complex 1:72-scale trucks I've assembled thus far.

Modifying the bonnet and posing one of the cab doors open was justified by the amount of detail on show. The truck should prove to be an eye-catching addition to a future diorama project.

The provision of separate parts to allow the dumper body to be raised was a welcome feature of this kit, along with the facility to pose the rear flap open.

CHAPTER FOUR

ON CIVVY STREET: DEMOBBING TAMIYA'S 1:48-SCALE OPEL BLITZ

The previous chapter illustrated the potential of the latest kits in 1:72 scale, but if you want something a little bigger, the modest range of 1:48 trucks may be worth considering. Sometimes referred to as 'quarter scale', 1:48 works out at ¼in to 1ft, and it also matches the US version of 'O'-gauge model railroads (the UK version of 'O' is 1:43.5 scale). It has a pleasing sense of proportion, allowing more detail to be incorporated without things feeling overly complex. The scale has also become increasingly popular with aircraft modellers, again due to the detailing possibilities over 1:72 and 1:76, without the prospect of completed models taking up too much space.

To complement the large range of 1:48 aircraft, kit makers have launched an array of military-themed support vehicles that can be readily altered to portray civilian or demobbed trucks. Tamiya, and more recently Airfix, have some very attractive, high-specification kits that require a varying degree of modification work to render them suitable for 'Civvy Street'. Indeed, some key World War II-era vehicles were based either on civilian platforms or were adapted to non-military use at the end of hostilities. For instance, the Opel Blitz may have been a favoured vehicle of the German military and its allies, but it was also prevalent in civilian use during and after the war. Due to its ubiquity in World War II, countless kits of the Opel Blitz have been released by numerous manufacturers, in various scales. Indeed, it offers a prime candidate for a post-war civilian conversion and forms the subject of this chapter.

There are some great truck kits to be found in 1:48 scale, particularly from Tamiya, while a few Airfix releases from recent years have been impressive. Although military themed, these kits can be readily converted to civilian condition.

At the heart of this German 3-ton cargo truck (aka the Opel Blitz) lies an attractive vehicle with elegant lines. Tamiya's kit offers great value.

Alas, there is only a very limited choice of exclusively non-military truck kits in 1:48 these days. However, back in the 1950s and 1960s, Revell launched a large range of road vehicles for the US market in 1:48, capturing the iconic pick-up trucks and tractor units of the day, both in civilian and military guises. Many of these moulds still exist, with some being recently acquired by Atlantis Models (see Useful Contacts), who are reproducing them as 'retro kits' in attractive packaging and with modern-grade decals. I haven't tried one myself, but the kits look to have great potential for a fun build or a super-detailing project, so I really ought to give them a try.

BLITZING THE OPEL

Tamiya has built a well-earned reputation for producing high quality models across the scales and modelling disciplines. It's no surprise, therefore, to find the parts in this 1:48-scale kit to be exquisitely rendered. Despite the fearsome associations of any World War II German military vehicle, the Opel Blitz is actually a very handsome truck with an elegant bonnet and cab design, while the curved wheel arches are surprisingly refined for a wartime utility vehicle. A little research revealed that post-war civilian versions did not look too dissimilar, albeit on a superficial level, so I made a quick list of the tasks required to 'demob' the kit's parts.

The most obvious alterations consisted of removing the tool mounting brackets from the front wings, along with the fuel-can brackets. I also trimmed away the mounting point for the triangular towing indicator on the cab roof, and the moulded windscreen wipers, as these would be repositioned at the top of the frame. The kit provides a choice of head-lamps, allowing wartime blackout shrouds to be installed or a pair of regular clear lenses, so I naturally opted for the latter.

I entertained the idea of portraying a split windscreen, which appears to have been a feature of civilian Opel trucks of the era. Once I realized how simple a modification it would be, with no need to alter the kit parts, I decided to go ahead with it. The central pillar would be created from a 1mm-wide strip of 10thou' brass strip, installed over the windscreen at the very end of the build.

It's a cliché to state that a kit 'builds itself', but that is partially true with Tamiya's products. The parts required very little tidying up before assembly, while a small but visually significant improvement was made by drilling out the nozzle of the exhaust pipe with a 0.5mm drill bit. This was a delicate task, as the plastic pipe can be easily broken, but clamping it securely and working patiently with sharp tools ensured success.

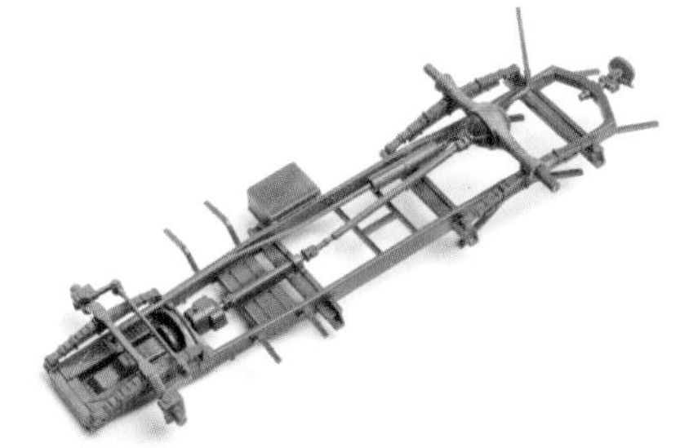

The kit features a single moulding for the main chassis framework, with the springs, axles, driveshaft and other smaller details slotting into place. As usual with Tamiya, the parts are crisply moulded, with just the minimum of fettling work required.

A trifling job, but one that makes a big difference, is to drill out the end of the exhaust outlet. Mark the centre of the nozzle with a sharp pin, and the indentation will guide the drill bit. Holding the part in a mini vice will protect the part from damage. I used a 0.5mm bit and bored the hole gradually, down to a depth of about 4mm (0.16in).

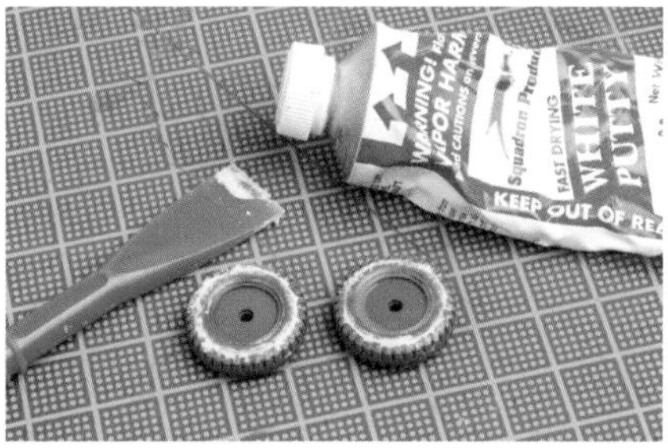

The wheels and tyres are moulded in two halves, with a seam within the inner face of the tyres. While the parts met neatly enough, it was still worth filling the joint with putty to ensure the joint would be seamless.

Having smoothed the tyre faces, a slight flat spot was formed on the base of each tyre to suggest a weighted effect. An attempt was made to ensure the flat spots were consistent across all wheels (except the spare!).

With the wheels temporarily fitted, the chassis was placed on a sheet of glass to test for alignment and consistency in the tyres' flat spots. The support framework for the load bed has been installed.

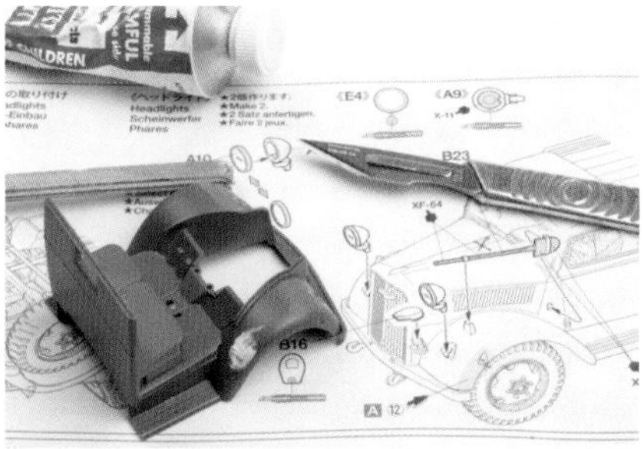

Part of the conversion to civilian use consisted of removing the tool mounting points on the front wings, filling the recesses with putty, and sanding smooth. I also flattened the hinge brackets on the cab roof for the warning triangle, and omitted the fuel-can brackets from the chassis.

To enhance the rear bodywork, a profile cutter tool was drawn along the recessed panel lines in order to deepen the seams slightly and make them more distinct. Apply only light pressure on the tool and pull it towards you gently, using a steel rule to help guide the blade if necessary. One or two cuts per seam will suffice.

After treating all the seams on the floor, sides and ends (inside and outside), the planks were scoured with a miniature brass wire brush, moving it longitudinally along the planks to create a texture similar to wood grain.

The shallow raised beading at the end was cut away and a flat extension piece created from 30-thou' plastic sheet. Plank and grain detail was scored with the profile cutter and wire brush before strapping was added with thin styrene strip.

ADDING TEXTURE

The area that received the most attention was the rear bodywork, in an effort to portray wooden components more effectively. Plastic kit parts can often appear too perfect, especially when they're moulded to such a high standard, as they lack the requisite texture of bare and painted timber. Trying to replicate wood with paint alone is difficult, and as we move up through the scales, compensating for a lack of surface texture becomes ever more important.

With this in mind, I used Tamiya's profile cutting tool to enhance the definition of the various planks, while a miniature brass wire brush scored a convincing grain effect into the plastic surfaces. This didn't take long to achieve, treating each part before assembly, and after cleaning away the debris, the body was assembled as per the instructions. The fruits of our labour will only be appreciated later, following the painting and weathering stages, but rest assured, it is well worth the effort.

Having cut away the shallow, wraparound coping at the front of the rear body, an extension panel was fabricated from a scrap of 30thou' plastic card. The profile cutter was employed to carve plank seams on both sides, with the wire brush adding the grain texture, as before. Strengthening straps were added from thin styrene strip.

PRIMING AND PRE-SHADING

Now that the various sub-assemblies were ready for painting, the chassis received a coat of Mr Surfacer black primer; the bodywork was treated to a grey priming coat instead. This helped to identify a few areas of the cab where the surfaces required filling and tidying before work could continue. An overall pre-shading undercoat of matt black was then airbrushed over the wheels and rear body, taking the time to ensure that the paint settled into the recesses and plank seams consistently.

The cab and doors, on the other hand, received the black paint in more specific areas, concentrating the pigment in recessed areas and around the edges of panels or raised beading – basically, everywhere that would logically boast a shaded appearance on the real thing. In contrast, those areas where highlights would appear – the centre of the roof, doors, wings and bonnet panels – were avoided, allowing the light grey primer to show through. This pre-shading approach can be hugely effective for creating a more nuanced paint finish, and removes much of the need for weathering *after* the topcoats have been applied.

A modicum of airbrushing experience is required, along with a good quality airbrush with a fine nozzle (such as 0.3mm diameter). The paint needs to be free-flowing and the air pressure set low (around 10psi or lower) in order to target key areas without causing runs or puddles. I used Mr Hobby's Mr Color lacquer-based paint for this, as it dries very quickly and has excellent flow characteristics when thinned correctly, thus making the task a little easier. If you're trying this technique for the first time, why not try the overall black undercoat approach to begin with, as you'll gain an understanding of how the process works when you come to apply the topcoats.

After cleaning, the main sub-assemblies were ready for priming. I treated the bodywork with a light grey primer, to help identify any blemishes. A few areas of the cab and bonnet needed attention, with Mr Surfacer 500 being brushed into the gaps and sanded smooth when dry.

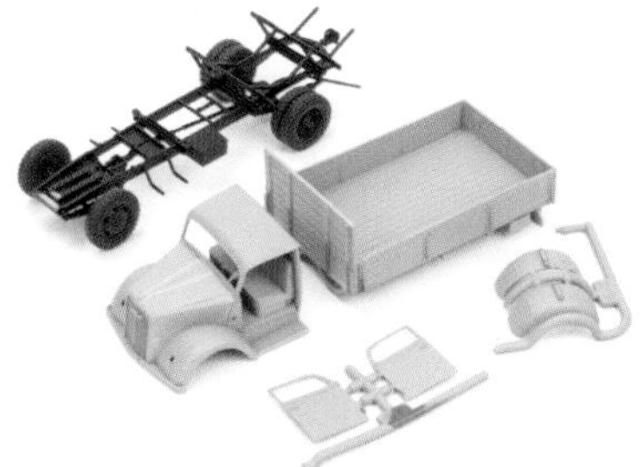

Further primer coats were sprayed on, and more checks made, before proceeding.

A pre-shading undercoat of matt black was airbrushed over the entire bodywork, as well as the wheels. The cab received a more targeted approach, leaving the grey primer showing through on areas of the roof, bonnet, wings and doors.

The red livery was also applied by airbrush, again working at a low air pressure to allow the tool to operate at close proximity. The paint is simply misted over the parts, working very patiently, so that the colour builds up slowly without obliterating the darker shading beneath. There is endless scope for customizing the finish, depending on the degree of shading required; keeping the nozzle perpendicular – rather than following the model's contours – will ensure a greater contrast with the darker recesses. The gradual application also allows the lighter areas to be tailored to your tastes, building up more of the topcoat colour in these areas to achieve greater opacity.

We can take things further and add a drop of white or light grey to the paint to treat highlight areas, but that can often be a step too far in smaller scales such as this. But experimentation is key: it is far easier to play around with the concept, working out for yourself what works and what doesn't, than trying to explain it on the page!

What is clear is how effective this approach can be for adding greater depth to the subtle panel seams and ventilation grilles of the bonnet. The combination of the earlier scribing and the pre-shading undercoat also brought extra definition to the planking on the rear body, avoiding the need to add a dark wash into the seams. The subtle shading that was retained around the raised strap and hinge detail also proved effective, and achieving the effect in this fashion is quicker and easier than attempting to add it after painting the topcoats, especially with an airbrush.

The red topcoat was then airbrushed on in light, misted coats, with little effort made to work the paint into recessed areas, as would normally be the case. This approach allows the black undercoat to show through, creating a shading effect. Where the pre-shading had not been applied, such as the centre of the cab roof, doors and wings, these areas appear lighter in comparison, thus providing an authentic array of tonality.

Both stages of the pre-shading process demand full control over the flow of paint from the airbrush, allowing it to be targeted into small, recessed areas without pooling or flooding. When adding the topcoats, allow each layer to dry for a few minutes to gauge the degree of shading more accurately; paint always looks different when wet.

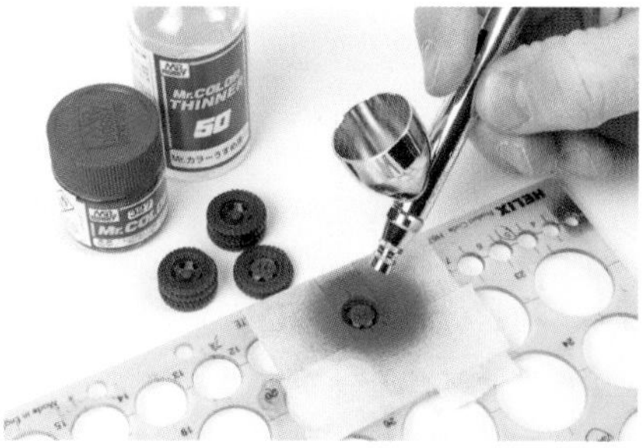

Circle stencils provide a simple means of masking tyres while painting wheel rims. A small amount of paint will inevitably bleed under the stencil, so I choose the circle that is slightly smaller than the rim, and mask off the adjacent apertures. Ideally the airbrush should be held perpendicular to the stencil to minimize the amount of paint that creeps under the mask.

While the bodywork dried, the chassis was weathered with a mix of dry pigment, which adhered readily to the matt paints applied to the frames and details.

A brush with stiffer bristles will create different effects, scouring the surface slightly and leaving behind a burnished aspect, which is perfect for wheel rims, mechanical components and the chassis framing.

TIMBER EFFECTS

With the red paint applied satisfactorily, the next task was to portray the bare timber of the rear load bed. Working over the black undercoat, we can limit the paint to the faces of the planks, thus maintaining the dark seams. Our aim is to layer several different paint shades in order to attain a random, natural pattern. A small flat brush is essential, and I find that acrylic paints are best, as they can be painted over within minutes and drying times accelerated with a hair dryer, whereas enamels require several hours before recoating is possible.

With a selection of brown and grey paints ready to hand, the brush is loaded and most of the paint wiped on to a piece of tissue before addressing the model. The brush is then run lightly over the surface, following the length of the planks so as to impart a distinct series of strokes to match the prevailing grain

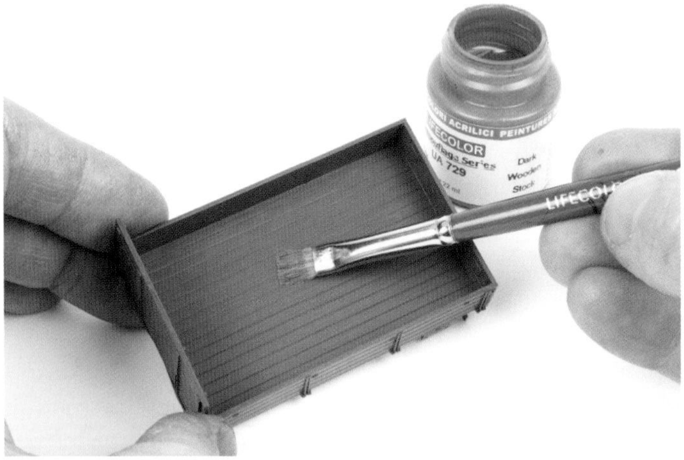

Working over a black undercoat, the timber decking was painted by hand, building up numerous layers of different brown and grey shades of acrylic. A small flat brush is best, with most of the paint removed on to tissue before stroking it along the length of the planks.

Successive layers of paint are built up in this way, always moving the brush in line with the likely grain direction of each area of planking. Only minimal paint is applied with each stroke, harnessing the bristles to impart a hint of grain texture. Allow each layer to dry for a few minutes before continuing, or use a hair dryer to speed things up.

direction. By repeating this process, using a varying array of shades and allowing each application to become touch dry, the surface will soon come to life. Yet again, this is a technique that rewards patience as it is easy to apply too much paint too soon, without imparting any suggestion of wood grain. Furthermore, the slight texture that we imparted into the plastic before assembly will come to our aid, helping to capture a less uniform pattern of pigment from the brush.

When the planks reach a point where their appearance is convincing, allow the surface to dry for a good six hours before applying a dark enamel wash to reinstate the shading within the planks, if necessary. Later applications of dry pigments and/or airbrushed weathering will add the finishing touches.

A dusty appearance can be created with dry pigments, working them into the corners with a brush and dusting away the excess.

The bodywork and chassis were enhanced with careful dry-brushing of a mid-grey shade. Virtually all the paint was removed from the bristles on to a piece of tissue before it was lightly run over the model. Any raised projections or texture will intercept traces of colour, thus enhancing the surface relief and highlighting the subtle grain texture imparted into the plastic with the wire brush before assembly.

To complement the subtle pre-shading effects, a thin weathering wash was run into the bonnet and door seam with a fine brush.

Dry pigments gave the cab interior a more lived-in appearance, especially the floor area.

DETAILING WORK

Tamiya's kit may not have a particularly large parts count, but it does provide plenty of fine detail straight from the box. However, I did decide to add a few extra items, including a set of mud-flaps cut from flexible metal foil. These were shaped to suggest a rickety appearance in order to give them a little more character. As the material is soft and pliable, I waited until the end of the project before fixing them in position, to avoid them being damaged or deformed. As the kit provides all-terrain tyres, the presence of the ramshackle flaps heightens the suggestion that this truck regularly sees service on rough ground, perhaps in a deeply rural setting. This pretence was further confirmed by stippling deposits of 'mud' (a mix of acrylic paint and dry pigments) on to the interior of the wheel arches.

An etched metal set of replacement windscreen wipers was installed at the top of the windscreen, taken from a 1:87-scale pack from the Automobilia range (see Useful Contacts), which, despite the scale discrepancy, happen to fit perfectly. Before these were fixed in position, a 1mm-wide strip of 10thou' brass strip was fixed to the windscreen to act as a central column.

Other detailing work involved the creation of a suitable payload. Tamiya's kit provided a few oil-drums, sacks and rolled sheeting, but they were accompanied by a couple of wooden packing crates, courtesy of a 1:35-scale set from Mini Art. The pack provides crates (in kit form) in a range of shapes and sizes, with a few of the smaller units looking well suited to this smaller scale. The parts feature a subtle timber-grain texture, so painting and weathering was a straightforward affair, using a similar technique to that employed earlier for the bare wood decking.

A set of mud-flaps was cut from a sheet of thin, flexible metal foil (from The Small Shop). The material was scrunched slightly to give it a little texture and character.

The foil flaps were painted and weathered in situ, with a mix of acrylic paints and pigments assembled over several layers to depict an accumulation of mud and grime.

As we neared the end of the assembly process, a final layer of dry pigments was brushed around the chassis and bodywork in an effort to blend the various sub-assemblies together. Apart from a smattering of dust along the lower edges, the cab was kept fairly clean.

A piece of 1mm wide, 10thou'-thick brass strip allowed the split windscreen to be recreated, being installed after the glazing had been fitted. A new pair of etched metal wipers were obtained from a 1:87-scale set from the Automobilia range of detailing components.

The wipers were fixed into small holes drilled above the windscreen beading, and secured with glazing adhesive.

Although aimed at 1:35 scale modellers, this set of packing crates from Mini Art includes boxes that are suitable for 1:48 trucks. After assembly, the crates were painted and weathered, along with the oil-drums and rolled sheeting supplied with the Tamiya kit.

FIRST, BUT NOT THE LAST

Marking my first foray into 1:48-scale trucks, the Tamiya Opel Blitz proved to be a highly rewarding project. Indeed, the finished results surpassed my expectations, creating an attractive vehicle that conjures up images of a hardworking truck belonging to a commercial haulier, operating somewhere in rural Germany in the early 1950s.

The proportions of this scale proved to be satisfying, allowing some fine extra details to be added with little fuss. There's clearly room to take things further, such as adding securing ropes to the oil-drums and designs to the cab interior. Tamiya's kit, like most in this scale, also provided a driver figure. Despite being clad in a military uniform, a little carving could have altered his appearance sufficiently to resemble a civilian driver. With a few more 1:48 kits on my shelf awaiting building, I'm tempted to take the detailing work further next time.

The packing crates look perfectly at home when loaded into the truck, proving that items from kits in one scale might also be suitable for use in another scale.

Close scrutiny reveals how effective the early preparation work on the plastic components was. A discernible grain effect is visible on the planked sides, highlighted by the various weathering processes.

Along with the tones and textures imparted during the assembly and finishing stages, the simple act of drilling out the end of the exhaust pipe adds greater realism. The shabby mud-flaps also look convincing.

Shorn of its military accoutrements, this civilian Opel truck now carries a more friendly appearance.

Tamiya's kits are always a pleasure to build, and with just a few simple tweaks, I've managed to create something a little different.

CHAPTER FIVE

POST-WAR WORKHORSE: ICM'S 1:35-SCALE MAGIRUS DEUTZ

Keeping with the theme of German wartime multi-purpose trucks, this foray into 1:35 scale features another kit from ICM. I'm only an occasional dabbler in this scale, despite its immense popularity with military and aviation enthusiasts, nevertheless ICM's range of 1:35-scale post-war European and Soviet trucks has consistently caught my attention over the past decade.

ICM's 1:35-scale truck kits can be great fun to build, with plenty of detail and parts that fit together well. Happily, for my interests at least, the Ukrainian firm offers a good variety of non-military vehicles.

Designed and manufactured in the Ukraine, ICM's 1:35 range includes some amazing examples of road vehicles, tanks, aircraft, figures and diorama accessories. Most of the recent releases that I've built have featured plenty of finely rendered parts that need minimal fettling before assembly. The kit featured here, a Deutz Magirus S330, impressed me so much that I went out and bought four more of them!

Aside from the endless choice of available kits, 1:35 scale offers manifold benefits. The subjects are of a size that can incorporate plenty of fine detail as standard, with full engine, transmission and cab interior renderings common. Finished models are not too cumbersome, either. Moreover assembly, painting and weathering can be a little easier compared to smaller-scale kits. That said, there is more opportunity to go that bit further with the detailing and weathering, so potential ease of assembly is often offset by an urge to try more complex techniques.

Parts counts are usually high, so modellers inevitably get plenty of plastic for their money, and kits can often be seen as an investment in terms of time and effort – they are not usually the type of kits that can be built in a couple of evenings. There's also a burgeoning range of after-market detail kits, providing resin and/or etched metal parts to refine certain elements, or to offer modellers the chance to perform conversion work. After building my first two Magirus kits, a couple of etched-brass upgrade kits appeared from the Polish detail specialists, Part (distributed by Jadar-Model – *see* Useful Contacts), one of which includes replacement parts for the bonnet, allowing the panels to be posed open.

MAGIRUS DEUTZ DESIGN

Unlike the Opel Blitz featured in the previous chapter, this ICM kit portrays a civilian vehicle straight from the box, with no need for any conversion work. The military heritage is still visible, however, with many spare parts in the box from previous iterations aimed at military enthusiasts. Of the various 3-ton general-purpose trucks built for the Wehrmacht, the Klöckner-Humboldt-Deutz (KHD) S330/S3000 was one of the most numerous. After the war, production restarted in 1948 under the Magirus brand, following a similar design but with civilian use in mind. A water-cooled 4-cylinder Deutz diesel engine was installed, with later models also offering an air-cooled version. Production continued until 1951, and like the Opel Blitz, they were handsome trucks, especially when stripped of the drab military façade.

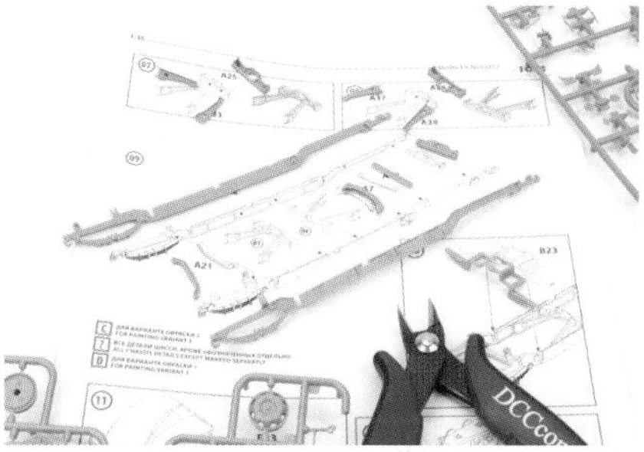

Having cut the chassis components from their sprue, they were laid out beside their respective locations in the instructions. This helped me to remember which piece was which.

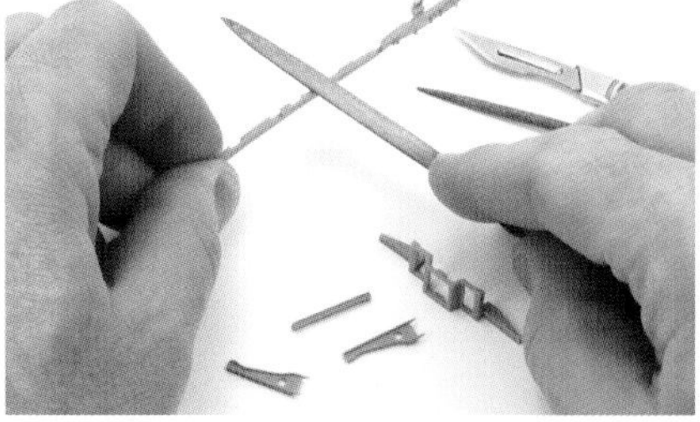

Generally the parts require minimal tidying up, save for flattening the sprue-gate stubs and any mould seams.

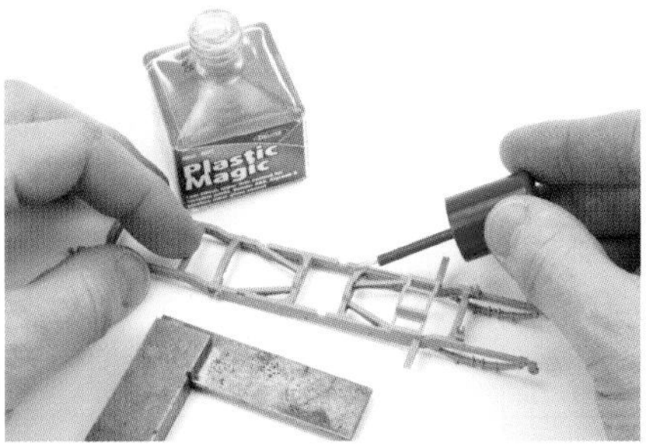

Erecting the frames was easy, although working on a flat surface is important. The cross-members slot into the side frames, and repeated checks were made to ensure that everything was square and true. After adding the last piece and double checking everything, the chassis was allowed to cure overnight, and developed into a surprisingly rigid structure.

The model's chassis is made up from separate side frames and various cross-members, each part slotting together neatly and combining to create an impressively rigid structure. Understandably, it's important to ensure that the frames are square and true, by working on a flat surface and checking that the parts are sitting at right angles to each other. Adding the axles and wheels comes later, so we can't rely on them to tell us if the chassis is level or twisted. Instead, a patient approach and a keen eye will have to suffice.

The rear axle and differential casing are rendered in two halves, which, thankfully, align positively. They were clamped tight while the cement was applied. When dry, the surfaces were abraded to create a seamless joint.

The front axle is fixed, but we can pose the model with the wheels steered by dipping one end at a time into hot water and bending gently. I used water from a kettle, which had been allowed to cool from boiling point for a minute or so, and the plastic was then submerged for 10 to 20sec at a time.

Remember that the outer axle (in this case the left-hand axle) ought to be angled slightly more acutely than the inner stub. Test the appearance by adding the wheels temporarily. When happy, the steering arm can also be bent before installation. Be careful, however, as this part is very fragile and easily broken.

The rear axle comes in two halves that meet up faithfully, and clamping pressure from clothes-pegs is enough to hold them still while the cement cures. Then the faint joint seams can be abraded smooth. Such an approach is necessary across a number of sub-assemblies, many of which can be primed, painted and even weathered before installation. Moreover, this is something that becomes more prevalent as we move up the scales.

The front axle is fixed, but with a minor intervention it can be modified so as to pose the truck with the wheels steered to one side. Immersion in hot water and gentle twisting will shift the axle stubs. The steering arm also needs to be modified, which needs to be done carefully, as the component is very delicate.

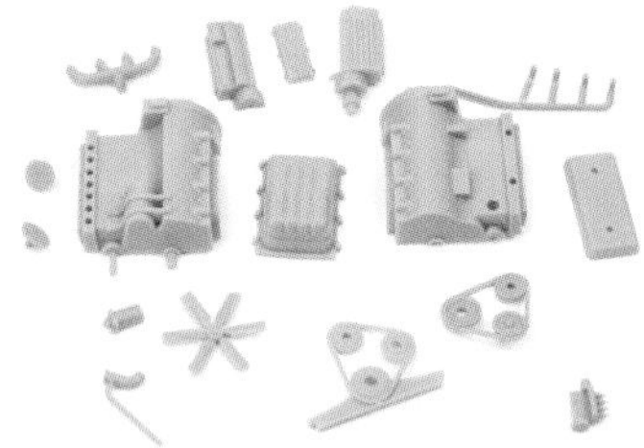

The comprehensive engine and gearbox are like a kit within a kit.

Assembled in no time, the powerplant can be treated as a separate sub-assembly from this point, allowing it to be painted, detailed and weathered independently. The cylindrical fuel tank also fits together nicely, and any visible joints can be hidden with some light abrading.

The tyres are acceptable, but there are pronounced seams along the tread faces that need to be rubbed away with a coarse sanding stick. The tread pattern is not very deep, so a gentle approach is needed.

The tyres form the 'meat' in the sandwich, with the wheel rims assembled around the vinyl mouldings. A slow-setting poly-cement was employed here, brushed on to the faces before they were pushed together. Alternatively, the rims can be painted beforehand and the bonds made with cyano glue.

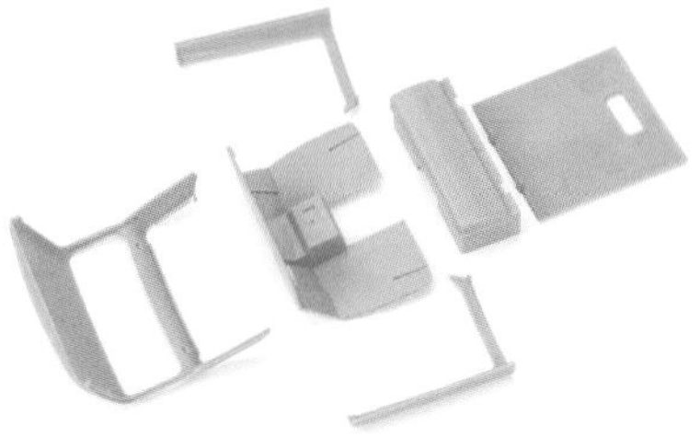

The cab is formed from a number of elements, which have to be aligned with care, especially the L-shaped side panels.

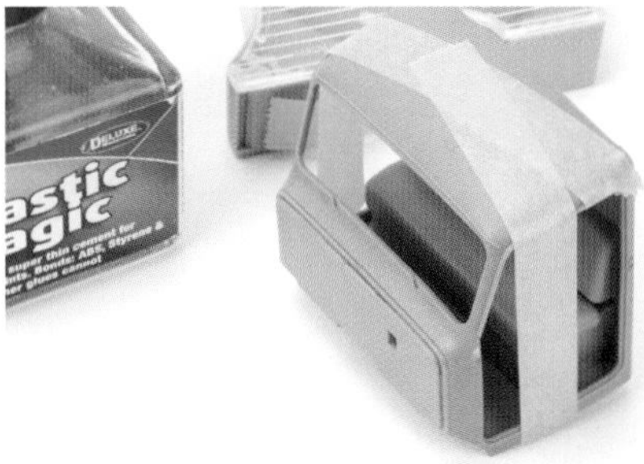

The dashboard and interior fittings should be fitted before the cab shell is sealed up. When you are sure that all the parts are aligned, clamp the assembly with masking tape while the cement dries.

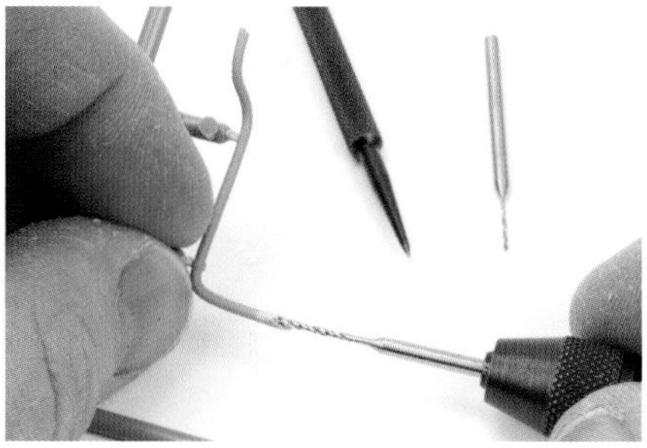

Opening out the exhaust nozzle is always worthwhile, but the angled end made it a tricky prospect. After marking the centre with a fine scriber, the hole was bored gradually, using successively larger drill bits.

The nozzle rim didn't escape totally unscathed, but a little work with Plastic Magic took care of it.

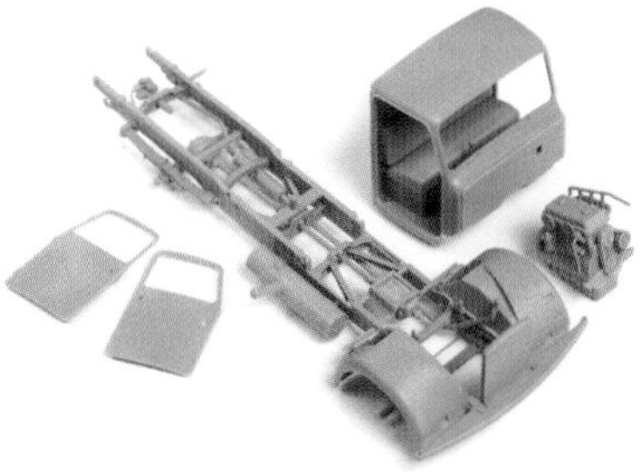

With the chassis, engine, cab and doors assembled, they could be cleaned and made ready for painting.

A full engine and gearbox are provided, made up of over a dozen separate parts. It's a very purposeful little powerplant, with a detailed radiator fan and drivebelts, and is crying out for a little extra work to add the finishing touches. Drilling holes and shaping various diameters of wire to form fuel injector pipes and electrical cabling doesn't take too much time, but it pays large dividends in terms of realism and reward. In fact it can be addictive, and I soon found myself adding extra details to the bulkhead too, crafted from scraps of plastic rod and strip, and connected with wire and occasionally a guitar string.

PAINTING AND WEATHERING

The pre-shading approach was used extensively on this project, employing either an overall or targeted coat of black undercoat to create a greater range of tones within the topcoat colours, as well as bringing attention to the plentiful surface detail. The topcoat colour was misted over the surface in very light coats, thus maintaining greater control over the process, building up opacity in the desired areas, especially around the cab and bonnet bodywork. While it felt laborious at times, especially when working on numerous sub-assemblies – big and small – it did cut down on the need for precise airbrush-applied weathering later.

When happy with the appearance of the topcoats, clear gloss was applied, which gave a deeper lustre to the

After a universal coat of grey primer, a matt black pre-shading undercoat was airbrushed over everything, leaving parts of the cab roof and rear with patches of grey showing through.

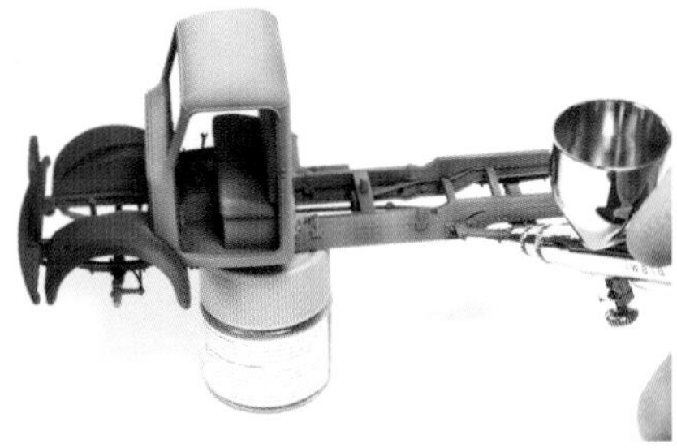

The light topcoat colour was then airbrushed over the frames and bodywork in light layers, allowing the dark shading to persist in key areas.

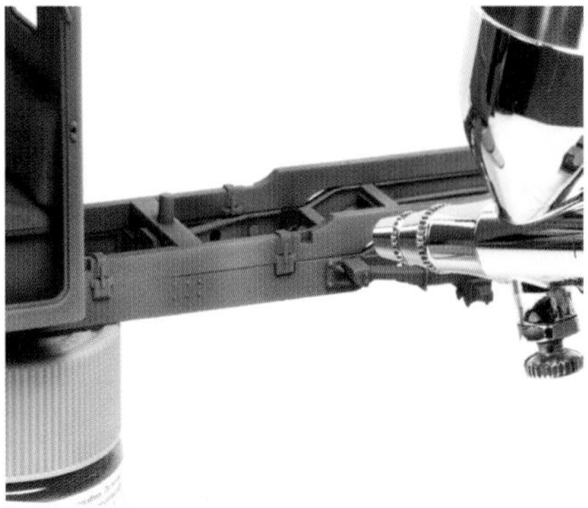

The colour was built up gradually, and targeted to create fuller opacity in certain areas, to bring highlights that contrast nicely with the shading.

After a few coats of clear gloss, enamel weathering washes were applied, allowing the pigment to settle within the frames; any excess was swabbed away.

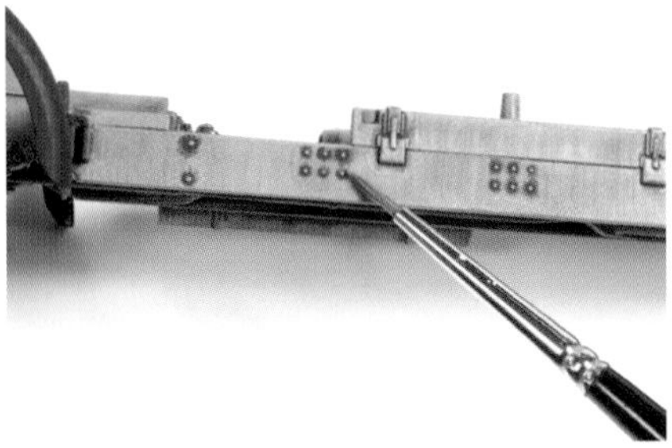

The washes were built up in layers, with deeper deposits applied around raised bolt-head detail and within deeper recesses.

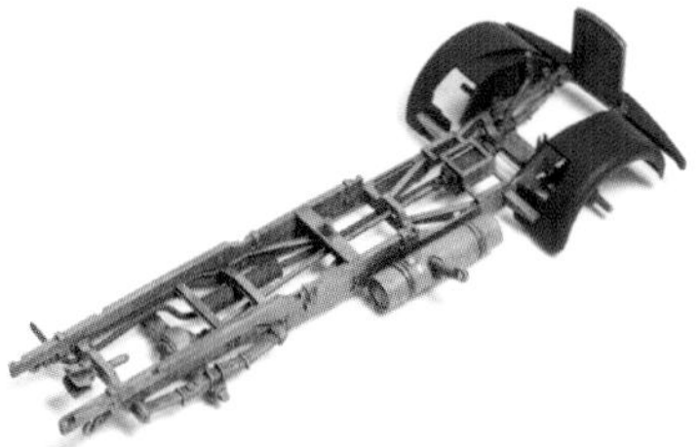

Building up the wash layers does take time, but they bring so much extra relief and realism to the chassis.

Having built a few of these trucks, I found that treating the cab separately made life much easier, installing it only once the wash stages were complete.

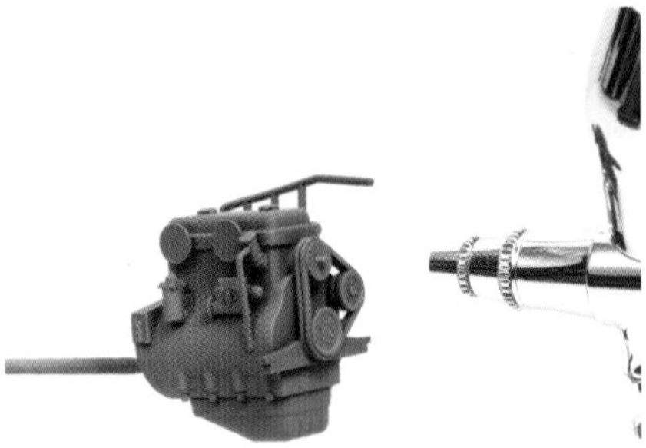

The engine block was mounted on to a wooden cocktail stick and airbrushed with a mid-green shade of acrylic, again allowing the black undercoat to bring a welcome degree of shading. After picking out certain details with appropriate colours, clear gloss coats followed.

Fine nickel wire was shaped and fixed into holes drilled into the engine block, injector unit and fuel pump. With a lack of reference images, I made some semi-educated guesses about what should go where.

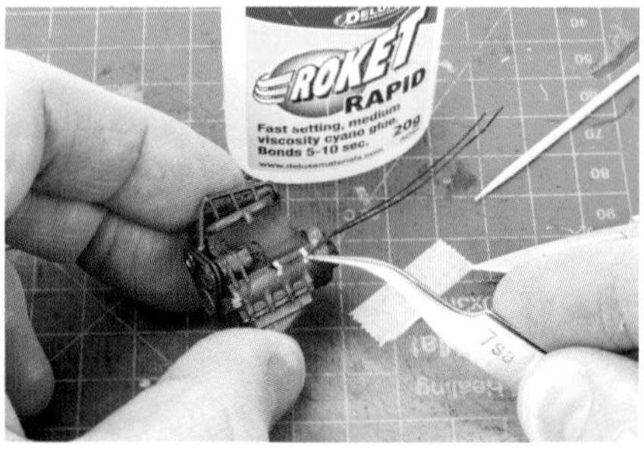

Black-coated nickel wire was added to the alternator, and cable clips were improvised with thin strips of masking tape, secured with cyano glue. The tape was then painted to blend with the surface.

Successive layers of enamel washes were applied, with the aim of creating a grimy, oily diesel unit.

Dry-brushing with AKI True Metal shades enhanced the fine detail and gave the surfaces a much more authentic appearance.

The finished engine does look rather careworn, but the extra pipework gives it a greater sense of purpose.

The oily sheen and texture of the engine block turned out well, while the dry-brushed metallic shades have highlighted the impressive level of relief.

Before installing the engine I improvised some extra equipment for the bulkhead, using scraps of plastic rod and strip, linked together with wire and a wound steel guitar string.

After painting and weathering the bulkhead, the engine could be slotted into place.

Dry-brushing added some highlights to the cab interior and suggested chipped paint and burnished steel from constant human interaction with the surfaces.

The cab floor also received a layer of dry pigments to provide a slightly dusty patina.

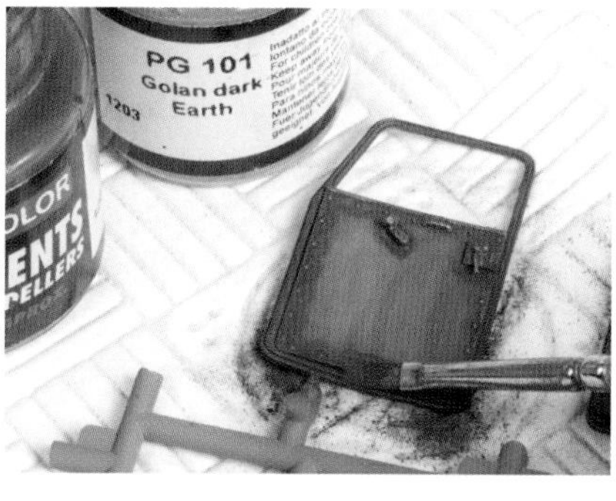

The inner cab door panels received similar treatment, with heavier deposits of wash and dry pigment around the edges. Dry-brushed metallic paint picked out the rivet heads and levers.

Layering the weathering always pays dividends. The bonnet sections began to look the part after a few coats of enamel washes, while the glossy paintwork beneath gave the panels a slightly oily sheen.

colour and softened the shading effect slightly. Enamel weathering washes followed, brushed liberally over the surfaces, then wiped away with swabs. This initial treatment brought greater definition to raised and recessed detail, especially the leaf springs, seams and bolt heads. When this had fully dried, more weathering wash was applied, but this time with a more targeted approach. Using a fine brush, the fluid was placed around the base of certain details and fittings, or within seams and recesses, and allowed to flow into position. Unless too much was applied, or the effect looked too severe – in which case, swabs came to the rescue – the washes were then left alone to dry without further manipulation. This increased the level of 'dirt' and shading in key areas, which again enhanced the surface relief considerably.

Once most of the sub-assemblies reached this stage, they were brought together, and where necessary, any paintwork or weathering was touched up after the bonds had cured. Further weathering followed, with dusty dry pigments creating a welcome contrast in sheen, especially around the wheel arches and within the cab. The spartan interior really benefited from the layers of washes and dry pigments, followed by dry-brushing to highlight surface edges and the detailed dashboard and controls.

Before the engine was installed, the bonnet interior was treated to several wash layers, using various dark and brown shades, along with a glossy 'oil and grease effect' formula. These washes were loosely stippled on to the interior surfaces and dabbed with swabs, rather than wiped, in order to create a more random pattern. Dry-brushing once again highlighted the relief of the scratch-built bulkhead detail in particular, resulting in a grimy but attractive engine compartment. With the powerplant installed and the pipes and cables tidied up, the overall effect was very pleasing.

GOING WITH THE GRAIN

By far the most time was spent on the rear bodywork, as I had a desire to recreate the look of unpainted, distressed timberwork, using a much more involved process than that employed on the Opel Blitz. Before assembly, a sharp, fine scriber tool was employed to engrave the grain texture into each individual plank, on the inside and outside of each component. If you're thinking that it would take forever, it did – or at least, it felt like an eternity. That said, I did anticipate the mind-numbing potential of this pursuit, and undertook the task in short bursts over a few days, usually while watching some trash on YouTube.

The hooked blade of Tamiya's profile cutter was drawn along each plank seam, using a steel rule to avoid wandering off course.

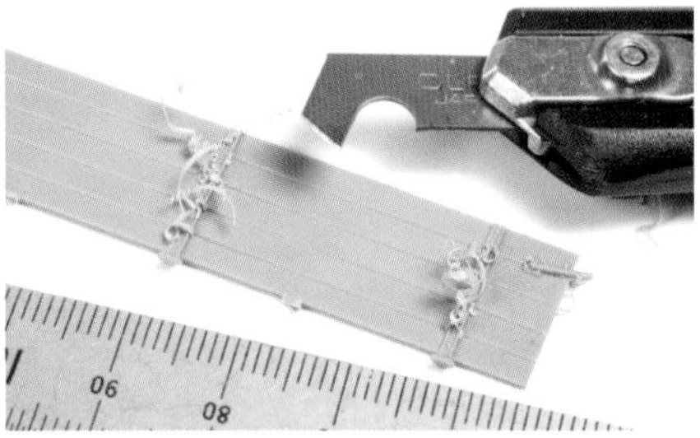

Only light pressure is needed if the blade is sharp, and care was taken not to damage the intersecting strap detail.

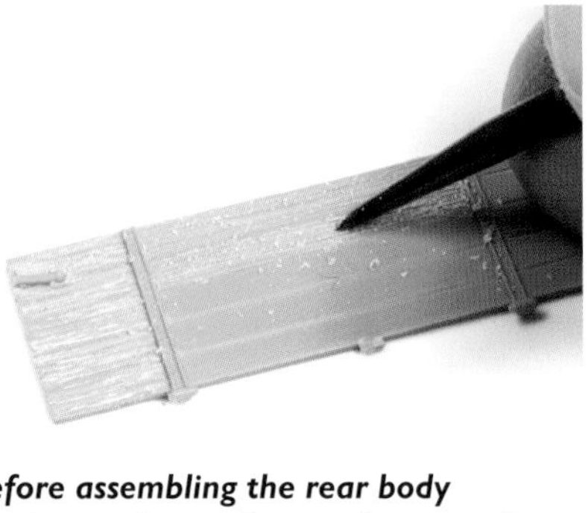

Before assembling the rear body sections, a fine scriber tool was used to engrave grain patterns into all the individual planks, on the interior and exterior faces.

The surfaces were then scrubbed with a small brass wire brush, working in harmony with the grain direction of the planks. This removed debris and imparted extra, more random grain texture.

The body could then be assembled according to the instructions. Unless the plank seams have been ploughed excessively, there should be no distortion of the parts, and everything should slot together nicely.

After priming, a base 'wood' shade was brushed over the bodywork, using a flat brush and following the direction of the planks with each stroke.

Using other shades in Lifecolor's Weathered Wood pack, a random array of tones was assembled, following the same procedure outlined in the previous chapter.

Greater definition was achieved with a coat of dark enamel wash, once the acrylics had dried completely. The pigment settled nicely into the recessed grain and plank seams.

Assembly of the truck could now continue, followed by some precision airbrush weathering to blend everything together.

Shading effects were airbrushed around the raised hinge and strap detail before glimpses of the livery colour were reinstated with the help of a simple stencil.

The stencil allowed the straps to be picked out accurately and with very little fuss.

The extra weathering work had resulted in parts of the bodywork appearing too flat, so the final sheen was tailored by airbrushing Alclad II's Light Sheen and Semi-Matte clear coats to various areas, keeping the spray away from the glazing as much as possible.

When the scriber had done its work, a profile cutter was drawn along the plank seams to deepen the recesses and enhance definition, before a small brass wire brush cleaned away debris and imparted some subtle, random grain detail. Take care with the profile cutter, especially if working on both sides of a component, as it's easy to weaken and distort the plastic. Just one or two light passes per seam should be plenty.

Once the bodywork had been assembled, priming and painting followed, using the same patient approach to the layering of almost dry-brushed coats of acrylic paints in longitudinal strokes, as showcased in the previous chapter. The greater surface texture of the distressed plastic makes the application of the paints much easier, and with subsequent layers of enamel washes and filters, pigments are readily retained within the recessed seams and grain.

ENDLESS POSSIBILITIES

The hand-scribed wood grain has added an eye-catching texture to the rear of the Magirus. The aim was to depict a humble and hardworking truck as it might have appeared in 1950s Germany, and I'm particularly pleased with the detailed engine and overall weathered finish.

With the number of unused parts left behind, there's plenty of scope for customization. Alternative bonnet parts are provided for an air-cooled version, and there's also a wartime-era radiator grille with Klöckner-Humboldt-Deutz lettering. A high-sided rear body is provided, complete with optional canvas roof rails, so the possibilities for demobbed or modified post-war variants are plentiful. It might have a business-like, utilitarian air about it, but I think this truck has some very attractive qualities, especially the rocketesque, stylized 'M' logo on the front grille. It's certainly a great kit to work with, with only the tyres being in need of an uplift, as the tread pattern is a little vague. Offering great value, superb detail, crisply moulded parts, clear instructions and endless potential for extra detailing – what more can you ask for?

Perhaps beauty is in the eye of the beholder, but I think the Magirus S330 is a handsome truck, helped by the stylish 'M' logo on the front grille.

The ICM kit was a joy to build, and the considered weathering work paid off with a convincingly grimy patina to the paintwork.

I was particularly pleased with the bare timber effects – which is just as well, considering how long the engraving work took!

Without the physical grain texture, recreating bare timber with paint alone is incredibly difficult.

Due to the fact that ICM offers a variety of trucks based on this common platform, there are plenty of spare bits in the box, allowing many variations to be constructed. This one is rather a hotchpotch of parts, my premise being that it has been repaired using earlier, wartime components, such as the original KHD grille.

CHAPTER SIX

UTILITY AND STYLE: MITSUBISHI CANTER IN 1:32 SCALE

I'd been meaning to try one of Fujimi's kits for some time, having heard many positive testimonials from modelling friends about this Japanese kit maker. A large range of road vehicles is available, including motorcycles and cars, as well as an interesting selection of diorama accessories. However, it was the attractive light-duty trucks that caught my eye, especially the ultra-stylish prototypes built predominantly for the Asian market in the 1960s and 1970s.

Not surprisingly, most of Fujimi's car kits are produced in the popular 1:24 scale, but many of the trucks are in the more diminutive 1:32. Once so common as to be referred to as 'standard scale', 1:32 offers the benefits of size and accessibility without the higher cost and intricacy of many 1:24/1:25 scale kits. Sharing the same scale as Gauge 1 railway models and Scalextrix slot cars, it has been especially popular with modellers in the USA and East Asia, as reflected by the range of kits offered by leading American and Japanese brands such as AMT, Esci, Monogram, Aoshima and Fujimi. Interestingly, many of the models aimed at the US market have been designed as snap-together kits, with the number of fiddly little parts kept to a minimum, making them especially suited to younger or less experienced modellers.

Some 1:24-scale trucks can appear huge when mounted on a display shelf, especially where long-wheelbase tractors or trailers are involved. In contrast, even the largest 1:32-scale trucks make a modest footprint, yet there's still plenty of scope for exterior and interior detailing work. Some excellent aircraft and building kits have been available in 1:32, along with a range of figures, from the likes of Airfix, Italeri, Eduard, Master Box, ICM and Tamiya.

Today there is minimal choice of European-outline trucks in 1:32 scale, yet fans of American and Australian vehicles can choose from a handful of Revell kits, featuring Peterbilt and Kenworth tractor units (*see* the following chapter), while rock music fans might like the special edition tour-truck packs, with trailers emblazoned with Kiss, Motorhead or AC/DC decals. In contrast, the market in Asia is rather more buoyant, with Fujimi and Aoshima offering a large range of excellent kits of medium and lightweight trucks and vans, depicting prototypes common across the southern hemisphere.

Looking outside the realm of plastic kits for a moment, 1:32 scale remains popular with manufacturers of ready-made die-cast and plastic models. The Siku and Britain ranges may be worth exploring, as their agricultural and plant vehicles offer plenty of potential for super-detailing and weathering projects, as well as offering suitable stablemates – and potential loads – for 1:32 kit-built trucks.

HOT TO TROT

It didn't take me long to find a suitable Fujimi kit, as I was quickly taken with the looks of the Mitsubishi Canter T200. The modest size and elegantly curved bodywork of the prototype immediately appealed. The Canter range of light-duty commercial vehicles first appeared in 1963, and the T200 was the third-generation version, appearing in the early 1970s.

An order was duly placed, and while I awaited the kit's arrival from Japan, I spent a little time researching the prototype online. Plenty of inspirational images were found, and these would eventually act as essential modelling references for a vehicle that I've never seen in the flesh. When the kit did arrive, I was instantly struck by the quality of the moulded components; there was very little flash and no tooling marks to be found, and the kit provides an excellent level of chassis and body detail, albeit without a full engine. The overall number of parts was fairly low, although this was reflected in the kit's price, making it a great value package.

Fujimi's 1:32-scale kit depicts the third generation of Mitsubishi's successful Canter, a versatile light-duty commercial vehicle platform.

BUILT AT A CANTER

Assembly of the kit progressed quickly, helped by the fact that the parts slotted together readily and with very little need for fettling. After just a few hours, the chassis and body sub-assemblies were ready for a straightforward paint. Although it's not an exact match to any prototype colour, Tamiya's AS-5 aerosol provided the attractive pale blue colour for the bodywork. Ultimately I was aiming for a faded, washed-out appearance, and this shade didn't look too dissimilar to images of a couple of real trucks I found online.

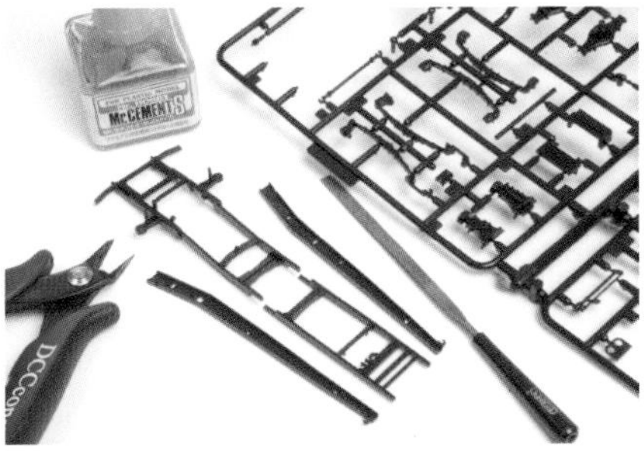

The main frames are rendered in two sections: front and rear. Side overlays help with alignment, and add rigidity to the chassis.

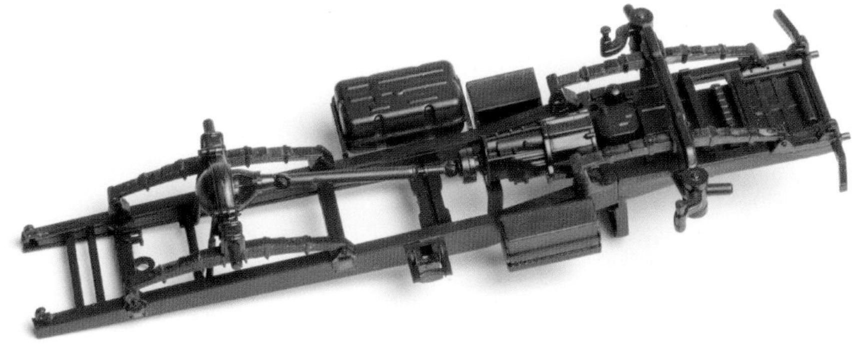

With minimal fettling required of the crisply moulded parts, assembly of the chassis was rapid.

Only the base of the engine is depicted, but the transmission and suspension components are impressive, while the chassis frames also boast some attractive detail relief.

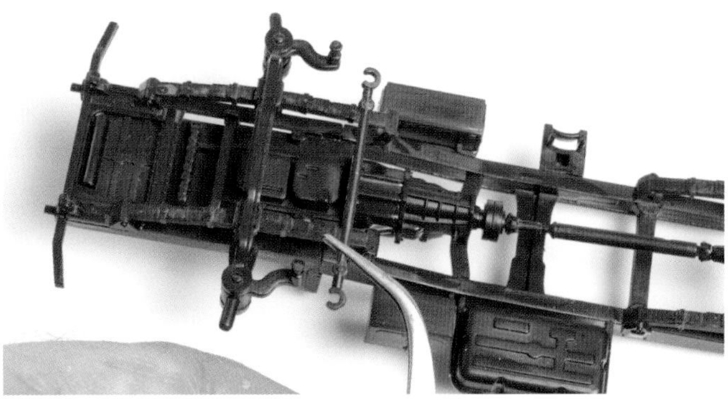

The steering connecting rod is designed to be a snap fit. However, the fit was very tight and I ended up breaking it: I should have fettled the inside of the cups beforehand.

The pivoting front axles took a little time to install, reaming out the holes slightly to ensure free play. After testing fit and alignment, the axle cross-member was fixed in position.

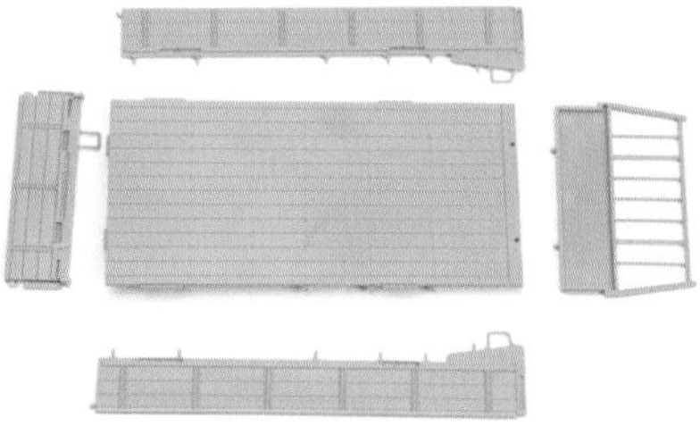

The rear body components were also exquisitely moulded.

Discreet tabs and slots are incorporated into the parts to aid alignment and add extra strength to the joints.

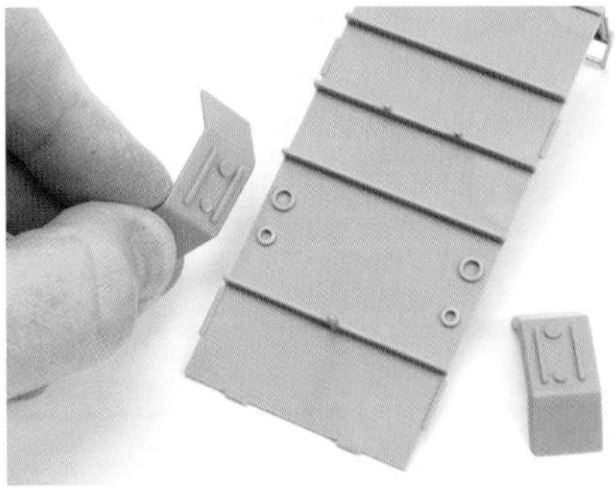

Helpful alignment aids are provided, including the mounts for the wheel arches, which prevent the parts being assembled incorrectly.

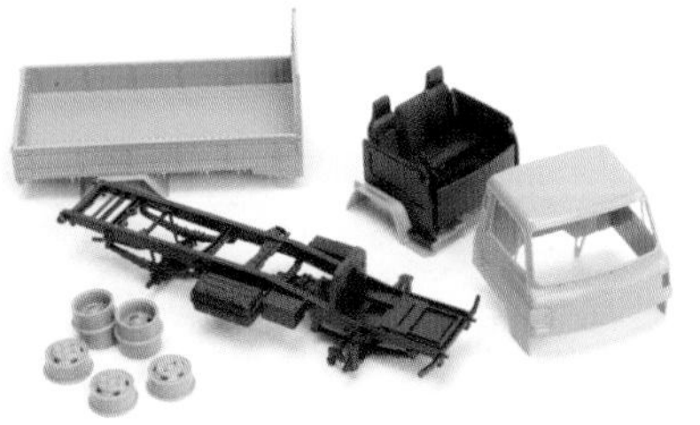

It took just an evening to get the various sub-assemblies ready for priming and painting.

Some detail work was required on the gearbox, chassis, interior and dashboard, along with a bare timber effect to the inside of the load area, but otherwise there wasn't much need for complex painting and finishing tasks. In fact far more time was spent on the truck's weathering than the assembly and painting stages combined. However, the kit's waterslide decals were a disappointment, being printed on a matt carrier film that is difficult to disguise, and some were prone to breaking up as they were slid from the backing paper. Reconstructing the decals proved a challenge, although some judicious weathering or touching in with a fine paintbrush managed to repair most of them satisfactorily.

The vinyl tyres are exquisitely rendered, with an impressive tread pattern and distinct Yokohama logos on the sidewalls. However, they carried significant traces of silicone from the moulding process and had to be scrubbed clean with hot water, detergent and a stiff brush before being fitted to the wheel rims. Once clean and dry, however, dry pigments had no problem adhering to the material. The vinyl really does look like rubber, especially after weathering, and Fujimi also provides a sheet of thin, flexible vinyl from which the front and rear mud-flaps can be cut. Full-size templates are included in the instructions, and Mitsubishi logos are provided on the decal sheet to finish them off (although I didn't bother with them). Once installed, they look fantastic.

AHEAD BY A NOSE

The front radiator grille, headlight clusters and fender are formed from several individual parts, each of which can be painted and weathered individually. The shiny, chrome-effect lamp bases are a great feature, giving the headlights and side lamps a realistic appearance without the need for any intervention on the modeller's part. The chrome

Once the basic top colour had been applied, the timber decking of the load bed was painted and weathered in the same manner as the Opel Blitz and Magirus trucks in previous chapters. While the brush strokes followed the longitudinal planks, the inside face of the bulkhead was treated with vertical strokes instead, as the real thing is lined with a sheet of plywood.

After a dark enamel wash was run into the recessed seams, various dry pigment shades added a welcome dusty texture to the interior, with darker tones creating shading in the corners and around the plank bolts.

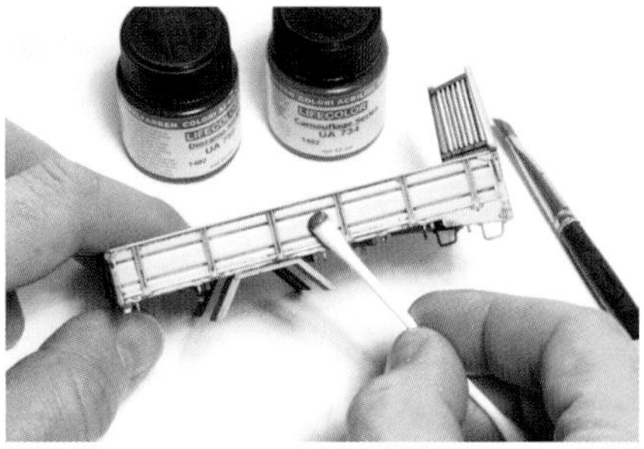

The exterior of the rear bodywork was treated to a wash coat of acrylic paints, mixed and thinned slightly before application. As usual, the excess was wiped away, leaving deposits within the panel seams and around the raised hinge detail.

Dry pigments, applied strategically with a fine brush, added a rusty, dusty patina to the hinges and strapwork. The pigment clung readily to the matt deposits left behind by the initial wash treatment.

After stippling the underside of the body and wheel arches with a couple of coats of dirty brown acrylic paint, a variety of dry pigments were brushed over the surface. Darker tones were worked around the edges of the framework to create a shading effect.

The cab body was weathered in a similar fashion, albeit with an aim for a slightly cleaner look. Stubborn deposits of the acrylic paint can be removed with Tamiya's acrylic thinners.

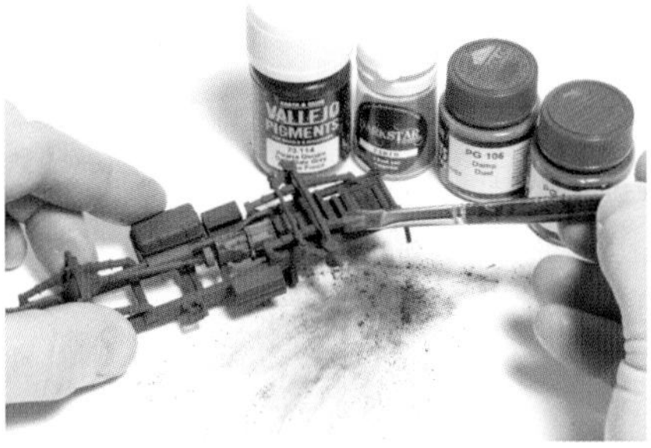

The painted chassis was dusted with a blend of dry pigments, the matt finish allowing the powders to adhere sufficiently, while any excess was brushed away. Varying the tones is important, to avoid a one-dimensional appearance.

More concentrated patches of corrosion were applied using AK Interactive's Rust Streaks enamel fluid. This can be built up over several layers to produce a pleasing, crusty appearance. It's also ideal for creating more delicate streaks, using a very fine brush.

Again, subtle patches of corrosion were added using the AK Interactive enamel wash, built up over two or three coats.

It's easy to bury the fine detail and contrasting colours of the chassis with the dry pigments, although brushing the surface with an old toothbrush will remove the excess while adding a convincing burnished appearance.

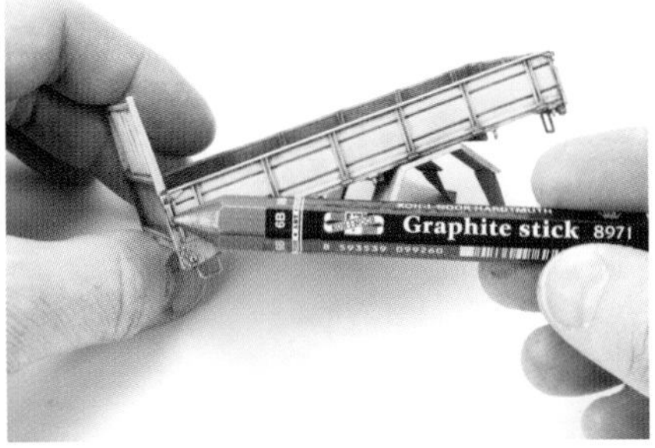

Finally, a burnished appearance was given to certain areas with a graphite stick, particularly the handles for the drop sides and end, along with the foot-steps and lashing hooks along the underside of the framework.

Tamiya's pointed swabs were useful for manipulating the rust streaks before the fluid dried. The tip of the swab can also be dabbed randomly on to the surface to suggest fainter deposits of rust.

The graphite stick was also deployed on the exhaust pipe and on other underframe surfaces to reinstate the wealth of detail relief. Running the edge of the tip against the edges of each component is enough to impart a metallic glint, which is highly effective.

After a thorough clean and degrease, the tyres were also treated with the same blend of dry pigments. The rims had already been prepared with weathering washes, in the same way as the bodywork.

The instructions include full-size templates for the front and rear mud-flaps, to be cut from the supplied sheet of rubber. Once secured with cyano glue, they were weathered with dry pigments to blend with their surroundings.

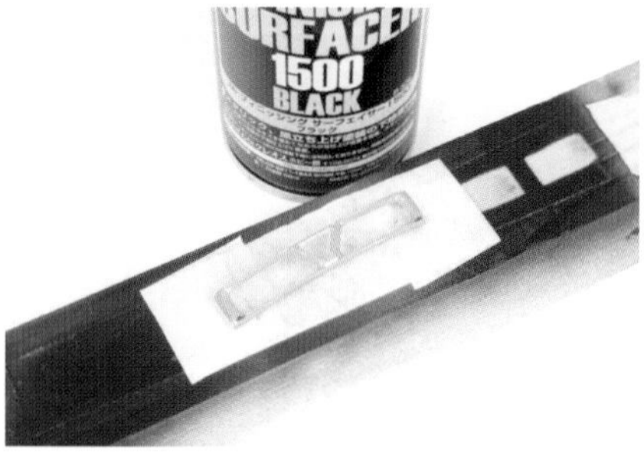

The chrome-effect front grille surround was deemed overly bright, and was lightly abraded to remove most of the shiny coating. When clean, it was sprayed with Mr Surfacer Black primer.

A coat of Tamiya silver paint created a more pleasing finish, and the various layers were weathered individually before being fixed together.

Following a dark enamel wash to add definition to the relief in the upholstery and dashboard, the cab interior was given a light dusting of dry pigments. Heavier deposits were added to the floor.

A quick on-line image search brought up a variety of Japanese newspaper, magazine and road-map covers. These were scaled down, printed and cut out, and then fixed inside the cab. Scrunching the paper slightly gives each item a realistically dog-eared aspect.

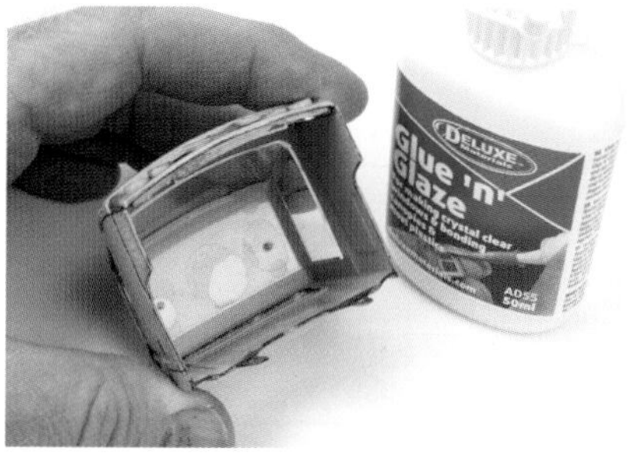

Glazing this truck was easy, thanks to the single-piece moulding for the windscreen and cab windows. The rear window is a separate unit that slots into place from the outside. No fettling was needed, as the clear parts were crisply rendered with an impressive level of transparency.

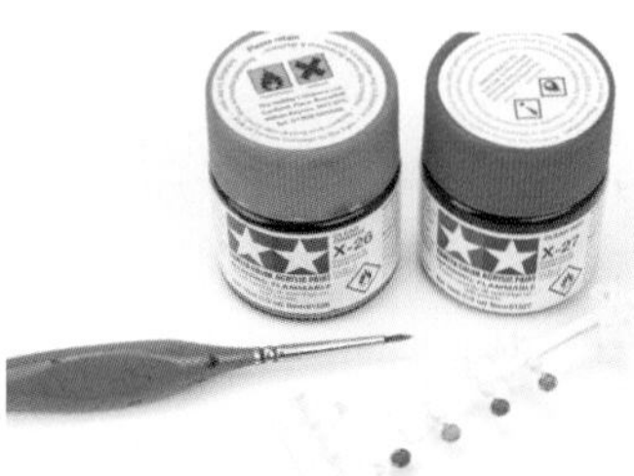

Tamiya Clear Orange and Clear Red acrylics were brushed on to the underside of the rear light lenses. Also, the orange segments of the front indicator/side-light lenses were treated in the same fashion. The lenses were secured with glazing adhesive.

finish is also applied to the top layer of the fender, but while the application is impressive, the part looked too glitzy for my work-worn truck. Initially I intended to simply rub the part with fine abrasives to diminish the shine slightly, but the chrome coating is so thin that the green plastic quickly showed through.

This wasn't a problem, however, and the part was duly rubbed down thoroughly and primed with Mr Surfacer Black, before receiving a coat of Tamiya AS-12 Bare Metal Silver, from an aerosol. The result was a subtle, slightly tarnished appearance that was perfect for my needs. I didn't bother applying a clear coat over the metallic paint, which is the conventional approach. Rather, I moved straight to adding a dark brown weathering wash, allowing the pigment to settle into the delicate profile and relief. Once all the layers had been sandwiched together and the unit fixed to the cab shell, the truck started to resemble the prototype.

ON THE HOME STRAIGHT

Final assembly of the completed sub-assemblies didn't take long, after the cab interior was given a suitably dusty outlook, and some interesting details were added, such as Japanese newspapers, road maps and paperwork. The kit's wipers and mirrors are all impressive, so I felt no need to try and improve them, and attention could then turn to creating a suitable load.

For the open load bed, Fujimi includes a number of sprues containing oil-drums and plastic crates. I opted for a quartet of the drums, and once they had been assembled, painted and weathered, they were glued together and covered with a homemade tarpaulin, crafted from a foil-backed paper biscuit wrapper. After wiping the wrapper clean with a damp cloth, it was scrunched into a tight ball and then flattened out again, revealing a wealth of texture on its surface, which the thin foil backing will retain. The paper was then trimmed and wrapped tightly over the load (foil side down), folding it over the corners and rubbing firmly so as to imprint the oil-drums' contours into the paper.

Ordinary printer-grade paper will suffice for this task, but it will lack the flexibility of the foil-backed material. This method can be employed to cover all manner of loads, from boxes and crates, to timber and steel, allowing the profile of the consignment to be seen through the tarpaulin. After diligent research,

Fujimi include a raft of oil-drums and plastic crates with which to create realistic loads for the Canter. I opted for the drums, building up the parts and smoothing the joint seams before priming. After painting and weathering, the motley quartet was glued together. I found a cast-resin sheet roll in my spares box (from Kit Form Services), but I also wanted to make my own tarpaulin, and a Tunnock's chocolate caramel wafer-bar wrapper provided the perfect material.

The foil-backed wrapper was scrunched up into a tight ball, and then flattened out again. The flexible paper took on a distinctive crumpled texture.

After trimming to the required size, the paper was wrapped tightly around the oil-drums, and the edges were folded over. Rubbing a fingertip over the surface will allow the profile of the drums to show through the sheeting. The wrapper can be secured with PVA or cyano glue.

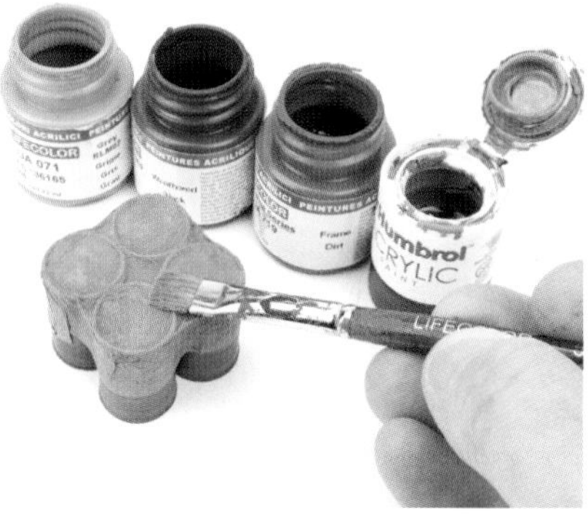

The tarpaulin can be painted in situ, with no need for priming. A blend of acrylic tones was employed to produce realistic shading and highlights. A final dry-brushed treatment of a lighter shade renders the paper's texture more visible.

Waterproof sheeting usually boasts a greasy sheen, and this was replicated with a light misting of clear gloss, sprayed with an airbrush. A subtle effect is desired, rather than a high level of shine.

I've found that the wrappers employed on Tunnock's chocolate caramel wafer biscuits (Scotland's finest!) are a superb resource for this task; the paper is just the right thickness, with the foil backing adding flexibility and resilience against tearing.

After trimming the paper to the desired size, allowing part of the drums to remain visible, the wrapper was secured to the load with a small amount of cyano adhesive, which also fixed the folded corners. When the glue had set, the paper was painted and weathered to mimic the look of a real tarpaulin, with a suitably greasy, grimy finish redolent of the hardwearing waterproof material. Various acrylic paints created the finish, applied by hand and working light and dark tones into key areas to create highlights and shading where appropriate. Dry-brushing with a much lighter shade will pick out the crumpled texture in the paper, creating an ultra-realistic appearance. Finally, a small amount of clear gloss was airbrushed over the sheet to give it the necessary sheen. Incidentally, this was one of only two instances when an airbrush was employed on this project.

Waxed cotton thread, as used for beading and jewellery work, was then

After fixing the load into the truck, extra ropes were added, secured with cyano glue and tensioned slightly at each stage, taking care not to put a strain on the plastic parts.

After securing the strips of timber, miniature leaves were fixed in piles around the load bed, using small drops of Glue 'n' Glaze. The resin rolled sheet was also installed, having been painted and weathered in the same way as the paper tarpaulin.

A smattering of Scatter Grip adhesive was brushed randomly on to the load deck. When it had turned tacky, dry sand was sprinkled over the top. After a few moments, the truck was upturned to remove the excess material.

A plastic toolbox and a variety of hand tools were assembled from a Tamiya 1:35-scale military diorama set.

Securing ropes were added using brown waxed-cotton thread, available from jewellery and craft stores. The 0.6mm-diameter cord is perhaps slightly overscale, but not by much. Small drops of cyano glue secure the ropes to the drums discreetly, allowing them to retain a level of tension.

Scraps of wooden coffee stirrers were broken roughly into small pieces and soaked in Weather All ageing fluid for about an hour.

The side mirrors and mounting stalks are extremely delicate, so they were installed at the end of proceedings.

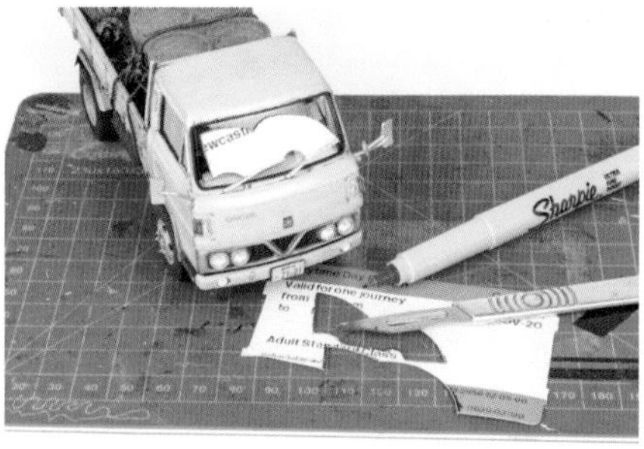

Wiper trails were created by cutting a template from thin card and placing it over the windscreen.

employed to act as a miniature rope. I only had a reel of 0.6mm thread to hand, which is probably slightly over-scale, but to my mind it doesn't look too incongruous. This thread is available from craft stores in a variety of colours, and has a close resemblance to real rope. The wax coating allows

A matt clear coat was then lightly airbrushed over the windscreen; this created a subtle dusty sheen around the edges of the wiper trails.

it to appear tensioned, with strategically placed drops of cyano glue holding everything taut, without putting undue strain on the plastic components. Furthermore, the cut ends are resistant to fraying.

To add further interest, a cast resin rolled tarpaulin was also painted, weathered and installed. This latter addition is actually billed as a 1:24-scale item, but there are no set dimensions for these items in real life, and it doesn't look out of place. A scattering of sand, scrap timber, autumn leaves and a loaded toolbox add the final touches.

A QUALITY KIT

Sometimes, when we've built up a level of anticipation about a kit, the reality can feel anticlimactic. However, this Fujimi kit didn't disappoint, providing a thoroughly enjoyable – and fairly quick – project. The truck's scale and subject matter has certainly added some variety to my truck collection, and I now can't wait to try a few more kits from the same stable.

The 1970s incarnation of the Mitsubishi Canter was a very handsome vehicle, and Fujimi's superb kit captures its character perfectly.

The sheeted drums and assorted detritus add plenty of visual interest to the load deck.

This kit provided a very enjoyable experience. I was particularly pleased with the weathering work, which was done almost exclusively by hand.

CHAPTER SEVEN

OPTIMUM TRANSFORMATION: IMPROVING REVELL'S 1:32-SCALE KENWORTH K100C AERODYNE

When I was a child in the 1980s, the animated television show *Transformers: Robots in Disguise* was very popular amongst my peers, and although I only watched it occasionally, I do recall that one of the principal characters, Optimus Prime, took on the form of a red Kenworth truck. I remember receiving one of the robots that transformed into a Lamborghini Countach for Christmas, but a school friend was lucky enough to have the more expensive Optimus Prime figure, which I couldn't help but covet at the time. Maybe that explains why the packaging of this Revell kit triggered a nostalgic response when I saw it on the shelf.

The iconic Kenworth K100 series of trucks has starred in a variety of 1970s and 1980s Hollywood films and US television series (including *BJ and the Bear*), so it's probably a familiar prototype for many readers of a certain age, whether or not they witnessed the real trucks on the highways of America. First launched in 1961, the K100 proved extremely popular in the USA, and the cab-over-engine layout was designed to squeeze as much haulage power and cargo within a restricted length.

Revell's 1:32-scale kit, which can be traced back to a Monogram release from 1981, depicts a K100C with the ground-breaking Aerodyne sleeper cab, a combination that was launched in 1976 and continued in production until 1984, when it was replaced by the K100E. The K100 series remained popular in the USA until the relaxation of length restrictions during the late 1980s, which led to long-bonnet trucks gaining a monopoly. K-series trucks also proved very popular in Australia, with a production facility being established near Melbourne in 1970, where trucks are still manufactured today.

A 1:25-scale Kenworth K100 has also been available in the Revell range since the early 1980s, both in original and Aerodyne format, but I was smitten by the low price of this 1:32 kit with its vibrant packaging. Aesthetics and cost aside, the low parts count should have given me prior warning of how basic the kit would be. Indeed, it was clearly designed as a snap-together affair for youngsters, despite the 3/5 difficulty rating printed on the box.

However, my aim is not to criticize this kit. In fact it proved to be a highly enjoyable project, although a substantial investment of time and effort was required to bring it up to a more acceptable level of realism. But I welcomed the challenge, and the many hours of super-detailing and scratch-building proved worthwhile.

Revell's 1:32 scale Kenworth Aerodyne is a cheap and cheerful product that depicts an iconic North American prototype.

HOW TO PROCEED?

The mission, which I freely chose to accept, was to see what could be done with a cheap and basic kit, in an unfamiliar scale, without spending too much on extra parts and materials. The existing parts would be retained and enhanced as much as possible, and any additions would be created mostly from 'stock' materials, such as styrene strip, rod and sheet.

Quite some time was spent in contemplation, wondering how best to proceed. The wheels and plastic tyres perplexed me initially: the rims and hubs weren't too bad, especially once the heavy 'chrome' paint had been stripped away (more of that shortly), but the tyres were hollow. And I mean hollow in a bad way, rather than a prototypical way. The tread patterns were also poor.

Having failed to devise a way to enhance the existing parts, I spent a few hours trawling the internet looking for likely replacements. Eventually I discovered that Fujimi offer various wheel and tyre sets as separate packages, so a few different sets were ordered direct from Japan. While I awaited their arrival, work began on the rest of the truck.

STARTING WORK

There's no shortage of prototype inspiration to be found on the internet, and I built up a dossier of images to help with this build. As is my usual preference when building models for my own enjoyment, I drew inspiration from a number of individual trucks, distilling the most interesting features of a dozen or so K100Cs of 1970s vintage into my model. Blue seems to have been a popular colour for owners and operators, so I decided early on that I'd follow suit, with the chassis frames to be finished in red.

First, however, I was faced with having to remove the chrome finish from all the parts on sprue E, including the fuel tanks, front fender and radiator cover, exhaust stacks and handrails. The coating appeared very uneven on this particular kit, being very thick in some areas but wafer thin in others. Coupled with the copious amounts of flash trapped beneath the chrome, the parts initially looked to be of dubious quality.

As I hadn't seen the replacement Fujimi wheels at this point, I also stripped the rims supplied with the kit, in case they would be needed after all. All the chromed parts were soaked in a bowl of household bleach, diluted slightly with water, and left in a safe place away from curious animals or children. Now and again I'd give them a poke with an old toothbrush to see if the coating was

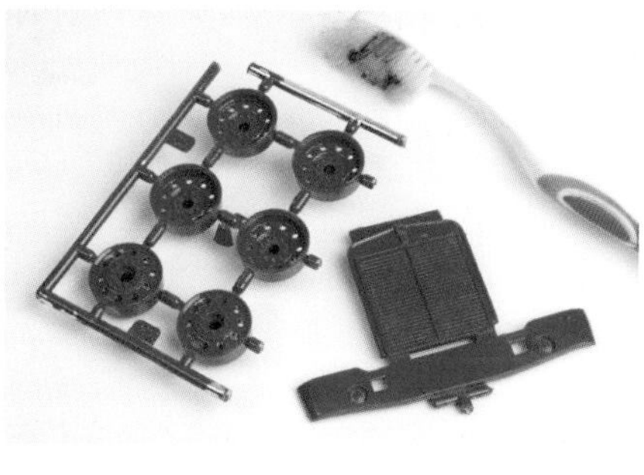

The first task was to remove the poor quality chrome-effect finish. After soaking the parts in a bowl of diluted bleach, they were scrubbed with an old toothbrush and a cream cleanser detergent. The fine abrasive particles within the detergent help to shift the remaining debris.

working loose, and after a few days, the bare red plastic began to show through.

With gloved hands and eye protection in place, the parts were scrubbed with a stiff-bristled brush to remove as much of the chrome finish as possible, followed by a thorough rinse in clean water. Any stubborn deposits that remained were dislodged with the tip of a scalpel blade or needle. There are more aggressive chemical agents that can be used for this task, but I was in no particular hurry and didn't want to risk damaging the plastic components, or my health.

Without the heavy chrome coating, and after clearing away the excess plastic, the various parts appeared much more refined than I'd expected, especially the horns, lights and radiator grille. Even the wheel rims weren't too bad. Thus I felt encouraged, and confident that this project would succeed.

THE CHASSIS FRAMES, SUSPENSION AND DRIVETRAIN

Countless hours were spent improving the spartan chassis frames, suspension and drivetrain. The parts might have been few in number, but they were all in need of significant work. Like the original plastic tyres, the axles and springs are moulded in hollow form, with the differential units being only half-formed. Plenty of Milliput epoxy putty was therefore mixed and sculpted to correct these shortcomings.

Although I tried to get the putty as smooth as possible before it cured, using damp swabs to help shape it, inevitably there was a need to file and sand the cured material to the required profile. Once that was done, the front leaf-spring detail was carved on to

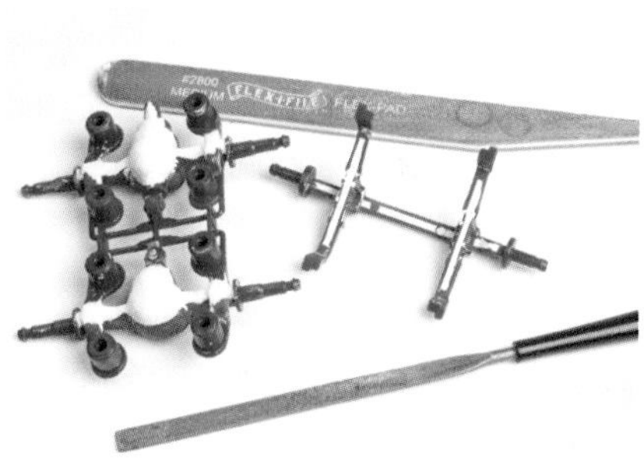

The axles and suspension units come as large, integral units, yet they're only moulded in half relief. Milliput epoxy putty was sculpted to fill the hollow channels and to complete the profiles of the differential casings and axles. When fully cured, the putty was tidied up with needle files and sanding sticks.

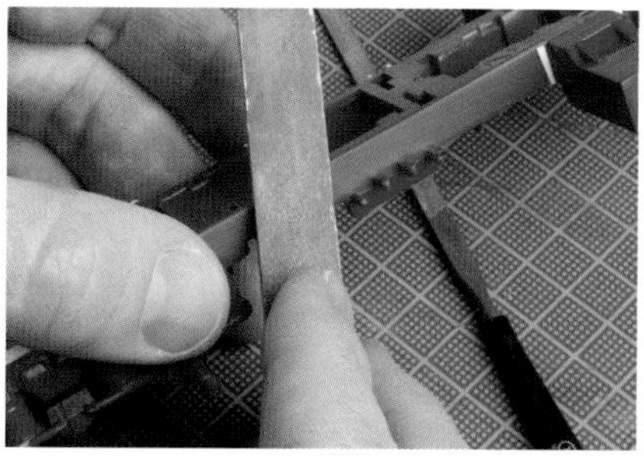

The single-piece chassis frame required a great deal of remedial work to remove moulding flaws. I also rounded over the outer edges of the main frame members with a file and sanding sticks.

the outer faces of the mouldings with a sharp scriber tool, albeit in a fairly rough fashion. Many of these parts will be barely visible once the truck is complete, but I decided that the effort invested here would be worthwhile.

An added bonus of the need for plenty of epoxy putty to fill out the underframe components was the fact that it gave the model some much needed ballast. With relatively few parts, the Kenworth is something of a featherweight model, although it did gain a more appropriate overall mass when the new rubber-tyred wheels were eventually installed.

IMPROVING THE REALISM

The underside of the single-piece chassis moulding features a rudimentary outline of an engine and gearbox, but very little else. After removing the many unsightly moulding marks, a more appropriate curved outline was given to the upper and lower edges of the side frames, taking away the sharp, square profile. Once the surfaces were smooth and free of tool marks, a plethora of individual hex nuts and washers was added. These were created from sheet styrene using punch-and-die sets from RP Toolz.

Punch-and-die sets are a worthy investment for any modeller who has ambitions of improving plastic kits. They work by clamping the styrene between two plates before a punch is driven through a guide hole using a small hammer. The shaped punch and die combine to form the styrene into round or hexagonal discs, which are ejected from the base of the tool. Each set offers a range of punch sizes, and although it can be a laborious task in some ways, it also has a certain therapeutic value.

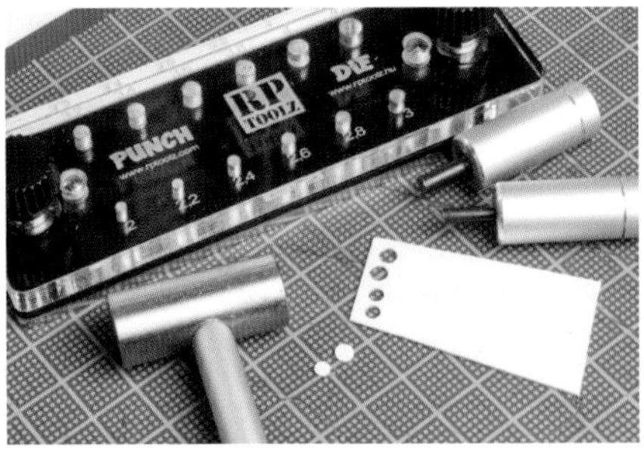

Circular punches are also useful, to create washers, tank filler caps, lamp lenses and countless other things. Various tools are available, offering a range of disc diameters.

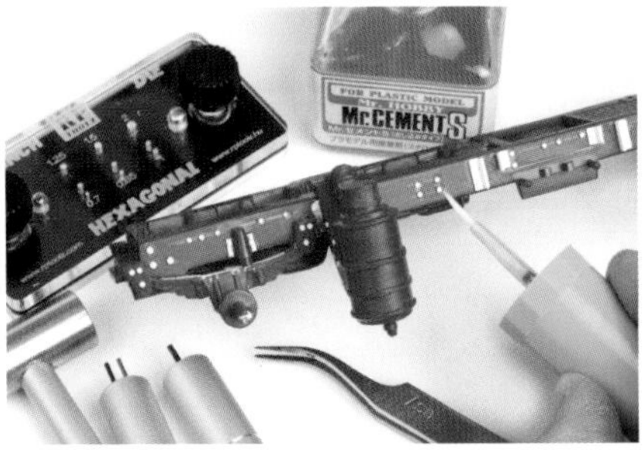

The punched details can be fixed to the surface with liquid poly-cement, applied with a fine brush. Alternatively, clear acrylic varnish is also effective. A variety of hex nuts were fixed in likely positions, where suspension or other equipment would be mounted.

Hexagonal punch tools are a great asset for super-detailers. Simply clamp a strip of plastic sheet inside the tool, and use the various size punches and mini hammer to knock out an endless supply of nut and bolt details.

The front leaf springs lacked relief, so I carved the individual layers on both sides of each component with a sharp scriber tool.

The punched discs and hex nuts were fixed to the chassis with thin liquid poly-cement, applied with a fine brush. Marking out their position with a pencil beforehand ensured that they were neatly aligned. It's a good idea to add a variety of nut and bolt-head sizes, chosen to reflect the nature of the parts they're supposed to be supporting (bigger nuts for heavier components). As well as being more prototypical, such an approach also adds visual interest.

On reflection, I think I may have chosen some slightly over-scale hex bolts for this 1:32 truck, but there's no denying the massive uplift in realism that they have brought to the barren frames. A little modeller's licence was taken in locating the fasteners, but I tried to make their positions look as authentic as possible, where cross-members and equipment mounting points would be. The engine sump, gearbox, propshaft, differential casings and suspension mounts were also treated to hex nuts and washers, while layers of plain discs added welcome relief to the air suspension units.

Styrene angle strip, of varying sizes, was employed to create mounting brackets for the air cleaner, fuel tanks, mudguards, front dampers and battery box, as well as for improving the fifth wheel mounting brackets. Punched hex nuts were then added to the brackets, which made them look even more realistic.

FIFTH WHEEL DETAILS

The original fifth wheel was to be retained, albeit with a revised pivot bracket and a release handle fashioned from brass wire. Meanwhile, considerable effort went into the fifth wheel's mounting area, with the upper edges of the chassis being cleared of the moulded clips and fitted out with various sizes of plastic angle and strip, plus bolt heads and washers, to mimic heavy-duty mounting brackets overhanging each side frame. A pair of slipper guides for the fifth wheel wedge pivot brackets were formed from a shallow styrene channel, before an adjusting mechanism was crafted from scraps of plastic rod and strip. Punched pivot bolts added extra relief, while a set of springs was improvised with short sections of a wound steel guitar string.

Online prototype research revealed a good deal of customization of fifth wheel mounting arrangements, but the images seldom told the full story, so I resorted to copying some of the visible elements and improvising the rest, to create something that I deemed convincing. This area was finished off with a pair of pronounced longitudinal weld seams, achieved by 'piping' acrylic putty through a syringe, in a manner akin to icing a cake.

IMPROVING THE FUEL TANKS

Even when the heavy chrome-effect finish was stripped and the parts were fettled, the halves of each fuel tank still didn't marry up particularly well. Part of the problem was the moulded locating pins, so these were cut away and the sections aligned carefully by eye. After applying cement, the tanks were clamped with masking tape and left to harden completely. Plenty of filling and sanding followed, to eradicate the joint seams – as they were to be given a new metallic finish, the surfaces needed to be as smooth as possible. Painting the tanks separately from the chassis meant that their cosmetic mounting brackets had to be aligned with the tanks temporarily in place, although care was needed to prevent the liquid cement from inadvertently fixing the tanks to the frames.

The tank mouldings are basic, so I added a set of retaining straps from 10×60thou' (0.3×1.5mm) styrene strip. These were cut roughly to length and

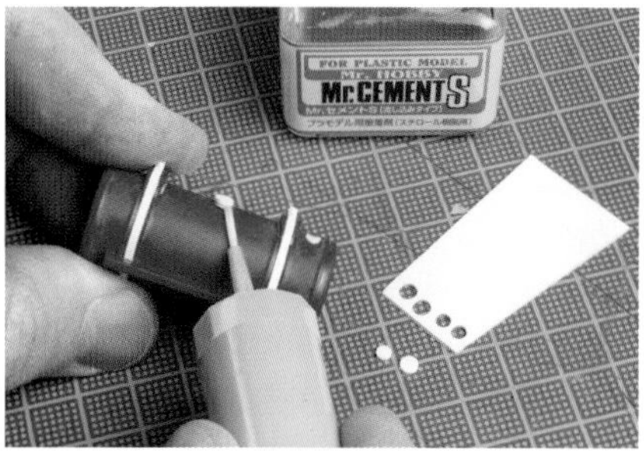

The straps were wrapped around the tanks and secured with liquid poly before being trimmed to length. Filler caps were formed from two punched plastic discs, one slightly larger than the other.

The halves of each fuel tank took some persuading to align correctly. After removing the locating pins, the mating faces were fettled and test-fitted until the parts sat together correctly. Masking tape held them together whilst gluing, and any gaps that did remain were treated with filler.

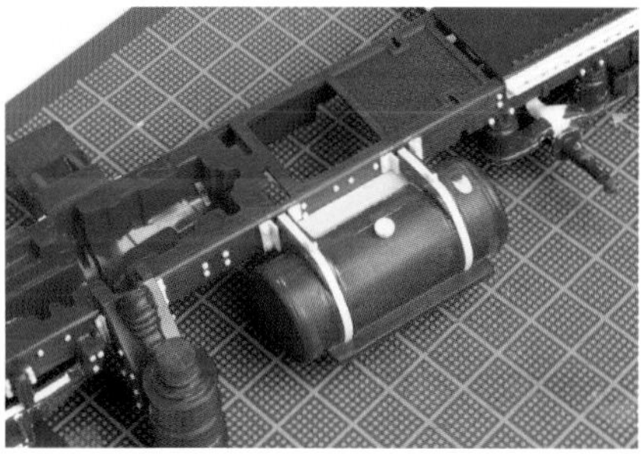

Using the tanks as a guide (but not fixing them to the frames yet), cosmetic mounting brackets were fabricated from plastic angle, adorned with more punched hex nuts.

To give the tanks more character, I made some retaining straps from 10×60thou' styrene strip, soaked in hot water for a few minutes before they were shaped with a thumbnail.

then curled gently with a thumbnail before being fixed into the moulded channels around the tank's circumference. The strip plastic can be prone to breaking, especially if it has been lying about in the workshop for a few years and has turned brittle. Soaking the styrene in hot water for a few minutes beforehand will significantly improve its flexibility. To enhance the straps further, I improvised some simple, cosmetic tensioning brackets from styrene angle, adorned with 1mm-diameter punched hex nuts and short tails of 0.9mm rod.

Many prototype images matched Revell's provision of a single horizontal step to each fuel tank, but a customized truck that proved particularly inspiring had extra steps. The same styrene channel used earlier on the fifth wheel mount was also utilized here, the steps being secured to the tank straps via small styrene brackets. Embossed chequer-plate sheet was cut and laid on each step. Once the new filler caps were formed from punched styrene discs, the tanks were ready for priming and painting. Incidentally, retaining straps were also added to the air-cleaner cylinder, using the same materials and approach.

The underside of the engine and gearbox were also improved with the addition of punched nut, bolt and washer detail. The open undersides of the battery box and air cleaner were covered with plastic sheet.

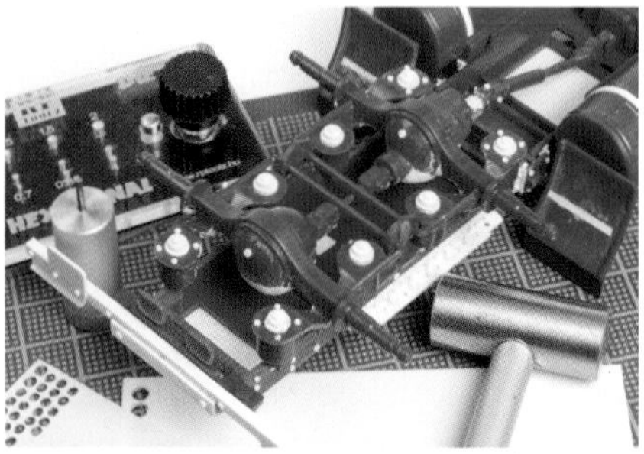

Oil drain plugs were added to the differential casings, and the air suspension units enhanced with punched discs and bolt heads. I initially crafted a tail-light boom, but this was subsequently removed. Having filled the hollow cavity on the inside faces, the forward driving axle's mudguards were installed, and a set of more convincing mounting brackets created.

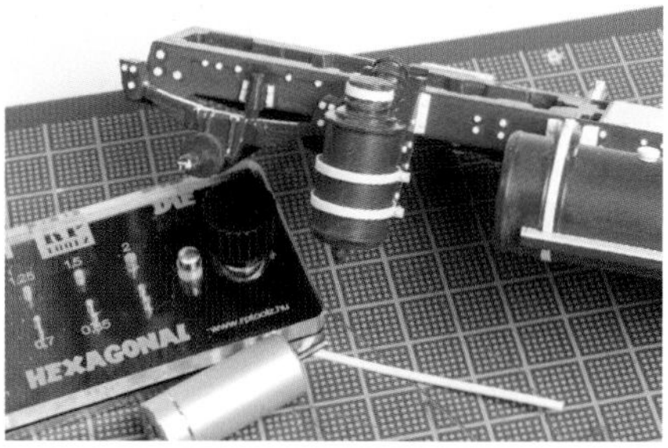

The air-cleaner cylinder received a set of superior retaining straps, shaped from 10×60thou' styrene after softening it in a bath of hot water.

TIDYING UP THE CHASSIS...

Embossed plastic sheet with a chequer tread pattern was added in separate panels to the top of the chassis frames, ahead of and behind the fifth wheel mount. The rear end of the chassis was tidied up with extra panels of plain plastic sheet, and I initially crafted a horizontal tail-light boom from square rod. However, as the project progressed, I changed my mind about this latter feature and cut the boom away during the painting stage.

After covering the battery box in embossed tread-pattern styrene sheet, plastic rod was fixed through the frames to act as mounting brackets for the front mud-flaps. Shallow channel strip formed the flap mounting points. The inferior kit wheels were loosely fitted to act as locating guides.

Styrene angle and strip helped to create brackets for the fifth wheel mount, with more punched hex nuts and disc washers representing retaining bolts. Acrylic putty was piped along the edges with a syringe and pinpoint tip, to create pronounced weld seams. The syringe can be cleaned afterwards with soapy water and reused.

The fifth wheel mount was embellished with pivot brackets mounted over the existing adjustment racks on each side of the frames. The mechanism was improvised with scraps of plastic strip and tube, while the springs were formed from a wound steel guitar string. The fifth wheel would be painted and weathered separately.

I added plastic channel to the underside of the fifth wheel to allow it to sit over the pivot brackets, while an operating lever was shaped from brass wire. More of the embossed tread-plate sheeting was used to create platforms on the frames.

The cab was test-fitted at this point to check that none of the new details would be in the way.

...MUDGUARDS AND MUD-FLAPS

The missing front mudguard brackets were fabricated from a length of 2mm-diameter plastic rod, threaded through a pair of holes drilled into the side frames. My thinking here was that a single rod would be more resilient than a pair of separate brackets fitted independently. Given that I have a nasty – and regular – habit of breaking mudguard brackets while handling truck chassis, I thought it would be worth a try. The mounting points for the flaps themselves were created with Evergreen shallow channel (3.2mm wide), fixed to the back faces of the rod and adorned with pairs of punched bolt heads; corresponding hex nuts were also added to the flaps to create a very small but convincing detail.

The flaps were cut from paper-thin 10thou' plastic sheet, although they wouldn't be fitted until the painting and weathering stages were complete. Like the tank retaining straps, the flaps were also gently shaped after immersing them in hot water, so they would hang with a gentle backward sweep. The kit-supplied rear mud-flaps were thinned with a broad flat file, which drastically enhanced their appearance.

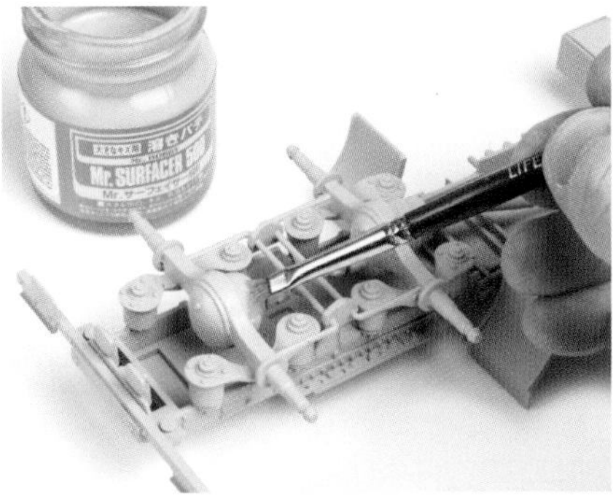

After an overall coat of grey primer, sprayed from an aerosol, Mr Surfacer 500 was hand-brushed on to the axles, gearbox and engine sump in order to provide a more realistic texture of cast metal. It also served to mask any imperfections after all the filling and sculpting done earlier.

A mix of Tamiya X-7 Red and XF-9 Hull Red was created, slightly darker than the intended final finish, and airbrushed over the entire chassis. Care and a patient approach were needed in order to target the paint flow around the various components, especially the axles and suspension.

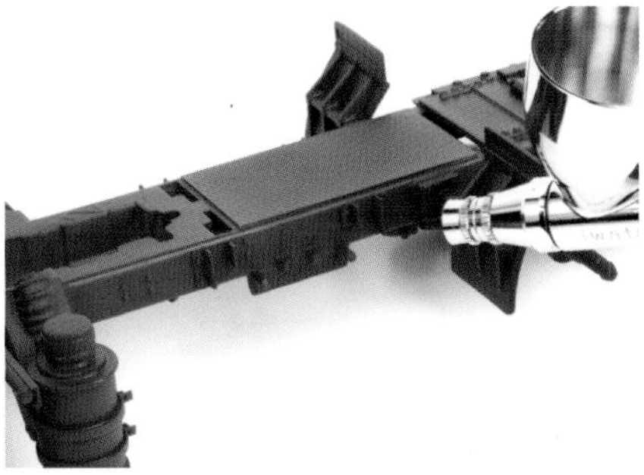

Once the initial layer was dry, a lighter shade of red was mixed (using a different ratio of the same two paints) and misted gently over the frames. By limiting the amount of paint applied and the angles at which the airbrush faces the subject, it is possible to allow some of the darker shade to remain visible, particularly within recessed areas and around raised details, thus creating subtle shading effects.

Once the red coats were complete, the engine and gearbox were picked out by hand, along with other details such as the rear air-suspension diaphragms and air-inlet trunking. AK Interactive True Metal Steel was applied to the air-cleaner restraining straps, using a micro brush.

A SUPERB SET OF WHEELS

It was at this point that the Fujimi wheels and rims arrived in the UK, and I could finally discern how they would fit and whether any modifications were required to the chassis. Apart from trimming the length of the truck's axles to allow the new hubs to fit, the only extra work needed was to fabricate a set of cosmetic brake drums. These were crafted from 20thou' plastic sheet using a compass cutting tool to create perfect circles. Conveniently, the locating pin hole that the tool leaves behind can act as a guide for the drill to cut the axle hole.

It has to be said that Fujimi's wheels are superb. The rubber tyres feature excellent tread and laser-cut sidewall detail, and they required no cleaning up of excess material whatsoever. The rims and hubs came with a chrome-effect finish that was light years ahead of many older kits, being subtle and natural looking. There is a high level of finesse to the moulded hub and bolt detail too, with only a modicum of assembly required.

What is important is to strip the chrome finish away from the mating faces of the rims and hub components, so they can be reliably fixed with liquid poly-cement or cyano glue (I used the latter). A choice of hubs was provided with my pack of 22.5in-diameter wheels, so I fitted the shorter units to one driving axle and the longer hubs to the other.

Work was interrupted by the arrival of the replacement Fujimi wheels and tyres, direct from Japan. Their superiority over the original kit wheels (lower) is clear to see. To fit the new wheels, the axle stubs needed trimming to about 8mm (0.3in) in length.

After test-fitting the new wheels, I realized that a set of cosmetic brake drums was required, so these were cut from 20thou' plastic sheet with a compass cutting tool. The centre of each disc was then drilled and reamed to a sufficient diameter to fit snugly on to the axle stub. The drums were primed and painted before fixing in place.

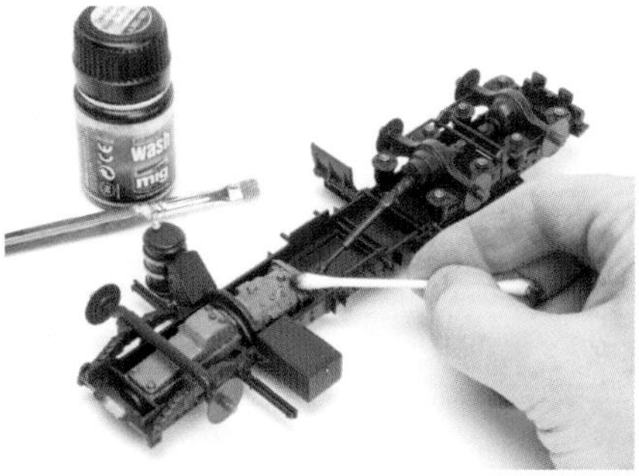

The weathering process began with a layer of MIG Dark Brown enamel wash, applied by brush and allowed to seep into all the recesses. After a couple of minutes, the excess wash was absorbed with cotton swabs.

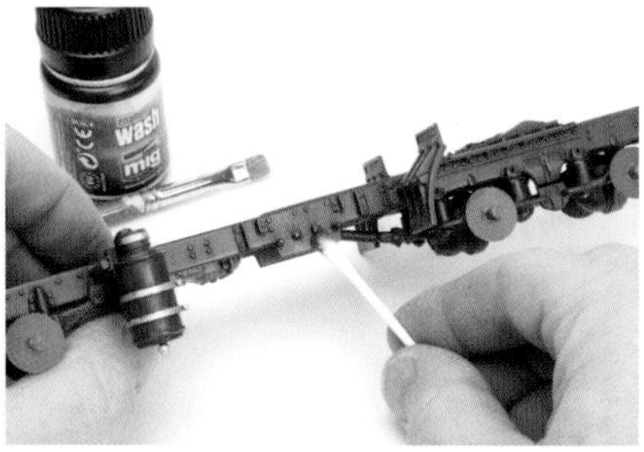

With a little enamel thinner on the swabs, the wash's pigment can be manipulated to create subtle streaking effects.

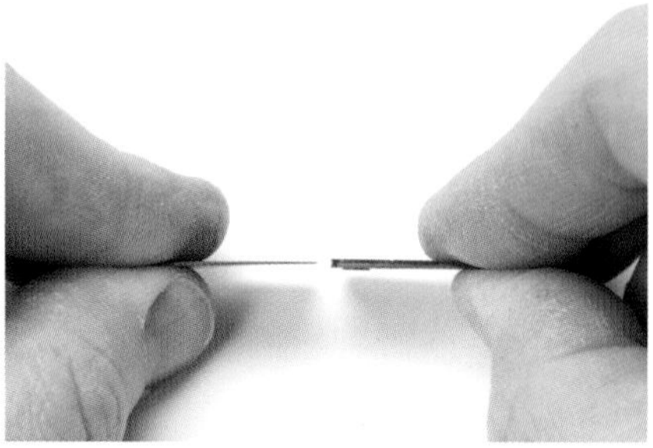

While the preliminary wash dried, I thinned the chunky rear mud-flaps to a more appropriate profile, using a flat file and treating both faces of each flap until a tapered shape was formed. After smoothing the plastic with abrasives, the flaps were primed and painted.

The rear flaps received the fetching Kenworth logos, courtesy of the Revell kit's decals, followed by a matt clear coat. The flaps and chassis were then treated with rust and dark earth-coloured dry pigments.

The fuel tanks had been airbrushed with Alclad II Chrome, with the straps and steps hand-painted with a darker metallic shade (Darkstar Steel). After a gloss clear coat, an enamel wash was applied, followed by a light brushing of dry pigments.

In order to highlight all the fine detail and surface relief that had been added to the chassis, a metallic silver paint was carefully dry-brushed over the surface. The bristles retained just a faint trace of paint, most of it having been removed on to a tissue. This is a very effective technique, but it takes a little practice, and a good quality, soft flat brush is essential.

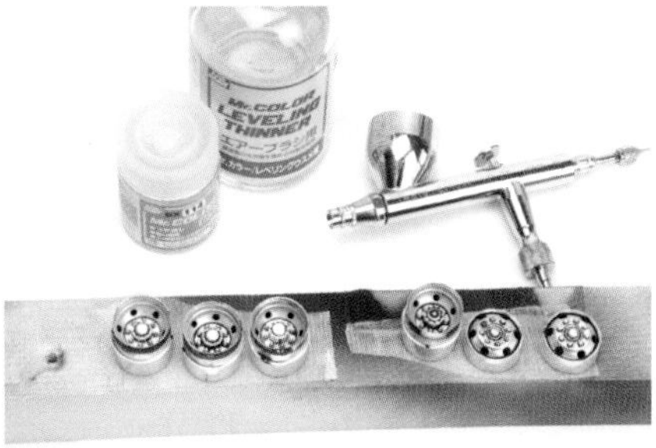

The assembled wheel rims were coated with a clear satin finish, which served to tone down the shiny chrome effect, producing a more lived-in appearance. Once dry, the same Dark Brown MIG weathering wash was applied, and the excess swabbed away.

With the tyres fitted, dry pigments were applied. The pigments adhere well to the rubber tyres and the treated rims, but a convincing burnished look can be achieved by scrubbing the surfaces with an old toothbrush.

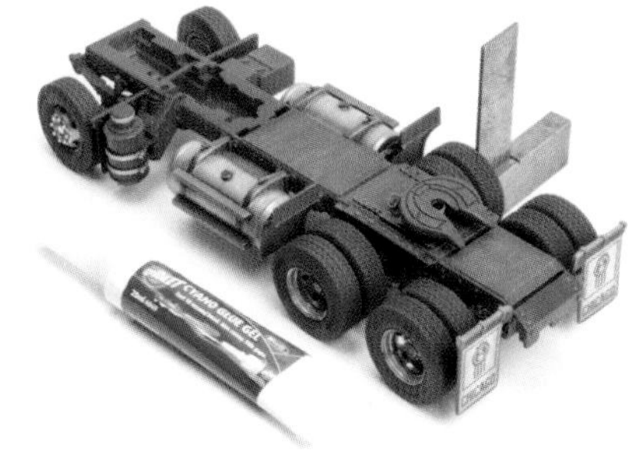

The replacement wheels were installed, one by one, using a cyano gel adhesive. This allowed plenty of adjustment time while also ensuring a secure bond for the slightly loose-fitting axles. Working on a flat surface helped to ensure that the wheels were correctly aligned.

A pair of front mud-flaps were cut from 10thou' plastic sheet, and a set of hex nuts and round discs represented the tails of the mounting bolts. These were spaced to align with the nuts fitted to the brackets earlier.

After painting and weathering separately, the flaps were installed.

The weathered chassis was refined with the airbrush, using a mix of brown and dark grey Tamiya acrylics. A very light misting was targeted to key areas where extra shading was required, or where the hand-applied pigments and washes looked a little heavy-handed. Less is more at this stage, as we don't want to obliterate the subtle effects that we've already applied.

Lifecolor's Reflective Agent is a fine graphite powder that can be applied with a brush. After dusting away the excess, the treated surface can be given a convincing burnished look with a clean brush. This worked particularly well around the fifth wheel's adjustment equipment.

IMPROVING THE TWIN EXHAUST STACKS

Like the suspension units and differential casings, the twin exhaust stacks provided another example of parts that were not rendered entirely accurately, as they featured large hollow sections behind the heat shields that were visible, even when attached to their mounting frame. Before this was addressed, there was plenty of fettling required to shift any last vestiges of the stripped chrome finish, and to form the pipes into a truly rounded profile (they were distinctly oval).

Milliput epoxy putty was mixed and inserted into the rear hollows, with short lengths of cocktail sticks pushed into the mounting holes to preserve their location. I also stuck some strips of masking tape over the heat shield's moulded dimples, to prevent them from being filled with stray putty. Once the Milliput had cured and final shaping had been achieved with files and sanding sticks, those dimples were then painstakingly drilled out with a 0.8mm-diameter bit to a uniform depth of 2mm (masking tape was wrapped around the bit to act as a depth gauge).

The air-intake column demanded a great deal of work, not least as the two sections didn't fit together very well. After filling and sanding, a grille was cut from a scrap of etched brass mesh sheet (from a model railway locomotive upgrade set), with a beading surround of plastic strip.

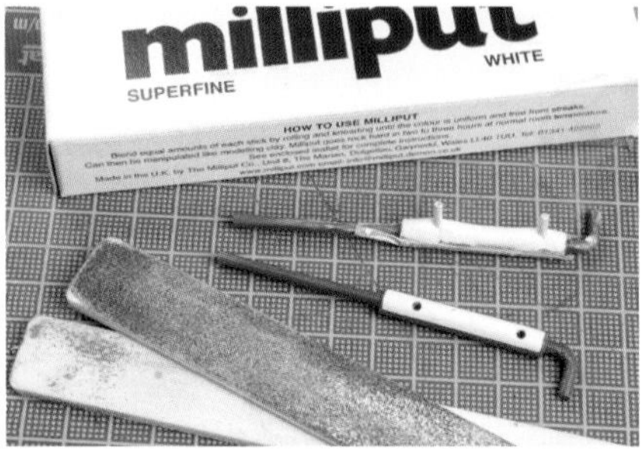

The exhausts also took time to bring up to scratch. The large hollow sections were infilled with Milliput, and the mounting holes preserved with wooden dowels (cut from cocktail sticks). The putty was left to harden for twenty-four hours; it was then shaped with files and abrasives.

The small moulded dimples were then drilled out with a 0.8mm bit to a depth of a few millimetres. There are over 100 holes on each exhaust, so this is not the most exciting job!

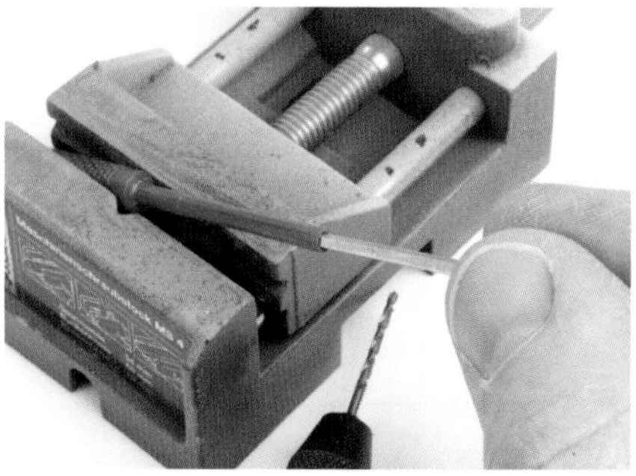

The exhaust-pipe outlets will be very prominent on the finished truck and the solid plastic will be obvious. The ends were therefore drilled and reamed very carefully to create as fine a profile as possible without damaging the plastic.

After priming and undercoating with gloss black, the stacks were airbrushed with Alclad II Chrome. Tonal variation and heat discoloration were achieved with subsequent use of Pale Burnt Metal, Hot Metal Sepia and Hot Metal Violet shades.

This is a task that needs to be done by hand, rather than with a power drill, but it is hard going for the finger muscles, so it was done in short bursts, which also minimized the monotony. The tops of the solid exhaust pipes were also drilled out, taking care to mark the centre with a fine scriber tool to act as a guide for the bit. I started with a 1mm drill bit, working to a depth of about 15mm, before opening out the hole in small increments, up to 3mm in diameter. Final profiling was achieved with a tapered reamer to get as fine a profile at the top edge as possible, without fatally weakening the plastic. The exhaust stacks are always a prominent feature of this kind of truck, so it's well worth going the extra mile to get them looking as good as possible.

Once the remedial work was complete, the stacks were sanded and polished, ready for the new metallic finish. After a coat of grey primer to check for any remaining blemishes, a gloss black undercoat preceded the Alclad II Chrome topcoat, applied with an airbrush. The metallic paint was applied in thin layers so as to preserve the dark shading in the heat shield's perforations, and when this was dry, the stacks were treated to faint targeted mists of Alclad II's Pale Burnt Metal, Hotmetal Sepia and Hotmetal Violet shades: these combined to create a realistically aged and heat-stained effect.

THE CAB

In contrast to the chassis, the Kenworth cab received only minimal attention. The single-piece moulding features plenty of fine surface relief, with just a few minor moulding seams in need of removal. Those on the front corners led to an inevitable loss of some of the rivet-head detail, but this was reinstated using a special Nutter tool. Having punched out rivet heads of the correct diameter from thin metal foil, they were fixed to the cab with clear gloss acrylic varnish (glues are too messy for this delicate job).

The same tool was also harnessed to add similar details to the front fender, before it received a new metallic finish, courtesy of Alclad II Aluminium. The same finish was also applied to the smaller cab fittings, namely the air horns, handrails and headlamps.

There is potential to go further with the cab than I did. The windscreen wipers and grab handles, for instance, could be

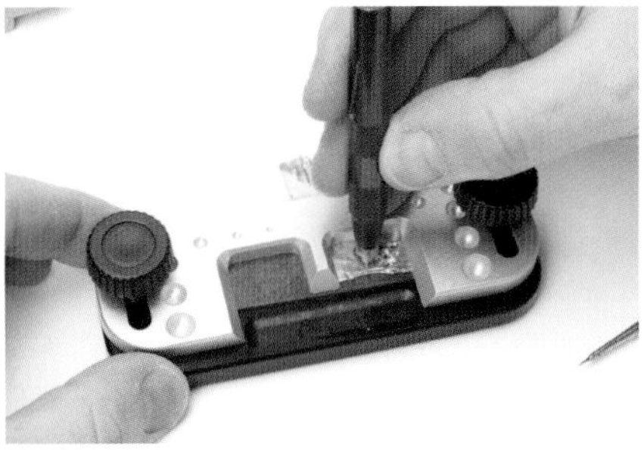

This Nutter tool, from The Small Shop, allows rivet and bolt heads to be punched from flexible metal foil. A set of punch tips is provided, of different shapes and sizes.

The Nutter proved invaluable for reinstating the rivet-head detail lost when removing the moulded seams from the corners of the cab. The punched rivets can be attached with clear acrylic varnish.

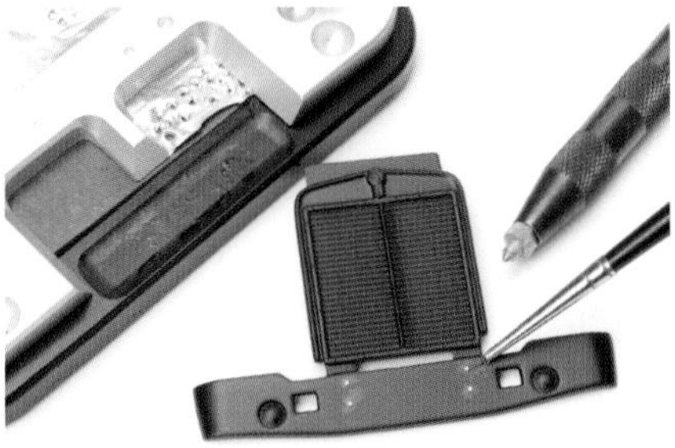

After cleaning up the radiator grille and fender moulding, these were given a coat of black primer, which revealed that the raised fastener detail was barely visible. The Nutter came to the rescue again, providing more authentic relief. When the clear varnish was dry, a second coat of primer followed.

replaced with finer components, but their location would necessitate very careful carving away of the moulded details, which I decided to avoid. Maybe if I build another Revell Kenworth I might feel inclined to give that a try.

PAINTING AND DETAILING

The gloss blue paint was built up with an airbrush, over several light layers, taking care to ensure even coverage. I rarely enjoy airbrushing gloss paint as its slow-drying nature invariably leads to errant dust particles landing on the surface. However, that's not a problem if you accept the inevitability of it. Indeed, for a deep and lustrous finish I prefer to build up the paint over two or three sittings, allowing each layer to cure fully for a few days before rubbing it down lightly with fine abrasives, washing and drying, then spraying another coat. Once the final layer was completely dry, the rubbing down is repeated, working from, say, 8,000grit abrasives down to ultra-fine grades of 30,000 or more. This will take care of any specks of dust or other imperfections, and the final glossy sheen will be restored in due course using clear coats.

Not surprisingly, it can take a few weeks to get the basic painting done to a high standard, but the effort will be repaid with a superior finish. After adding painted details, such as window seals, door handles and so on, clear gloss was applied from a spray can (Mr Hobby's Premium Topcoat). This dries rapidly and the glossy surface was soon ready to be adorned with decals. Some of the Revell decals were employed for the information panels and licence plates, but the truck needed a corporate identity. Luckily I found some Mason-Dixon Line logos that appeared tailor-made to fit the cab doors.

Taken from a Gofer Racing decal sheet for 1960s-era 1:24 US trucks, the light blue and white logos really suited the Kenworth, so I employed modeller's licence to suggest that this company should have painted its trucks blue rather than red, as they did in reality! I don't think they employed Kenworth K100Cs either, but never mind, I really like the look of the finished vehicle.

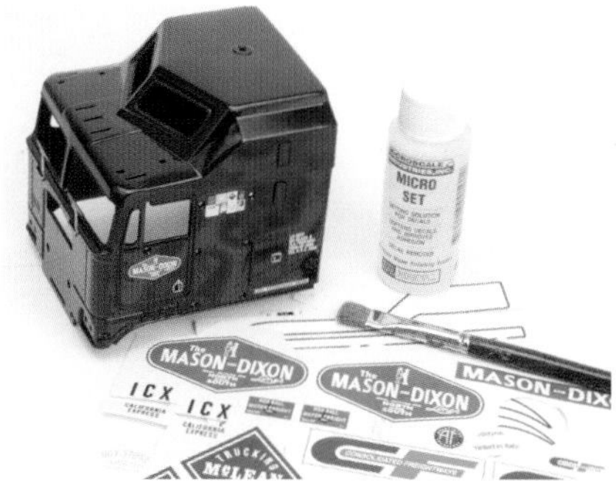

Once the cab had been painted and treated to a clear gloss coating, the decals could be applied. Revell's kit provides plenty of small infographics but I felt the plain blue cab needed some interesting logos. A Gofer Racing decal sheet, designed for 1:24-scale trucks, happened to include a set of Mason-Dixon Lines logos that fitted perfectly on the cab doors. Not prototypical, but they look nice!

A further gloss clear coat sealed the decals before the weathering process began. As with the chassis, work began with enamel washes, using a mix of Dark and Brown MIG shades. The swabs were rubbed in vertical strokes to create lifelike streaking, and there is plenty of surface relief in and around which the pigment can settle.

After the washes had dried, I used the airbrush again to refine the weathered effects without making the cab appear too dirty. Using a low pressure and correctly thinned paint, a very fine mist was aimed mostly around the door frames, along the lines of rivet heads and along the lower edges.

All the small detail fittings that had been stripped of the chrome-effect finish at the outset were carefully fettled to remove mould imperfections, and repainted with Alclad II Aluminium over a black primer coat. The headlight lenses were sprayed a slightly darker metallic shade (Stainless Steel), using a circle stencil as an improvised mask.

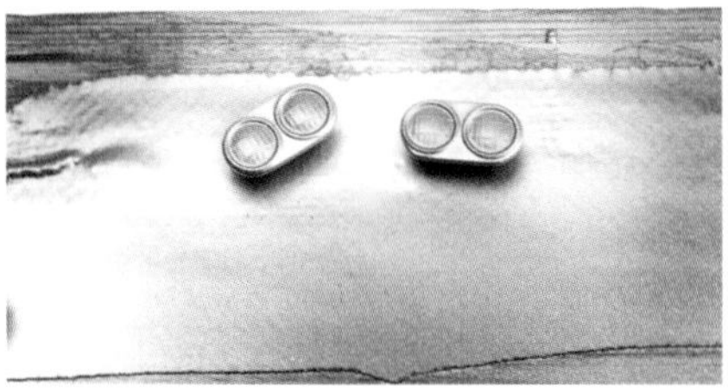

The tonal difference is not stark, but it is effective.

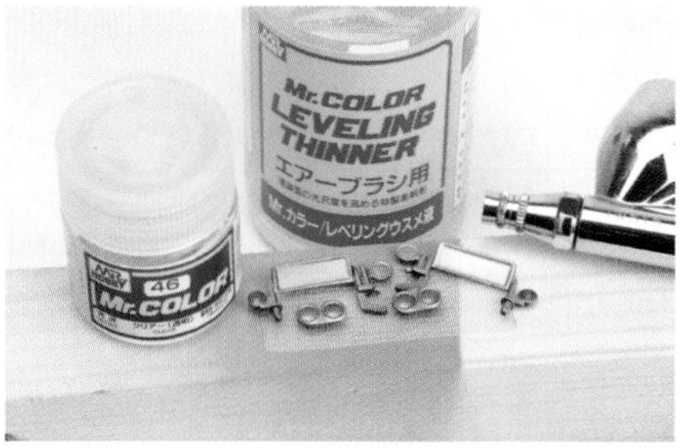

While most of the detail parts received a semi-gloss clear coat over the metallic paint, the headlight lenses and mirror panels were coated with a much higher gloss finish to mimic glass.

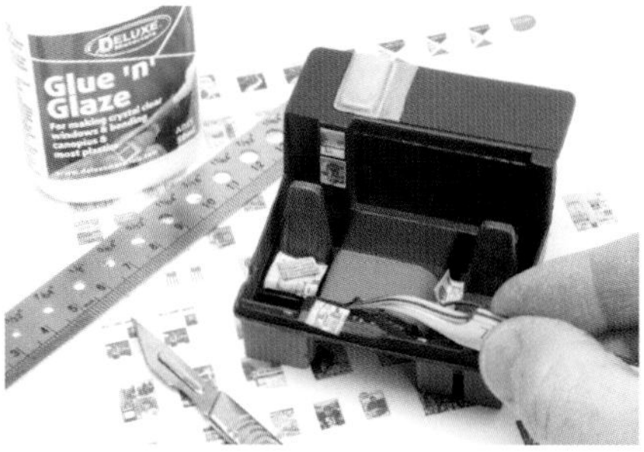

The one-piece interior moulding didn't look anything special to begin with, but once painted and detailed, its appearance was much more convincing. I found plenty of newspaper, magazine and road-map covers online, dating from the late 1970s and early 1980s. These were cropped, scaled down using design software, and printed on to paper. Cut out, folded and fixed within the cab, they bring a bit of life to the scene.

The red chassis created a pleasant contrast to the blue cab, and in order to accentuate all the added detail, I took the time to introduce some shading and highlight effects with the airbrush, following the application of a dark base colour (a mix of Tamiya X-7 Red and XF-9 Hull Red). On top of this, a much lighter mix of the same two colours was lightly misted over the frames, allowing some of the darker colour to show through, mostly within recesses or around raised details, thus creating a subtle and natural shading effect. This initial stage was followed with weathering washes and the application of dry pigments, after which the detailed chassis frames really came to life.

CONCLUSION

While I was cautiously optimistic at the outset, the finished Kenworth K100C looks even better than I'd hoped, and it has certainly fulfilled my initial goal of creating something lifelike for minimal financial investment. Taking a very basic kit as a starting point, my original brief was adhered to in the sense that the original parts were retained almost entirely. It helped that the cab moulding needed little work, with about 95 per cent of my energies being targeted towards the chassis, exhausts and detail fittings. Apart from the Fujimi wheels and tyres – which are fantastic – all other additions were made from stock materials.

Final assembly is easy, with most of the cab fittings simply snapping into place without the need for glue. A pair of aerials were formed from thin wire and fitted into holes drilled into the top of the mirror brackets.

The RP Toolz hex nut and disc punch tools, plus the Nutter, each proved invaluable for the upgrade work, but apart from those, there was no need for any other specialist tools and devices.

There's a real sense of achievement to be gained from creating a realistic model from a less auspicious starting point. There was certainly a lot of time and effort involved, and I did question my sanity at one point, but once the paint started to flow on to the components, I began to feel vindicated in my belief that this plan could work.

As an exploration of the potential of cheaper, less comprehensive kits, this one has certainly taught me a number of lessons along the way, not least the benefits of patience. That said, I must admit to rushing the final stages: after over two years of working intermittently on this truck, the nearer I got to completion, the sooner I wanted it finished. The use of the Mason-Dixon Lines decals was convenient, but I now wish I'd created some more authentic logos. However, with a second Revell kit in stock and the ease with which the cabs can be interchanged, maybe I'll have a second attempt in future, with a more authentic identity.

The transformation from a cheap, basic kit into a lifelike model has proven to be a very rewarding process.

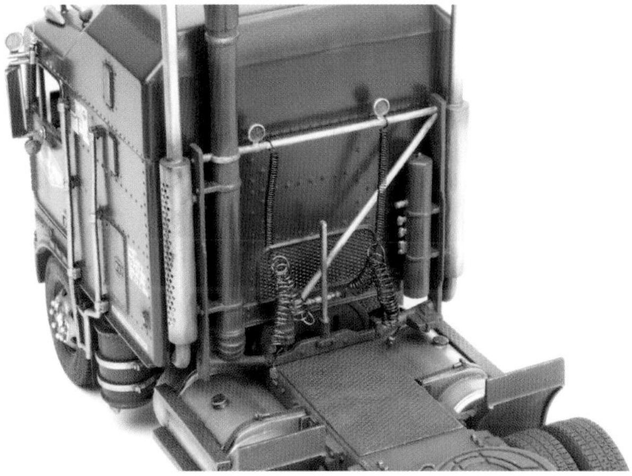

A pair of susie cables and sprung retaining cords were formed from coated copper jewellery wire, wrapped around the shaft of a drill bit. The plugs at the end of the cables are simply lengths of plastic rod, drilled for the wire to pass through and painted with an aged metallic brass shade.

Fujimi's replacement wheels and tyres are excellent, featuring laser-cut sidewall and tread detail.

Kenworth's K100C Aerodyne was undoubtedly an attractive truck, and Revell's kit captures the character of the prototype, even if it does require many hours of extra detailing work to achieve a faithful replica.

CHAPTER EIGHT

PLOUGHING THROUGH: A MERCEDES-BENZ UNIMOG IN 1:24 SCALE

Wiping the condensation from the window one February morning, I was greeted by the sight of an orange truck clearing the town's market square of several inches of snow. A large steel plough was installed on the front of the chassis, and as I sat in the little café drinking my coffee, I reflected on how exciting it would be to drive such a vehicle amidst the blizzards and snowdrifts that were wreaking havoc in the Derbyshire Peak District.

Of course, it's always easier to dream about these things than actually do them, and as my hot oatcakes arrived, I immediately revised my opinion and was thankful that I was safely ensconced indoors beside a roaring fire. However, the sight of that Derbyshire County Council snowplough did leave a lasting impression, and within a couple of weeks I'd bought this Revell kit.

The kit's subject is a very different vehicle to the DAF truck I'd seen in Chapel-en-le-Frith, but I'd been interested in the Mercedes-Benz Unimog for some time. Furthermore, it had been a while since I last built a 1:24-scale kit, so I was attracted to the package for a number of reasons – though I'll admit that the box's portrayal of an orange snowplough-fitted truck did clinch the deal!

The earliest slot car systems in the USA featured 1:24-model vehicles, and the scale has remained popular with car and truck enthusiasts ever since, becoming the 'standard' scale for this genre in many peoples' eyes. There's certainly a huge selection of automobile kits on the market, thanks to brands such as Revell, Italeri, Hasegawa, Fujimi, Tamiya, Airfix, and many more. As for trucks, Revell, Italeri and AMT boast a particularly impressive array of kits, while Emhar, Heller and Meng are also key players in the market. Figures and diorama accessories are widely available, and Airfix has produced a number of 1:24-scale aircraft over the years, too.

The scale means that vehicles, and especially trucks, are of a size that permits a wealth of detail to be incorporated into the kits as standard, without the parts feeling too fiddly. Furthermore, adding extra detail such as brake pipes, electrical cable and hydraulic hoses becomes a viable option for modellers with a modest amount of experience. Much depends on the nature of the prototype, but finished 1:24-scale trucks can be fairly big, especially modern tractor units and trailers, making for a striking addition to any modeller's display shelf.

OLDER THAN IT LOOKS: A 1980S VEHICLE

Despite the modern packaging, Revell's 1:24 Unimog actually dates back to the mid-1980s, with a number of different versions appearing over the years. The first iteration of the snowplough-equipped vehicle appeared way back in 1987, when I was still a child, barely into high school. The fact that I'm now midway through my forties puts the kit's age into perspective.

It really does pay to do a little research before buying a kit, to avoid any unpleasant surprises and to gain a rough idea of what work is likely to be involved. I had an inkling that the Revell kit had been around for some years, but that didn't stop me buying it – it was a whimsical purchase, after all.

I love attractive, colourful kit packaging, and couldn't resist the snowplough theme of this Revell Unimog. The kit dates back to the 1980s, and the moulding quality is variable, to say the least. The instruction booklet is comprehensive, but some of the diagrams could be a little clearer.

The single-piece chassis avoids the need to build up a ladder frame from individual parts, but the poor quality of the mouldings means that there is plenty of fettling to do before assembly can begin.

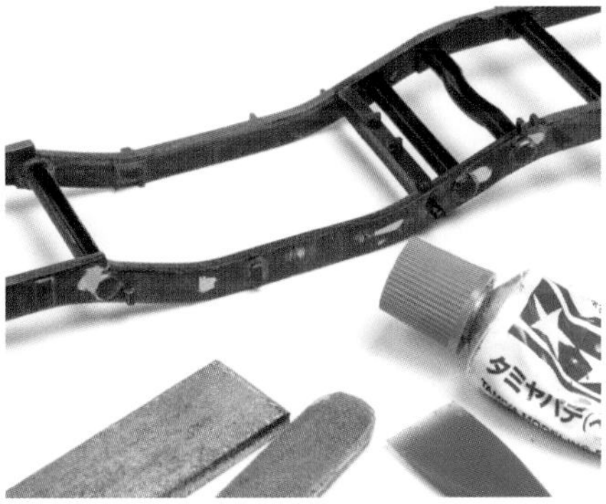

A few hours were spent filling sink holes and filing away raised mould seams and excess material. Much of the side frames will be visible, so it's important to get the frames cleaned up.

Naively I had envisioned a fairly quick and simple build. Alas, once I opened the box and took a close look at some of the components, it became clear that a significant investment in time would be necessary in order to produce a model of a high standard. A good number of the moulded components were showing their age, with the engine and chassis parts requiring a great deal of remedial work before assembly could begin. Mould seams, sink marks, flash and rough surfaces abounded, and after a while, the constant fettling before and during assembly became monotonous.

However, once the chassis frames were assembled and the mechanical gear installed, there was finally a sense of reward for the hours of work. Indeed, the bodywork components demanded much less intervention and progress soon accelerated.

A GOOD INTRODUCTION TO 1:24 SCALE

As I mentioned, prior to building this Unimog, a few years had passed since I last built a 1:24 kit and I was a little apprehensive at the outset, especially as I'd been working on a number of 1:76-scale kits. This Revell kit, despite its challenges, proved to be a great reintroduction to the larger scale, thanks to the one-piece chassis frame and relatively low parts count. As we'll see in the following chapters, other 1:24 truck kits feature a much more complex array of components and assembly methods, yet the techniques and processes adopted here apply equally well to any larger-scale plastic truck kits.

The raised stance of the Unimog means that the underframe is clearly visible, so there is ample opportunity to add extra detail in terms of hydraulic and air hoses and electrical cable. The kit even includes an array of air reservoir tanks and valves, plus some rudimentary moulded plumbing, along with lengths of vinyl tube to form the hydraulic lines to the plough and gritting equipment. However, I decided to keep things relatively simple with this endeavour, concentrating my efforts on improving the existing parts and adding a small number of extra details, in the hope that a good quality paint job and weathered finish would also enhance the kit sufficiently.

Indeed, the kit does have a number of good points. The tyres are acceptable, the decal sheet is extremely generous, and the cab and bodywork mouldings are fairly clean, with most of the flash and moulding imperfections confined to the black plastic sprues that contain the chassis components. The front axle is steerable, the cab interior is well appointed, and the plough and gritter equipment feature plenty of detail.

A UNIVERSAL IMPLEMENT

Initially conceived at the end of World War II as an agricultural vehicle, the first Universal-Motorgerät ('universally applicable motorized implement') – or 'Unimog' – appeared in 1948. Initially they were not actually built by Mercedes-Benz, but once the trucks had also become popular with civilian, industrial and military customers, Daimler Benz soon took over production, with the famous Mercedes logo first appearing on a Unimog in 1953.

A highly versatile design, Unimogs could be adapted for all manner of undertakings, with the powerful engine, all-wheel drive, high ground clearance and flexible chassis allowing it to cope with the roughest terrain. The design and specification continued to evolve over the subsequent decades. Revell's kit is based on a short-wheelbase version that first appeared in the mid-1970s, featuring an angular truck-style cab. Three different wheelbase options were available at that time: 3,250mm (128in), 3,700mm (146in) or 3,850mm (152in). Having measured the kit's chassis, the model appears to be based on the short-wheelbase version, although the kit is actually twenty-five times smaller than the prototype, rather than the stated 1:24.

THE CHASSIS

Having realized that the kit wouldn't be built in just a few weekends, I decided to enhance the truck slightly, by replacing certain parts with scratch-built details and introducing missing features, particularly to the cab interior. The chassis, however, received only minimal extra detail work. In fact, more than enough time had been spent fettling the parts before assembly, so I was getting a little impatient. Besides, without an opening bonnet, the upper half of the engine would not be visible once the bodywork was installed, so there seemed little point in adding fuel lines, electrical cable and hydraulic hoses.

However, I soon regretted not adding one extra detail to the engine, as one of the lower drive-belt sprockets hangs in thin air. I didn't think it would be visible once the snowplough was installed, but alas, it was quite evident when viewed from either side. Eventually, a simple solution was improvised towards the end of the project.

Thanks to the high ground clearance, the chassis frames, exhaust system, transmission, suspension and brake discs are all clearly visible, so I channelled a lot of energy into getting these areas looking as good as possible. The main ladder frame is moulded as a single component, but there were so many unsightly moulding marks on the

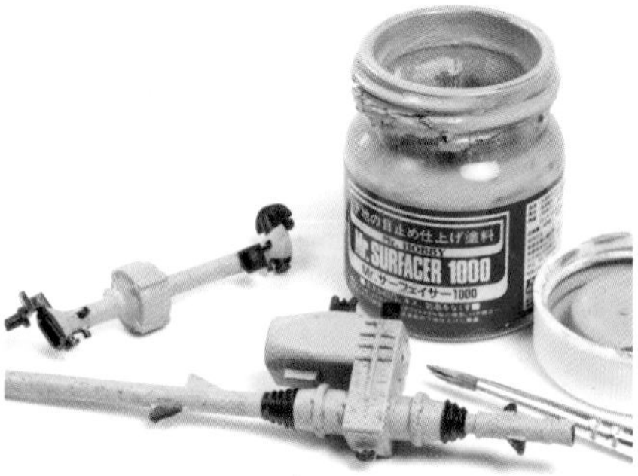

Both axles and the driveshafts are created from half-relief mouldings. After gluing and clamping each section, they can be fettled to remove any traces of a joint seam or other unsightly imperfections. Mr Surfacer was once again employed to add a cast texture to the transmission elements, applied over several coats with a brush, using a stippling action. This also serves to hide any remaining traces of joint seams. Remember to keep the material away from the rotating front axle stubs and the moulded rubber gaiters at each end of the gearbox drive outlet.

The front wheel mount stubs are designed to swivel within the main axle units, so all four elements need to be fettled carefully until they fit together neatly and move freely.

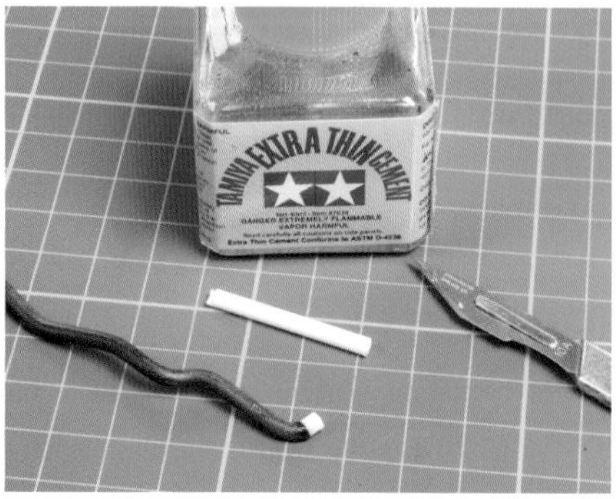

Test-fitting of the exhaust pipe revealed that it was a few millimetres too short (a common feature of 1:24 kits, as we'll see throughout the rest of the book). A scrap of a similar diameter plastic rod was found, and a short length fixed to the end of the kit's pipe.

With the stub axles slotted between the two halves of the drive axle unit, the parts were clamped and liquid poly-cement applied sparingly, keeping it away from the moving parts.

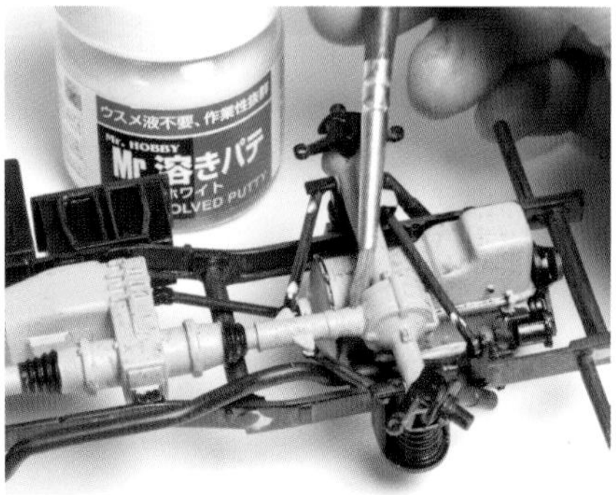

The engine was also treated to a stippled coating of Mr Surfacer before both it and the transmission components were installed to the chassis. Any small gaps between the parts were filled with Mr Dissolved Putty.

The extended exhaust was then installed, Mr Dissolved Putty again serving to create a seamless joint.

sides that it took an hour or two of filing and sanding to get them square and smooth.

The axles, driveshafts, gearbox and engine also demanded several hours of remedial work to get them looking neat and tidy. In order to give these components a more authentic texture, the smooth plastic parts received a couple of coats of Mr Surfacer 1000, stippled roughly over the sub-assemblies with an old brush. A number of layers were built up until the desired effect was created, and after painting and weathering, the results were very effective.

The steering rod is meant to be retained by melting the tips of the protruding plastic lugs with a hot screwdriver blade. I'm not always keen on this approach, and as an alternative, I found some plastic tube of a suitable diameter to slot snugly over the lugs. A tiny drop of poly-cement was applied, ensuring that the rod and axles could move freely.

The rear suspension units are made up of various sections, each requiring a great deal of filling, filing and sanding before assembly.

Small panels of etched brass tread plate were cut and fitted to the cab footsteps with a drop of cyano glue.

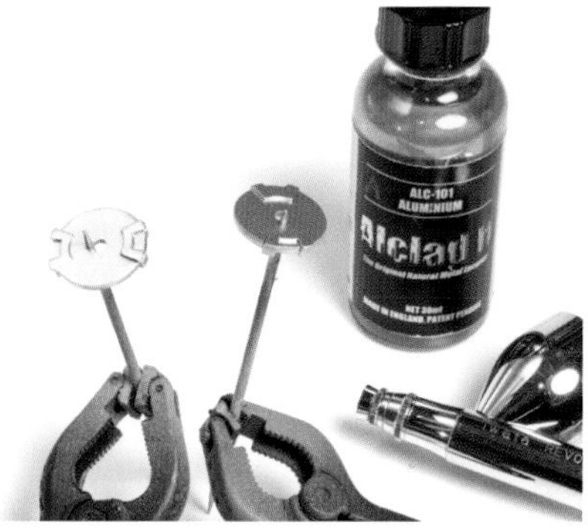

After a black primer coat, the brake discs were airbrushed with Alclad II Aluminium. Once dry, the metallic coating was buffed with a soft cloth to remove any loose particles before a clear satin coat was sprayed on top.

The brake discs were fixed to the axles, and the hubs and edges picked out in a rust-brown shade. An authentic texture was introduced by adding some dry pigment to the paint. The calipers were also painted, using a slightly darker shade of metallic paint.

The exhaust outlet section was made up of two halves, and after bonding and fettling, the end of the pipe was carefully opened out with a tapered reamer. After installation, the exhaust system was treated to a stippled coating of Mr Surfacer, then the whole chassis was sprayed with Mr Surfacer Black aerosol-based primer.

The engine and transmission units, as well as various other detail fittings, were hand-painted in appropriate colours. When dry, various layers of enamel weathering wash were applied, including MIG's Oil & Grease Effects.

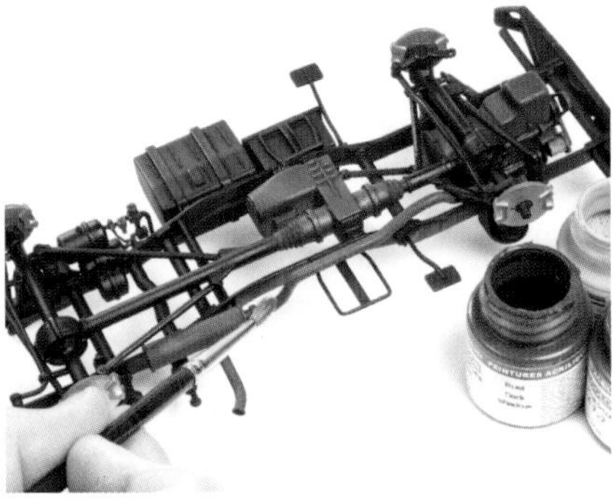

The exhaust pipe could then be painted with a mix of rust shades, built up over several coats and applied with a stippled action to avoid too smooth a finish.

The texture created by the stippled coats of Mr Surfacer and acrylic rust shades can be highlighted further by dry-brushing the exhaust pipe with traces of metallic paint. I used two shades of Darkstar acrylic, Pewter and Steel, to create some tonal diversity.

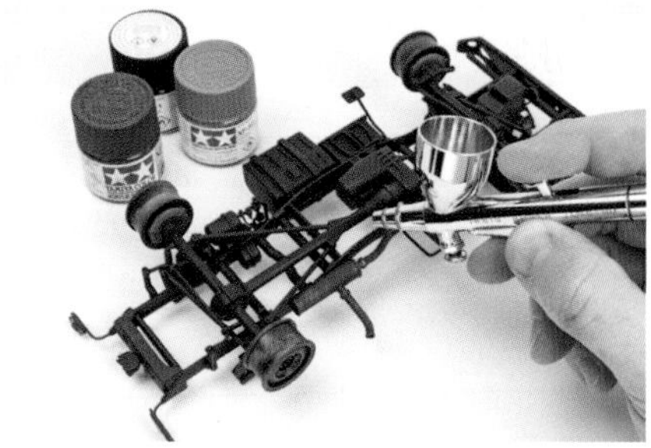

The chassis then received some finessing work with the airbrush and a fine misted layer of Tamiya acrylics.

The chunky tyres are well rendered, but the tread faces needed abrading to remove moulding flaws and to give them a more realistic patina. After washing and drying, these too were airbrushed with the mix of Tamiya paints before being fitted to the chassis.

The plastic tail-light mounting brackets were very flimsy, so I replaced them with 1mm stiff brass wire, shaped with a special wire bending tool from Expo Tools.

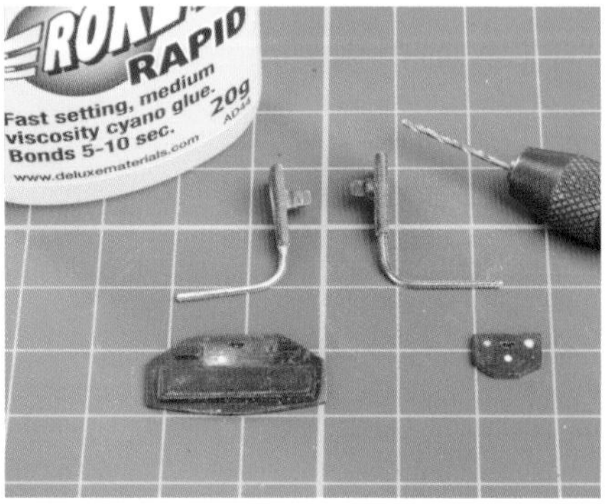

The shaped wire was fixed into holes drilled into the bases of the original brackets. The other ends of the wire will then be fixed to the rear of the tail-light boards.

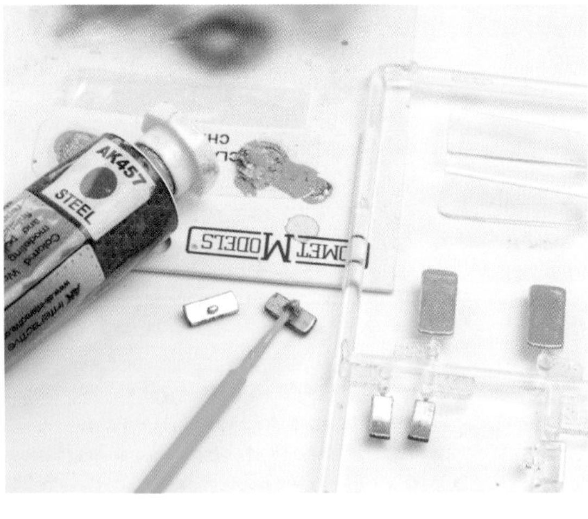

The rear faces of the lenses were painted with Tamiya's Clear Orange and Clear Red acrylics. When dry, a metallic silver paint was overpainted – in this case AK Interactive True Metal Steel – to act as a reflective backing.

The modified light units look good, and importantly, the brackets are much more resilient.

The lower drivebelt pulley lacked any form of mooring, so I crafted a simple assembly of styrene rod and strip to suggest a likely piece of apparatus. I wasn't aiming for anything too specific, but when painted and weathered to blend with the surroundings, it made the engine appear much more believable.

Initially I toyed with the idea of replacing the exhaust outlet pipe with a short section of brass tubing, as the kit's original component was rather coarse. It didn't help that the two-part assembly didn't marry up neatly, and the edge profile was overly thick. However, with judicious use of filler, abrasives and a tapered reamer, the plastic part was vastly improved. Again, a few stippled coats of Mr Surfacer 1000 introduced a suitable surface texture and removed any last vestiges of a seam between the two halves.

Aside from adding a metallic finish to the brake discs and calipers, the only other significant additions to the chassis were small rectangles of etched brass, chequer-tread plate fixed to the tops of the footsteps, and replacement of the flimsy plastic tail-light brackets with brass wire; these two simple modifications introduced a more refined appearance to the underframe.

With the chassis assembled and painted, the wheels were secured to the axles with small captive styrene plugs, which fit between the inner and outer wheel-hub sections. In theory, the plugs should be a push fit on to each axle, but I had to secure them with a small drop of cyano glue, applied to the inside of the plug and taking care not to get any adhesive on to the wheel hubs. Just enough slack was allowed for the wheels to rotate freely, and after tidying up the tyres with abrasive sticks, they were gently pushed on to the wheel rims.

THE CAB INTERIOR AND FITTINGS

Attention then turned to the bodywork. The cab interior is highly visible, thanks to the large windscreen and opening doors, so it made sense to enhance the dashboard (which in the kit is rather poor), seats and flooring. The 'dash' took a couple of attempts to get right. I originally drilled and reamed out the moulded dials, and having applied the supplied decals to a sheet of plastic card, I intended to fix this behind the facia.

However, the thickness of the plastic was excessive, so I simply drilled and cut away the entire section from the dashboard moulding and inserted a replacement facia cut from thin plastic card. The dial apertures were carefully marked and drilled before the facia was installed, and the warning lights, switches and levers were added with various sizes of plastic strip and rod. After painting the dashboard and adding a sheet of clear styrene behind the apertures, the plastic sheet adorned with the dial decals was inserted behind, making for a very convincing appearance.

Various other interior fittings were created from scratch, including seat-adjustment knobs and levers, plus a set of seatbelt anchors. The featureless floor was given a non-slip covering, using embossed plastic sheet, along with a set of ribbed floormats, also cut from sheet plastic. The inner faces of the

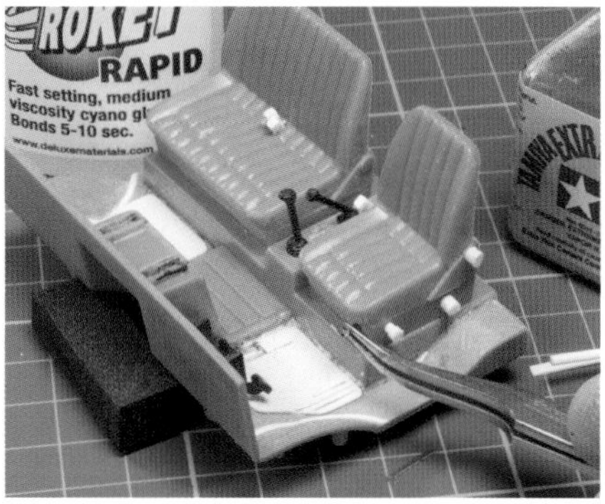

Embossed plastic sheet, from Slaters and Evergreen, provided the textured floor covering and ribbed mats, while seat adjustment controls and seatbelt anchors were improvised from plastic rod and strip.

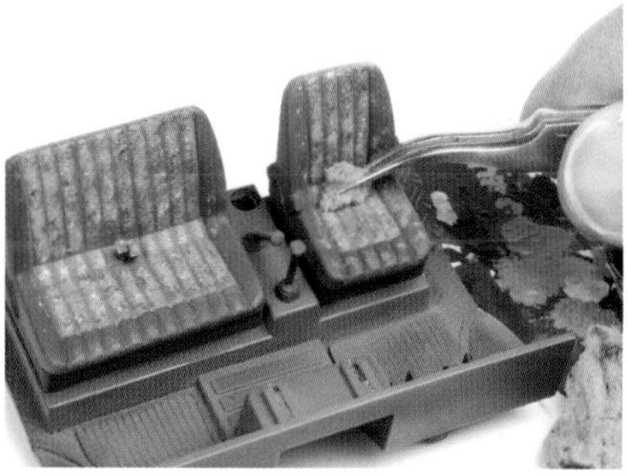

After priming and painting the interior, the seat fabric was initially treated to a base layer of dark grey acrylic, mixed with a little talcum powder, which gave the finish a distinctive texture. A scrap of natural artists' sponge was dipped into a variety of acrylic shades and stippled on to the seats to create a random pattern.

After tidying up the contrasting edges of the seats, a dark enamel weathering wash was run into the ribbed seams to add shading. This will dry to a flat matt finish.

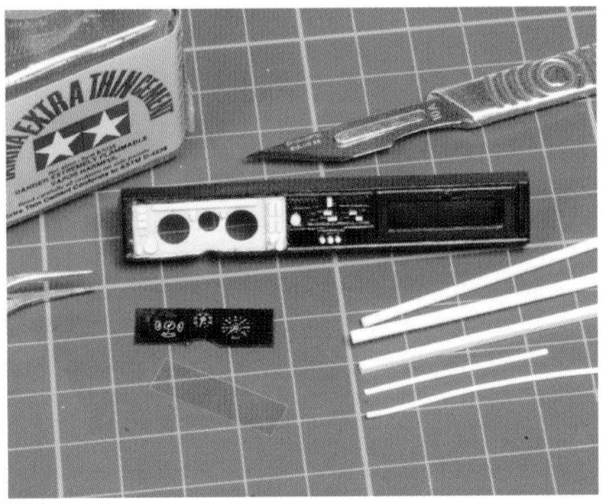

The dashboard moulding was disappointing, so I drilled and cut out the driver's facia and inserted a sheet of 10thou' plastic card, having pre-drilled and reamed apertures for the dials. Extra controls were formed from plastic strip, and the kit's decals included a set of dials – these were applied to another piece of plastic sheet that will sit behind the new facia, separated by a strip of clear plastic.

The modified dashboard, after painting, looks much better than the original layout. The steering wheel is just awaiting a Mercedes-Benz logo. The grubby cab floor was created with various shades of dry pigment.

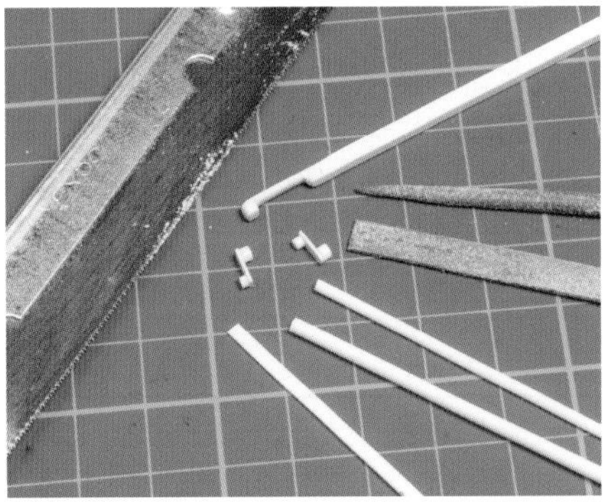

The inside of the cab doors was also in need of a detail uplift, so I created pairs of grab handles and window-operating arms from plastic strip and rod.

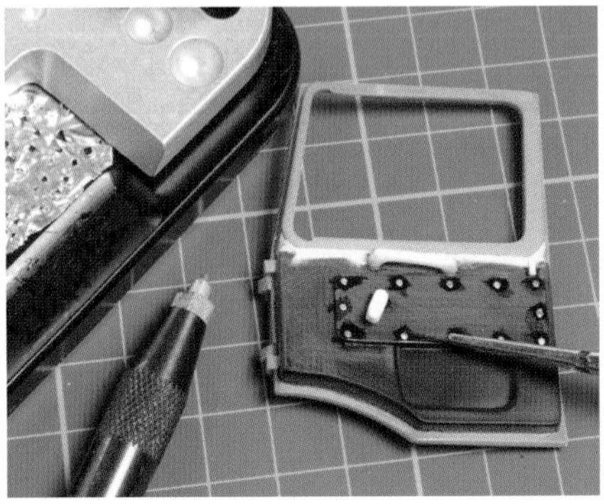

After adding the new handles, the trim panels received a set of fastener heads, courtesy of the Nutter punch tool.

Painting the seat upholstery was good fun, with scraps of natural sponge employed to provide a random application of various shades of paint, which had been laid out on a palette. Prior to this, doors received scratch-built grab and window-operating handles, plus raised hinge bolt heads and fasteners for the trim panels, fabricated using a Nutter punch tool, as described in the previous chapter. The exterior door handles were carefully carved away with a miniature gouge, and replacements created from a bespoke detailing set that I commissioned from PH Designs for another of Revell's Mercedes trucks, which I've yet to build.

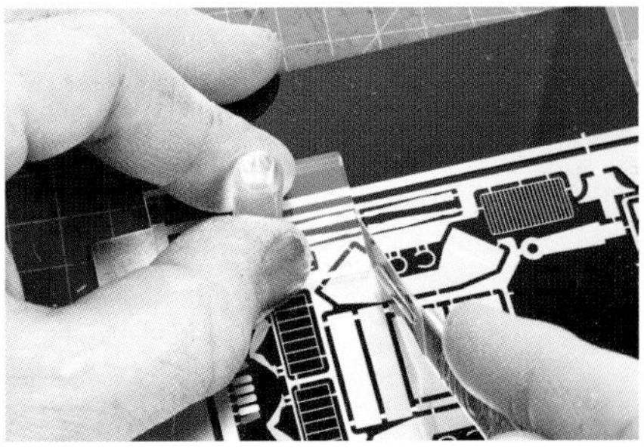

I decided to carve away the moulded cab door handles and replace them with a set of etched metal parts that I'd commissioned from PH Designs for a different 1:24 scale Mercedes truck. As the parts were common across various vehicles of the period, the metal parts were a perfect fit for this Unimog, so they were cut carefully from the fret with a fresh blade. A photo-etch cut-out kit, from The Small Shop, helps to hold the parts securely while the cuts are made, avoiding any distortion of the metal.

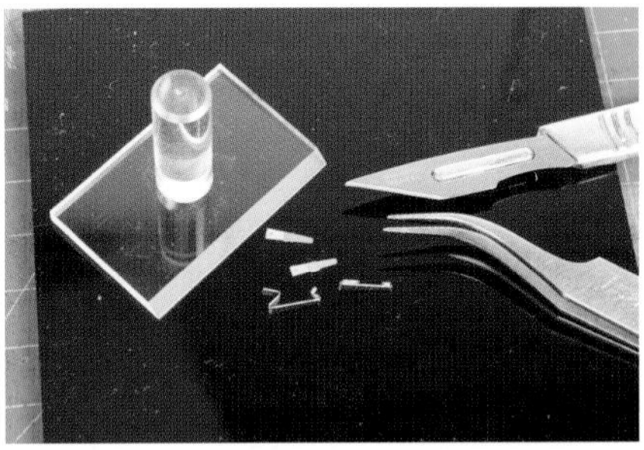

The parts are designed to be folded in order to achieve the necessary profile. Separate overlay pieces feature the lock button detail, and each handle was assembled with the help of cyano glue.

Once painted, the handles were fixed to the doors and a little weathering work made them look realistic.

the seats had been hand-painted with a mixture of matt acrylics and a little talcum powder. This created an ultra-matt, textured coating, and once the random patterns had been created with the sponge, the seats were further enhanced with a dark weathering wash, run into the ribs to add subtle shading effects.

IMPROVING THE BODYWORK

While the hopper mouldings lacked the unsightly flash and other imperfections of the chassis parts, the ends in particular featured visible traces of the milling bit employed to create the moulding tools. It took plenty of work with abrasive pads to create a smooth finish before the parts could be married up.

The cab bodyshell didn't need much in the way of remedial work, especially when compared to the chassis, although I did add greater definition to the bonnet seams using a profile cutting tool.

The snowplough blade also demanded a great deal of remedial work, the outer face having a large sunken crater along its length, while the inner face featured a number of circular injector-pin marks in highly visible places. The opportunity was also taken to replace the solid hydraulic pistons that control the lower edge of the blade with plastic rod.

Time was spent in ensuring that the main hydraulic rams were assembled, filled and sanded carefully, prior to the application of metallic paint, which can be unforgiving when applied to less-than-perfect surfaces. The main pistons are designed to move within the outer cylinders, allowing the snowplough to be posed at different angles. Therefore, the telescopic elements needed to be fettled to allow smooth movement, without excess 'slop' but with sufficient clearance to prevent the paint from being chipped away as the parts interact.

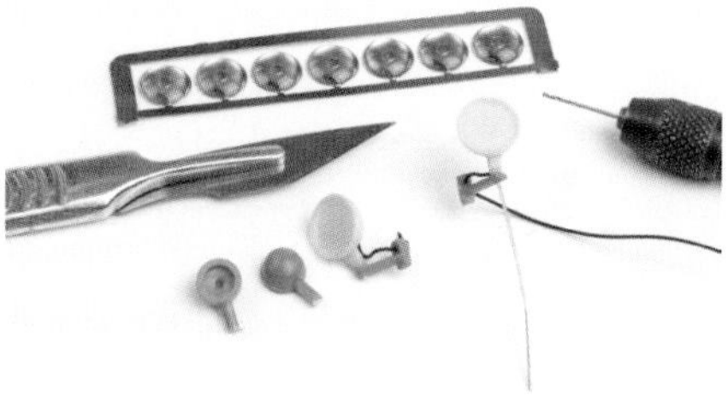

Because the snowplough obscures the Unimog's main headlamps, extra lights are attached to the cab. Those provided in the kit are poor, so I employed a pair of resin castings from Kit Form Services, using the mounting brackets from the original kit parts. Lengths of brass wire were employed as mounting dowels, secured with cyano glue.

The small, inferior front spot-lamps were replaced with resin units from Kit Form Services (KFS), using the original mounting brackets. Brass wire was inserted into drilled holes to act as a dowel and greatly strengthen the glue bond. The KFS lamps include realistic lenses, and these were installed after the lamps had been painted. The small spot-lamps that sit on the snowplough blade were retained, but vastly improved by the addition of 5mm-diameter clear and red lenses from AK Interactive.

ISSUES WITH ORANGE PAINTWORK

Orange is one of my least favourite colours to apply to scale models, especially over large areas such as this Unimog. Treating the occasional element of a broader scheme isn't too bad, but when orange is the main overall colour, I begin to feel a sense of rising dread. A small consolation came in the fact that the livery wasn't yellow, which I utterly detest, but a few issues with the orange paintwork were encountered, nonetheless.

The main problem was getting the shade correct. After studying a host of prototype images, it was clear that many orange Unimogs appear to wear a slightly faded shade, especially those that were clearly a few years old. This tallied with my own observations of service vehicles in similar colours. Indeed, those snowplough-fitted DAF trucks belonging to Derbyshire County Council that had initially inspired me, all carried a slightly washed-out shade of orange.

Revell's instructions suggest a mix of 60 per cent orange, 30 per cent yellow and 10 per cent mud brown, but I wanted something a little different. After mixing Tamiya X-6 Orange and a small amount of X-2 White in different ratios, I finally found a shade that was acceptable. There's a convention that states that orange (and yellow) paint benefits from application over a pale pink undercoat, but I opted for a white primer in order to maximize the colour's luminosity and maintain a slightly faded look. As it transpired, my orange shade didn't look too promising when first applied, but following a deep clear gloss coat prior to adding the decals, the hue of the orange began to turn a little deeper, which improved the situation.

Revell provide a generous array of decals for seven possible schemes, all but one being for an orange livery. There are markings for German, Austrian, Swiss and Dutch trucks, and I chose one of the former identities, for the Stadt Olsberg municipal authorities, a town in the Hochsauerland district of the North Rhine-Westphalia, in the northwest of Germany. One issue with the decals surrounded the red and white warning panels for the rear of the hopper. These were slightly too big and needed trimming beforehand with a sharp pair of scissors (it's much easier to trim the decals before they've been soaked in water).

The weathering was carried out over several stages, with the chassis, main bodywork, hopper and plough all treated separately. The first act was to apply a general wash coat, and instead of enamel washes, I mixed my own from two shades of Lifecolor acrylic paint: UA734 Worn Black and UA758 Blackened Umber. The aim was to create heavy, dark deposits of grime, trapped in and around the various raised and recessed elements of the bodywork, hopper and plough. I'd noticed that snow can become very dirty as it begins to thaw, and when mixed with grit and road dirt, the resultant staining on vehicles can be worse than usual. The grimy deposits will invariably contrast with the bright orange livery, and there would also be a need for streaking and splashing effects.

Therefore, the mix of the two Lifecolor acrylics produced a dark and dirty shade of grey-brown, and this was brushed on to small sections of the bodywork at a time, without thinning. Immediately, most of the paint was removed with swabs, leaving heavy deposits of grime in key areas and creating vertical streaks. If the paint proved stubborn, the swabs were dipped in Tamiya's acrylic thinners. It took some time to work round all the separate sub-assemblies, but employing this process on a gloss surface is important. The gloss finish allows the weathering layer to be manipulated much more readily than a matt surface, on to which the paints will cling more tenaciously.

With this stage complete, I could add greater concentrations of dirt in specific areas, using dry pigments. The pivot points of the plough assembly are a prime example, with the lubricated joints invariably capturing more of the filth. Accordingly, a Grimy Black shade of pigment was brushed on to the surfaces with a small brush, after pre-treating the areas with a light coat of pigment fixative fluid. A fixative is not always required when applying dry powders, but for more concentrated deposits, or when working on a gloss substrate, it greatly improves adhesion. The gritting chute and spreader was first treated with a coat of light grey textured acrylic paint, before building up layers of dry pigments. Again, a fixative fluid helped the layers of powder to adhere effectively.

Dry-brushing with metallic paints (light and dark Steel shades) brought out the relief contained in the plough assembly and gritting apparatus, suggesting areas of chipped paint and burnished metal. An airbrush was employed next, loaded with a mix of dark brown/grey Tamiya acrylics, and a fine mist was aimed around those areas where the Lifecolor paints had been

After painting the bodywork, the windscreen seal and radiator grille were masked off and painted with Tamiya's XF-85 Rubber Black.

Following a deep coating of clear gloss, the Revell decals could be applied. To help the warning panels conform to the ribbed sides of the rear section, Micro Sol softening solution was applied. After a few minutes, the decal film will become more flexible and can be helped to settle with a damp brush. It might take two or three applications of Micro Sol, but it's important not to rush the process, lest the decal be damaged.

Once the decals had been sealed with a further clear gloss coat, the bodywork received its initial weathering treatment by brushing on and wiping off a mix of Lifecolor acrylics, leaving behind traces of the pigment in key areas and using swabs to create subtle streaking effects.

deposited. This served to soften any hard edges, and to provide a smoother transition between cleaner and grimier areas. By moving the airbrush a little further from the surface, a more diffuse spray pattern was achieved, mimicking the appearance of dirt splashed or sprayed up from the road. At this stage the weathering process paused, with attention turning to assembly of the various elements of the truck.

GLAZING AND FINAL ASSEMBLY

A really disappointing aspect of the kit was the sheet of clear glazing parts, which were certainly not up to scratch. The main windscreen was significantly smaller than the aperture in the cab, and if the large gaps weren't enough, the mounting tabs were highly obtrusive. No glazing is supplied for the twin rear windows, nor for the cab doors, save for the quarterlights, which were in fact fairly good. With no alternative, I had to cut my own windows from clear styrene sheet – tedious work involving a great deal of fettling and checking until the parts fitted perfectly. The clear styrene's transparency was passable, and was greatly improved with a coat of Johnsons Klear acrylic floor polish on both the inside and outside faces. When dry, the Klear also provides a resilient coating for the plastic, reducing the risk of scratches or other blemishes.

Assembling the plough to its bracket proved a little more complicated than I'd anticipated, due to some modifications I made to improve the look and operation of the parts. I wanted the plough to pivot slightly from side to side, but some of the supplied parts weren't capable of this. Drilling and inserting stiff wire dowels provided more secure pivoting points, while the hydraulic rams were carefully prepared so they would move smoothly, as well as look realistic, with a polished metallic finish. The plough itself was greatly improved, with some extra detail, including a new set of lights and superior hydraulic lines, using Tamiya's flexible vinyl hose.

To improve the clarity of the glazing and to afford protection from scratches, each panel was treated to a coating of Johnson's Klear floor polish, applied with a soft, flat brush. Both the inside and outside faces were treated.

The supplied glazing – what there is of it – is very poor. The main windscreen is too small and the mounting brackets are clumsy and unsightly, so that had to be replaced. Alas, no parts are provided for the rear windows or the cab doors, save for the quarterlights. Several hours were spent cutting and fettling clear styrene sheet to fit the various apertures. Once a good fit was achieved, the edges were polished with fine abrasives.

After priming, the wing mirrors – still partially attached to the sprue – were sprayed with Alclad II Chrome, followed by a clear gloss coat.

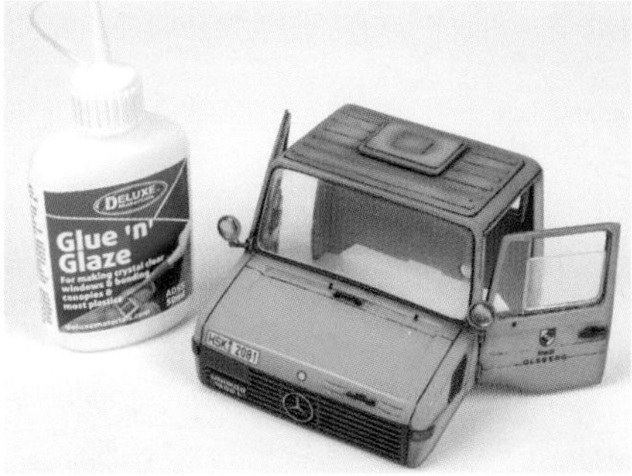

The new glazing was installed one section at a time, using Glue 'n' Glaze. A fine bead was run around the aperture using a needle-tip applicator. A few minutes were allowed for the glue to turn tacky, then the window was pressed into position. Each was allowed to dry for an hour or so before the process was repeated with the next window.

The mirror panels could then be masked, using a mix of tape and masking fluid, before the brackets were sprayed black.

The rear-view mirror was fixed to an offcut of foil, which was then cut flush with the outside profile.

The hopper is assembled from several separate sections, and it is important to check that the corners are square.

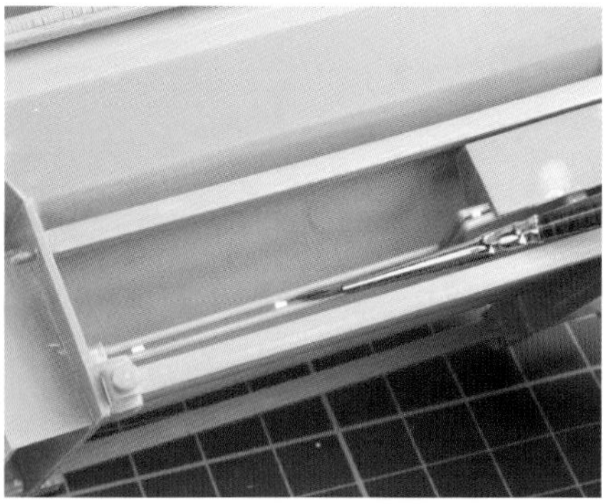

A small enhancement to the hopper was the addition of small sections of plastic strip, which gave support and added realism to the two parallel pipes.

Parts of the gritter chute and spreader unit featured pronounced ejector pin marks, which required filling and sanding prior to assembly.

The snowplough mount needed a little intervention as the forward vertical support was too short. A length of plastic rod was cut and inserted in its place.

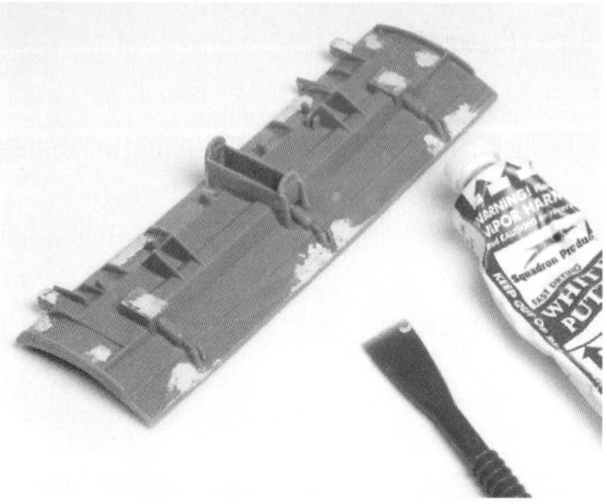

The plough blade needed plenty of work to fill ejector pin marks and remove moulding seams; this was a little tricky in places thanks to all the raised details. The front of the blade had large sink marks, so these were also filled and the surface sanded smooth.

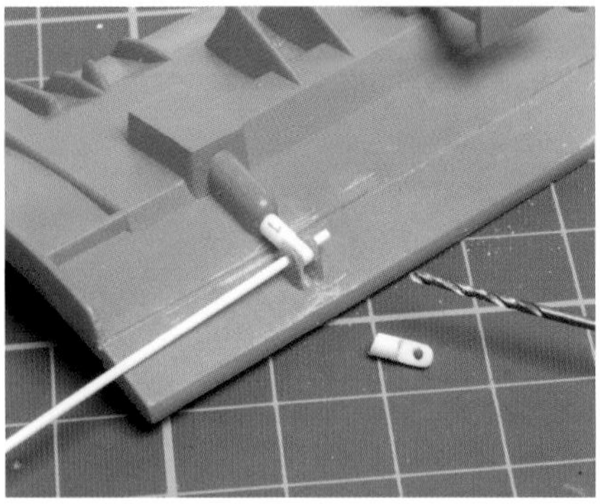

The small, lower hydraulic rams were disappointing, so I carved them away and crafted replacements from plastic rod, including the mounting pins, which were slotted into drilled holes.

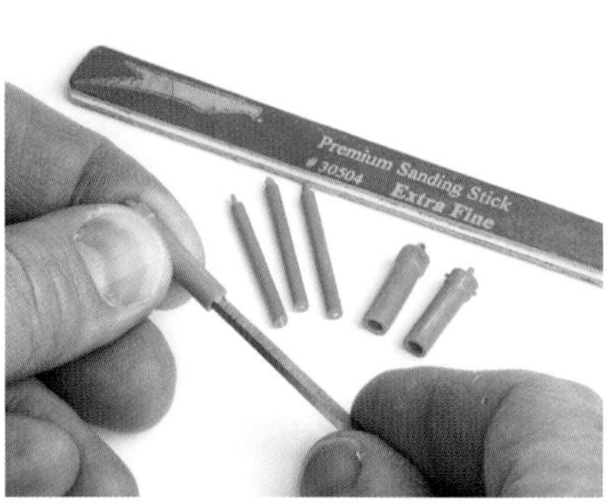

A trio of hydraulic rams control the pitch and angle of the snowplough; these are made up of several sections, each of which required careful fettling before and after assembly.

Alclad II's Chrome lacquer was applied to the pistons, over a gloss black undercoat. The pistons were sanded as smooth as possible before priming and painting, to remove any imperfections, which would otherwise be magnified by the shiny metallic finish.

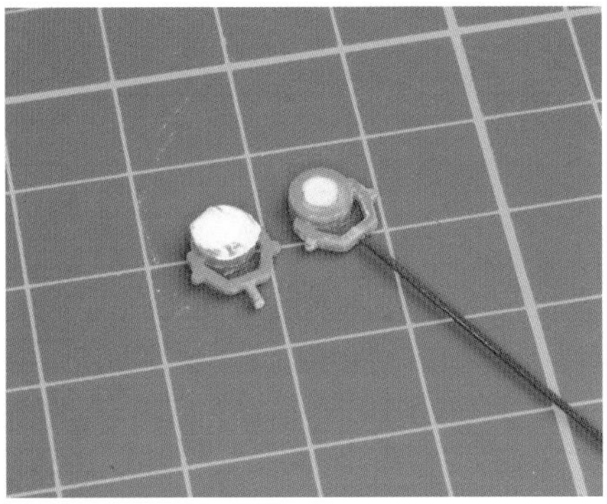

Again, the lamps provided to sit on the plough blade were deemed inferior, although I did retain them. The lens faces were filled and sanded flat, while new mounting brackets were formed from stiff brass wire.

Heavy deposits of black dry pigment were applied around the pivot points of the blade and bracket, to mimic heavy deposits of dirty grease. Pigment fixing fluid was employed to ensure good adhesion and to allow multiple layers to be applied. When dry, the surfaces were dry-brushed with the metallic paints.

Like the rest of the bodywork, the hopper was weathered initially with an acrylic wash before the airbrush added finesse. Dry-brushing followed, to highlight the edges of the panels and the spreading equipment.

After the lamp bases were painted, AK Interactive 5mm-diameter jewel lenses were installed to the modified lamps. A clear lens is fitted to the front and a red lens to the rear.

The hydraulic rams were then installed, and the plough fixed to the bracket with stiff wire dowels fixed into pre-drilled holes. Airbrushed weathering added the final touches, softening any hard edges left by the earlier wash coats.

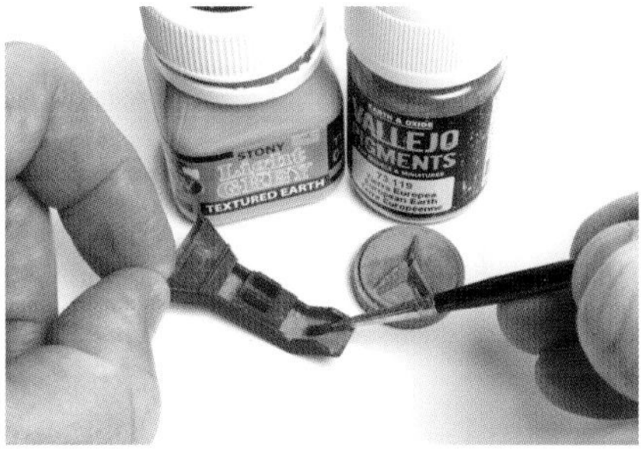

The chute and spreader outlet received a heavy coating of Wilder's textured acrylic paint, followed by a generous dusting of dry pigments.

Once painted, the plough blade received a heavy wash treatment with Lifecolor acrylics, before the detail relief was enhanced with dry-brushed metallic paints.

When the plough had been mounted to the chassis, hydraulic hoses were installed. I discarded the bulky grey hose supplied with the kit in favour of Tamiya's 1mm flexible black cable. Mounting holes were drilled and the hose fixed with cyano. Etched cable ties from CTM were added to keep the hoses tidy.

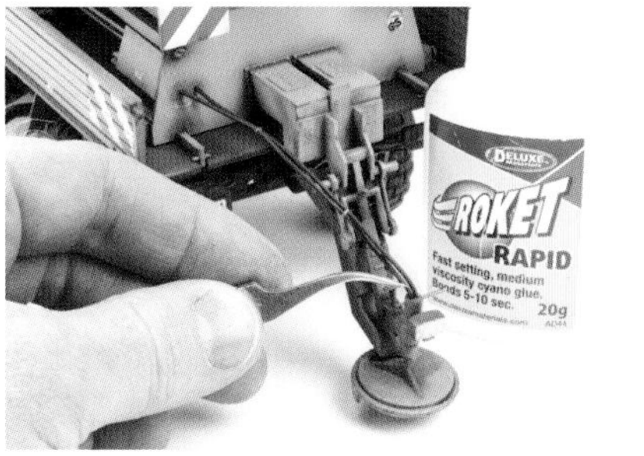

Tamiya hose was also employed for the rear hydraulic hoses, with a few more of CTM's etched cable ties keeping them neat and tidy.

SNOWY MEMORIES

I lost track of how many hours were spent on this truck, with work being spread over the best part of a year. Revell's kit is labour intensive, particularly in terms of the amount of remedial and detailing work undertaken. The rather fussy nature of the prototype, with complex plough and hopper equipment, meant that the painting and weathering of various sub-assemblies inevitably made for slow progress. The lack of decent glazing also added to the workload.

But grumbles aside, I thoroughly enjoyed the process as a whole, and the finished Unimog is a striking addition to my collection. One of my reasons for building the kit was to rekindle my love of 1:24-scale trucks, and in that respect it definitely had the desired effect, with a couple of other kits started and finished while the Unimog was still in progress. It may not be a Derbyshire County Council DAF, but my faded orange Unimog does remind me of that snowy morning as I waited for my hot breakfast in Chapel-en-le-Frith.

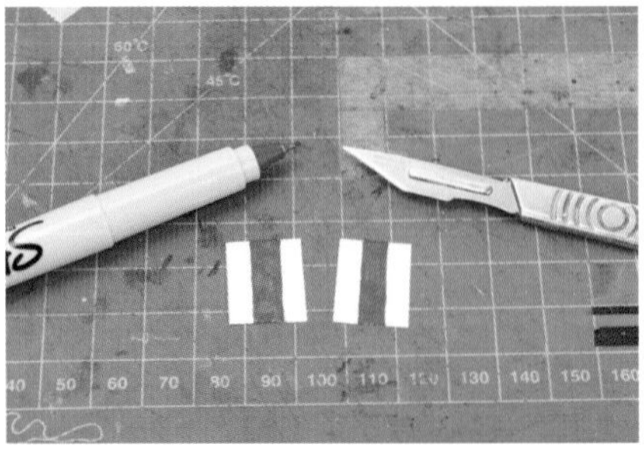

Rather than fiddle around with decals, I made my own flags from small rectangles of paper and a red Sharpie marker pen. The stripes and the edges of the paper were purposely rendered a little less than perfect.

Although not without its challenges, Revell's Unimog is an interesting kit that captures the character of the real thing admirably.

The rear flap was a little difficult to install, with no mounting points for the chain. Therefore I wrapped the chain round the frames, securing it with fine wire, twisted through the links.

The flags were scrunched up slightly before fixing to the plastic poles, whereupon they were weathered slightly with the airbrush. The front snowguard was mounted with a pair of wire pins, fixed into holes drilled into the plough brackets.

One day I'll build a snow-scene diorama on which to pose my finished Unimog!

CHAPTER NINE

BUILD BIGGER, BUILD BETTER: 1:24-SCALE DAF 95 CANVAS

Italeri first released a 1:24-scale DAF 95 in 1989, as a 6×4 tractor unit. Featuring extended chassis frames, this long-wheelbase canvas-bodied version appeared in 2016.

After the trials and tribulations of the Revell Unimog, the following project is offered as an introduction to more conventional 1:24-scale heavy trucks. There is a large number of possible kits I could have chosen for this chapter, as many share a common design of components and method of assembly, whether they be European or US outline prototypes. Based around a ladder-style chassis, with highly detailed engine, transmission and suspension components, along with tilting cabs (or hoods) and a fully appointed cab interior, this is an approach adopted by virtually all the main kit manufacturers in this scale.

Italeri's canvas-bodied DAF 95 kit was deemed a suitable subject as it poses a number of interesting challenges for the modeller, although most of the assembly is straightforward, with nothing too perplexing or complex. In common with a number of long-wheelbase US tractor units, the lengthy chassis frames have to be assembled carefully in order to create a sound foundation for the rest of the vehicle.

Furthermore, with any kit that contains hundreds of individual components – many of which require fettling before installation – there's an increased risk that key elements might not fit together correctly during final assembly, so knowing how to make any necessary corrections will help any building project progress more smoothly. This is something that we'll face with each of the large-scale trucks throughout the following chapters, with some kits posing greater problems than others.

Happily, this DAF 95 project called for minor interventions only, and in contrast to the Unimog, the need for extensive pre-assembly remedial work was limited. Italeri has offered only a handful of different versions of the DAF 95 (and later DAF 95XF) since its first release in 1989, all featuring a three-axle tractor unit. Also boxed under the Revell brand during the early 2000s, the kit made use of a number of chassis components from the older DAF3300/3600 kits, which date back to 1983. This canvas-bodied, long-wheelbase version appeared in 2016, and comes complete with a large decal sheet for the colourful Transports Chevrier truck seen on the cover of the box.

Like any kit that derives from moulds of the 1980s era, it has a number of good points and a few disappointments, most notably amongst the latter the lack of detail on the engine and gearbox, and the roughly moulded wheel rims. On the plus side, a good amount of detail is provided. Indeed, this is a kit with huge potential and plenty of scope for customization. While a tractor unit posed without a trailer allows the frames to be admired in detail, with this canvas-bodied truck the chassis is hidden beneath the bodywork, so I didn't see much point in adding any great number of brake lines, valves and so forth. However, the tilting cab would reveal the engine and gearbox, so I did decide to put in a little extra effort and improve these features. In the main, though, I set myself the brief of making the best of the kit's components, with the only major upgrades being a new set of wheels and a switch to right-hand drive.

PLAYING IT STRAIGHT

Work began on the pair of long side frames. There was plenty of tidying up to do, as the outer faces were blighted by various moulding defects, and a pronounced, raised seam along the upper and lower edges of the shallow channel profile. Furthermore, several vertical seams revealed where the original tractor unit frames had been extended on the tooling, which was interesting, but they needed to be flattened. After a couple of hours of patient filing and abrading, a smooth, blemish-free surface was achieved. Modellers who are more perfectionist might also want to address the inside faces of the frames, which are peppered with ejector pin depressions, and even a row of raised numerals.

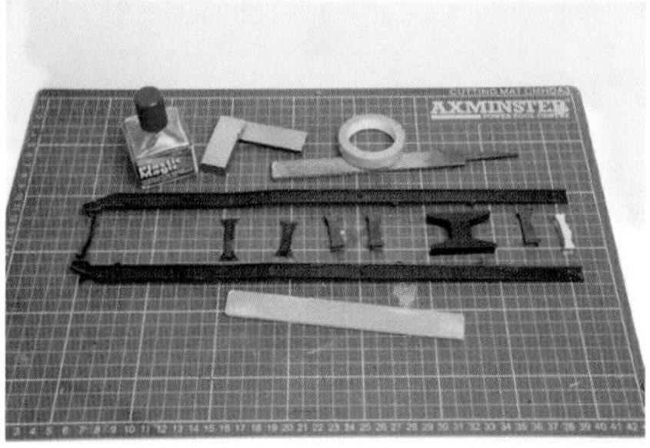

The impressive ladder-frame chassis is nearly 370mm (14.5in) long, with a varying array of cross-members. All parts require a degree of fettling to remove seams and other imperfections.

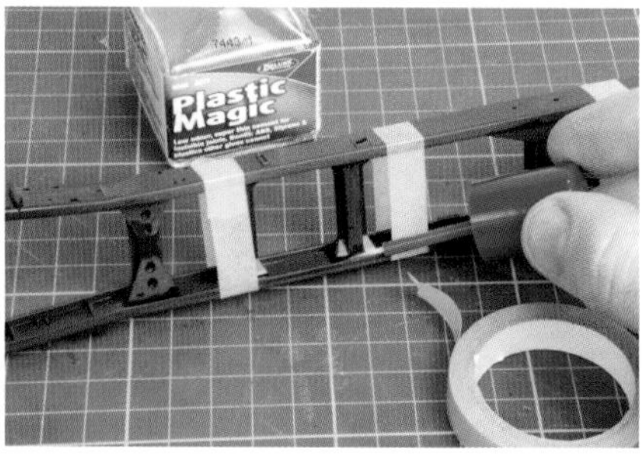

The chassis elements can be assembled without adhesive, using masking tape to clamp everything together. Check that the cross-members sit correctly, and that the side frames show no signs of bowing inwards or outwards, which might suggest that one of the braces is too short (and requiring shimming) or too long (when extra fettling is required). Only when you're sure that the frames sit together squarely should the adhesive be applied. Run liquid poly-cement into each joint, leaving the masking-tape clamps in position.

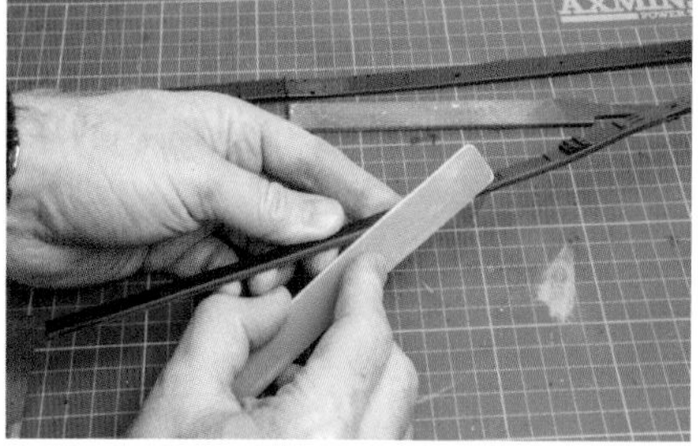

The side frames featured pronounced seams along their length, so these were flattened with a flat file and sanding pads, creating a gentle, rounded profile at the upper and lower edges.

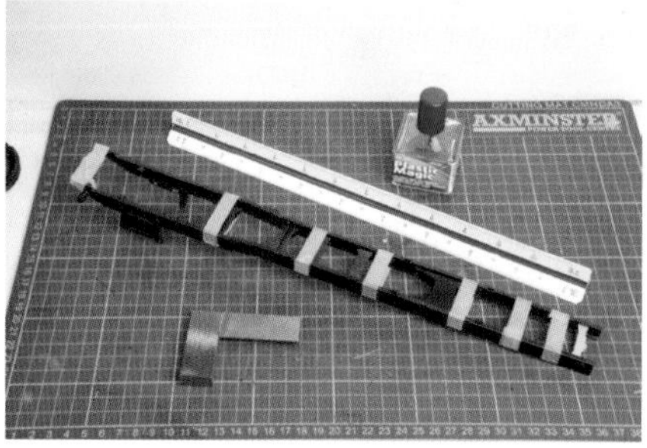

Keep checking the angles of the frames and testing for overall straightness as you make each glue bond, to ensure that the parts are not moving out of true.

When cleaning up the cross-members, it's vital to ensure that the mating faces are square and true. This helps to achieve correct alignment, as well as maximizing the surface area over which the adhesive can work.

A particular challenge of long-wheelbase trucks is the need to erect the frames squarely, as any twisting in the chassis or misaligned parts will hinder the subsequent assembly stages and prevent the bodywork from fitting correctly. The fact that the various cross-members required a great deal of remedial work introduced a higher risk of things going awry, so care was needed to ensure that the mating faces were square; also the overall length of the parts must be consistent.

Temporarily assembling the frames without glue, using masking tape to clamp the side frames and hold the cross-members in place, is an effective means of identifying any potential problems. The sides of the DAF frames are almost parallel, save for the flared front ends that accommodate the engine, so any kinks in the outer faces from an overlong or short cross-member will be readily apparent. Errant members can then be removed and fettled or shimmed, before repeating the 'dry' assembly and re-checking. Only when you're sure that everything fits correctly should the glue be applied.

WORK ON THE SUSPENSION SYSTEM

ALIGNMENT OF THE AXLES

In addition to getting the frames nice and straight, correct alignment of the three axles is also vital. All the individual suspension components required fettling, and the tandem-drive axles needed building up from several parts, and any gaps or imperfections filled and dressed along the way. The leaf-spring assemblies feature mounting pins that slot into holes in the chassis frames, thus ensuring a degree of accuracy, for the front axle at least. However, the rear springs feature a single, central pin, so these have to be installed with extra care, so that the four mounting points for the axles are level and concentric. Again, the need to remove pronounced moulding seams from the mating faces increases the margin for error, so be prepared to add plastic strip as shims during assembly. It really does pay to have a stock of styrene strip on hand, of various widths and thicknesses, when building kits such as this.

I deemed it prudent to fix the front springs and axle in position first, as this was an easier prospect to align. The distance between the axle and the frames

While waiting for the frames to harden, the axles and suspension elements can be fettled and assembled. Like the Unimog in the previous chapter, each differential casing is made up of two halves. The moulded locating pins didn't allow the parts to align correctly, so they were flattened with a file, along with the whole mating face of each component. I still couldn't get the parts to align perfectly, so I clamped them as best I could and resolved to improve the parts once the glue had cured completely.

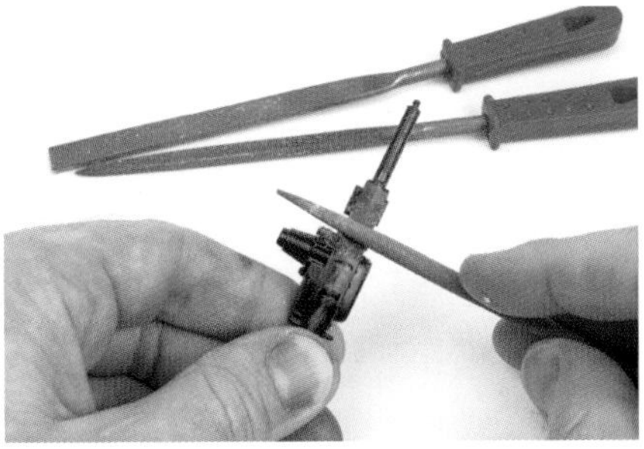

Round, flat and square profile files were needed to carve the correct profile to the differential casings, with the aim of creating a seamless joint between the two halves. The axles were also smoothed and any gaps filled with putty. Special care was taken to ensure that the mounting faces for the suspension were flat and square.

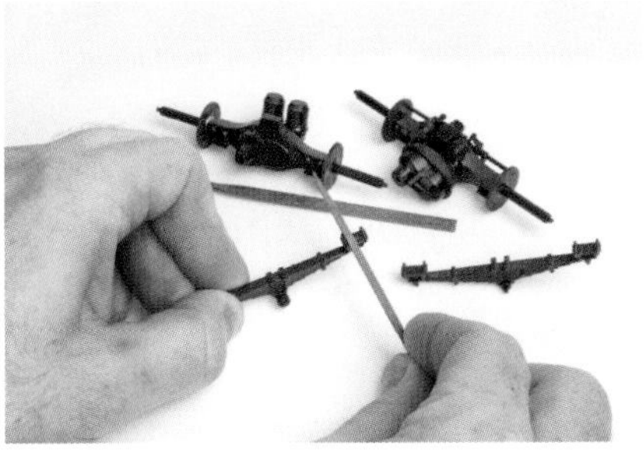

The rear axles can then be fitted with the brake drums and chambers, along with the extra transmission box. The leaf-spring units also need to be fettled, again paying special attention to the mounting brackets.

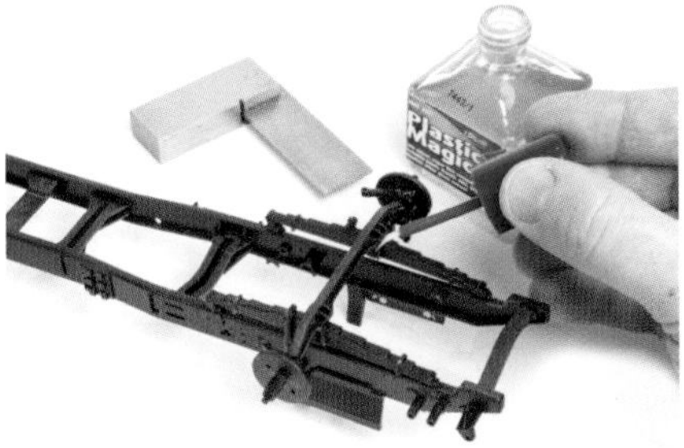

I installed the front axle and suspension first, as this is a straightforward task. Just check that the axle sits at the same distance from the frames on each side, adding a shim of styrene strip where necessary.

The rear spring assemblies are mounted to the frames by central pivots, allowing the axles to flex slightly. These units were dry-fitted initially, with the axle units being fixed to the springs after checking that the angles were correct and that the axles stood level with each other and perpendicular to the side frames.

The frames were then flipped over and a set of wheels fitted loosely over the axles. Working on a flat surface, checks were made to ensure that each tyre was in contact with the surface and that the chassis appeared straight and level. Adding a little weight to the frames put the suspension units under a small amount of stress and helped iron out any discrepancies. When all appeared correct, the spring units were secured to the frames with liquid poly, and the chassis was set aside to cure overnight before continuing.

The shock absorbers and other suspension fittings could then be installed, helping the assembly to become fairly rugged. Note the bolt and washer detail added to the driveshaft yokes, created using the punch-and-dye tools featured in previous chapters.

was checked on each side to confirm that it was sitting level, whilst a set-square revealed whether it was oriented at 90 degrees to the chassis. Moving to the rear, the spring units were pushed into the mounting holes but not glued just yet. Thankfully they were quite a snug fit and stayed put, although I'd been prepared to hold them in place with tape or a mini spring clamp if necessary. The two drive axles could then be slotted into their respective positions between the leaf springs and the dampers (having placed the short driveshaft in position), which held them securely enough to allow the frames to be upturned and the wheels temporarily placed on to all three axles.

Working on a flat surface, I could gauge whether all the tyres were in contact with the ground, or whether any shims were required between the suspension and the axles. The central pins of the two rear leaf-spring assemblies allowed a degree of movement in order to get the axles level and the frames sitting correctly in relation to the ground. After several checks with a set-square and a set of callipers (to ensure the rear pair of axles were equidistant from each other and the frames), I felt confident enough to apply liquid cement to the axle-spring interfaces. A few more checks were made before the spring mounts were secured to the frames. The chassis was left on its temporary wheels, weighted slightly over the axles, to ensure that no twisting occurred while the glue cured.

INSTALLING THE REST OF THE SUSPENSION SYSTEM

Several hours later, the rest of the suspension system could be installed. There were no moulded fixing points or guides on the chassis to help locate the rear shock absorbers; presumably they'd been lost while I fettled the frames earlier. It wasn't too difficult to work out their position, double-checking that the pitch was consistent on all four units. Once the rest of the suspension is in place, the framework takes on an impressive level of rigidity.

As the chassis progresses, it's worth taking a moment and considering whether some components should be fitted now or later. Items such as fuel tanks, battery boxes and reservoir tanks may hinder the finishing process, especially when airbrushing or spraying aerosols, as it's not easy to work the paint evenly around them. In the case of the DAF 95, the fuel tank and the exhaust unit were treated separately, but I did install the mudguards, battery box and the spare-wheel rim.

ENGINE AND TRANSMISSION

While most of the chassis components can be improved by simply tidying up the moulding flaws, the engine and gearbox elements offer a stark reminder of their 1980s heritage. The engine block and gearbox are formed by combining several components, with the two main elements refusing to marry up correctly without intervention. After fettling the mating faces and clamping the parts together, a neat glue joint was finally achieved. Once the visible seams had been cured with filler, the smaller components could be installed.

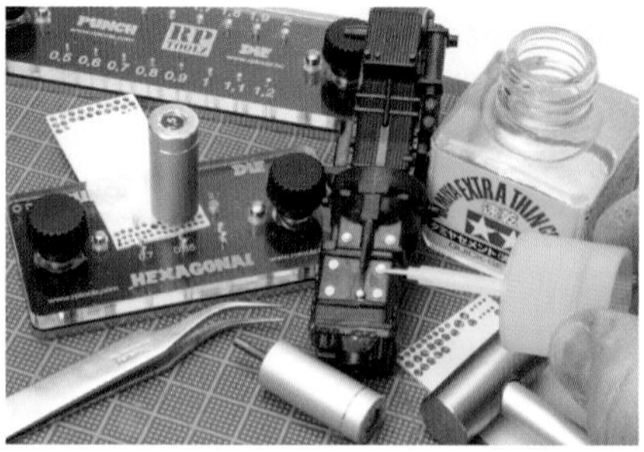

The powerplant is made up of a number of components. Like the differentials, the locating pins were useless and were removed, and the parts were aligned by eye and clamped securely while the cement cured. The joint seams were smoothed, and any gaps filled before attention was turned to improving the detail. Bolt and washer detail was applied to the gearbox and engine casings using a mix of hexagonal and round punch-and-die sets.

The drivebelt pulley and alternator were enhanced with punched detail and thin strip styrene, while a mounting bracket for the alternator was improvised from plastic strip.

After a couple of hours, the engine and gearbox began to appear far more purposeful.

The engine was test-fitted into the chassis, while other parts were prepared and installed permanently, including the battery box, various reservoir tanks, mudguards, spare-wheel bracket and tail-light booms.

As a means of addressing the relative lack of surface relief, the engine, transmission and driveshaft yokes were bedecked with punched styrene washers and hex nuts. The various case covers, oil-filter mounts, fuel pump and injector rail all benefited greatly from the punched details, creating a much more purposeful powerplant.

The crankshaft drivebelt unit is a very basic moulding, but the addition of punched discs and hex bolts had a transformative effect, while fine styrene strip – wrapped around the crankshaft pulley wheel and alternator body – helped to soften the spartan mouldings. The alternator also benefited from the addition of a mounting bracket to attach to the side of the engine, plus a pair of cable terminals, all created from scraps of styrene strip and angle.

PAINTING AND WEATHERING

A CHIPPED PAINT FINISH

After upgrading the powerplant, I was eager to get on with the painting and weathering stages, so the assembly was the first part of the DAF to receive any paint. My aim was to create a chipped paint finish, with the bare metal showing through, indicative of an engine that had been lifted out of the frames at some point. Work began with a coat of Mr Surfacer black aerosol primer, followed by Alclad II Aluminium lacquer, applied with an airbrush and taking care

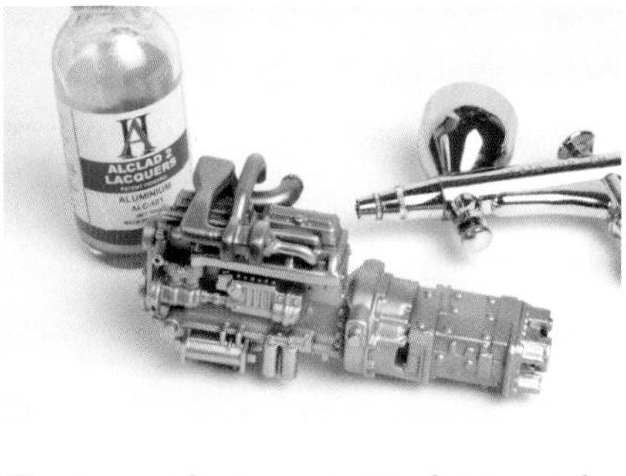

The powerplant was painted separately, first with a gloss black undercoat, then the metallic Alclad II Aluminium lacquer. A clear gloss coat followed.

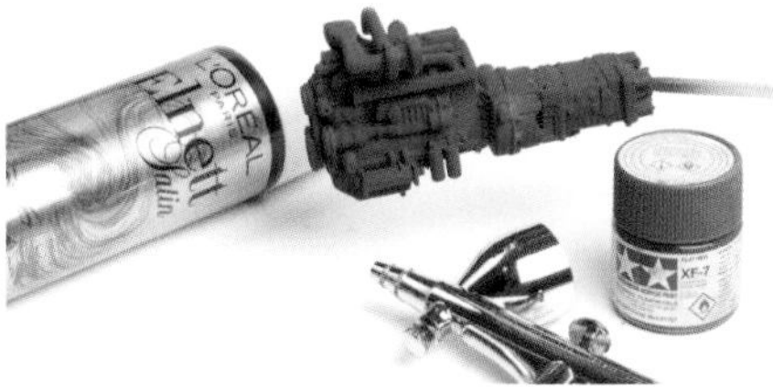

When the clear coat was completely dry, the engine and gearbox were sprayed with a few light coats of extra-hold hairspray. After about ten minutes, the assembly was sprayed with Tamiya acrylic paint.

The Tamiya paint was given an hour or so to dry, then the surface was touched over with damp swabs and brushes. The water softens the hairspray, causing the red paint to chip away and reveal the metallic finish beneath.

A special rubber (Mr Hobby) was also used to create a greater variety of chipping effects.

to work the paint patiently into all the nooks and crannies. After sealing the metallic finish with a clear gloss coat, the assembly was sprayed with a few light mists of extra-hold hairspray.

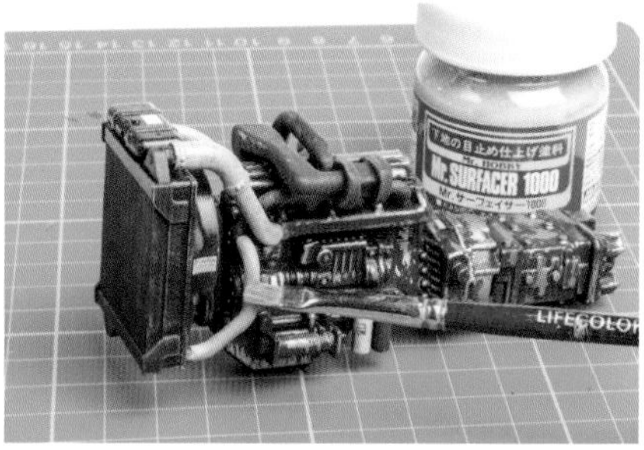

Once you're happy with the amount of chipping, the effects can be sealed with a clear coat. After adding decals, and detail painting the pipework, filters and fan belt, the powerplant can be enhanced with weathering washes. Assembly of the rest of the engine components can follow, with the coolant hoses primed in situ with a brush-applied coat of Mr Surfacer. This will fill any small gaps between parts and give the hoses a realistic texture. To add some visual interest, I later decided to paint the gearbox green before the unit was fixed in place.

After ten minutes or so, the acrylic red topcoats were airbrushed, again in light coats, aiming the paint into the various recesses. The Tamiya paint was left for an hour or so, before being disturbed by a flat brush dipped in water. Using a dabbing or scrubbing action will soften the layer of hairspray and allow the metallic basecoat to appear. As much or as little paint can be removed as you wish, and other implements can be employed to create various other effects, such as a stiffer brush or dampened cotton swabs. Anything from a vaguely worn effect to heavy chipping can be achieved by varying the amount of moisture and pressure applied, and a little practice is worthwhile to help familiarize oneself with the technique.

Alternatively, a special chipping rubber tool or a brass wire brush can create similar effects, with or without the use of the hairspray as a random masking medium. When you're happy with the results, allow the engine to dry overnight; then apply a sealing clear gloss coat. If you're not happy, wash the engine in warm water, and when fully dry, start again with the hairspray and topcoat colour. Applying a slightly different shade of paint, or even a different colour altogether, presents the opportunity to add further interest, as the previous colour will be revealed in patches, along with the bare metal finish, suggesting an article that has been repainted at some point in the past.

This is a technique that can be used on all sorts of truck elements, not just the engine, and it may take a few attempts to get things to your satisfaction. The results will look a little stark to begin with, but once layers of weathering washes, oil and grease effects and dry pigments have been applied, the overall effect should be more cohesive. That's the hope, anyway. While I was mostly happy with the results, I did later repaint the gearbox in a different colour and omitted the chipping process, which provided a pleasant contrast with the engine.

DECALS AND DETAILING

Other enhancements to the engine included the application of decals, featuring a serial-number plaque and various warning legends. Once these were in place, detail painting of the engine components could follow, including the drivebelts, turbocharger and air ducts, exhaust manifold, radiator fan and oil filters.

THE CAB INTERIOR

CONVERSION TO RIGHT-HAND DRIVE

Despite the Continental-style outline of the truck's canvas body, it was my intention to model a UK-based DAF 95, and this would inevitably entail a conversion to right-hand drive (RHD). Given that the vast majority of truck kits are produced in left-hand drive (LHD) format, this job is something I've become accustomed to over the years. In most instances, shifting the controls across the cab can be achieved with a small amount of cutting and rebuilding, as illustrated in Chapter 11. However, this particular project made use of a cast resin replacement dashboard, courtesy of Kit Form Services (KFS), who offer an impressive range of parts to convert a host of 1:24 trucks to RHD.

Designed as a 'drop-in' fixture, all we need do is site the steering column and pedals in the appropriate positions. The resin casting needed tidying up before installation, ensuring that the joint face was flat and square, maximizing the

Conversion to right-hand drive was made easy thanks to a resin casting from KFS. This is designed to be a direct replacement for the kit's dashboard, and after a little fettling work to get the mating faces flat and true, it was fixed to the interior moulding with a slow-drying cyano glue.

After painting, the overlay was fixed over the decal, which had been treated to a heavy clear gloss coating to mimic glazing panels. Note that the seats and bunks have yet to be installed: this makes it easier to paint the interior.

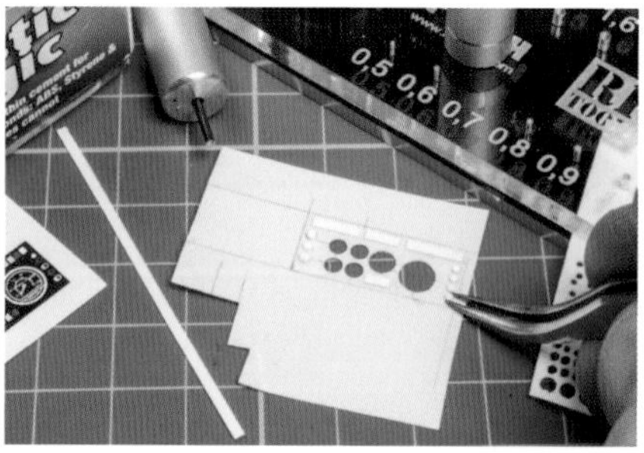

The resin dashboard features a flat surface on which the kit's decal can be applied, depicting the various gauges and controls. To add a sense of relief, I created a thin plastic overlay, similar to that fashioned for the Unimog in the previous chapter. Plastic strip and punched discs made up the lighting strips and buttons, while the apertures had to be drilled and reamed carefully to align with the decal's gauges.

The seats and bunks were covered with a fetching leopard print, courtesy of a waterslide decal sheet from KFS. The surfaces were given a deep gloss coating beforehand, to aid adhesion, with a matt clear coat added afterwards to help seal the film securely and provide a more authentic texture. An airbrush was used to mist some subtle shading over the seats and bedding, which is just about discernible, giving them a more lived-in appearance. Printed maps, papers and magazines added the finishing touch.

amount of surface area on which the cyano glue could form a strong bond with the plastic (epoxy adhesive is also suitable, and provides longer adjustment time). There was still a need for gap-filling here and there, which was achieved with epoxy putty that was mixed and sculpted into the gaps with the aid of a damp swab.

Resin is a useful material, and its soft nature makes it easy to work with – perhaps a little too easy, so take care when filing, drilling or cutting to avoid removing more than you intended. It's important to wear a facemask when filing or sanding resin (and wash your hands afterwards), as the dust can be harmful. Furthermore, the surface of the resin is likely to be contaminated with silicone residues from the moulds. After fettling, give the component a thorough wash in warm soapy water, using an old toothbrush to scrub the surface. Rinse and dry thoroughly before applying adhesives or painting.

DECALS AND DETAILING

The KFS dashboard features a flat driver's facia, allowing the kit's decal to be applied after the painting stage. For greater realism, I crafted a simple overlay from thin plastic sheet with holes cut out to reveal the decal's dials. Getting these spaced correctly took careful measuring, drilling and reaming, while extra relief was created with thin strips of plastic and punched discs to act as warning and instrument lights. For the sake of an hour or so of extra work, the results proved to be very satisfactory.

To ensure easy access to the cabin interior during priming and painting, the steering wheel, seats and bunks were treated separately. A smart set of leopard-print seat- and bed-covers was created using a waterslide decal sheet from KFS, which certainly makes for an eye-catching interior. Cut slightly oversize, the decals were laid over a high gloss clear coat, and with the aid of Micro Sol decal softening solution, they were patiently formed over the moulded components. The corners were cut and folded over, in a similar way to gift-wrapping a box, with any excess decal material cut away *in situ* with a fresh scalpel blade.

When the decals had dried out fully, they were sealed with a further layer of clear gloss, followed by a matt clear coat to give a flatter sheen more appropriate to fabric. Extra visual interest was created by a range of scaled-down magazines, newspapers, road atlases and posters, along with a blanket and sleeping roll, both sculpted from epoxy putty.

ASSEMBLING THE CAB

The assembled cab interior module served as a useful former, around which the exterior body panels could be taped together temporarily, while their fit was assessed. The cab elements sat together nicely, the moulded locating tabs helping with alignment, and they were duly 'tacked' together with a few drops of liquid poly-cement at strategic locations. After an hour or so, the interior was removed and the panel joints were glued properly, applying the cement from the inside. The next day, any gaps between the panels were filled with acrylic putty, administered via a syringe and a pinpoint tip. A damp cotton swab tidied up the exterior before the putty dried, leaving very little abrading work to do later.

PAINTING THE CHASSIS

The painting process began in earnest when the chassis was treated to an initial primer coat. The frames had been washed and dried beforehand, and despite my efforts to tidy up the assembly with fine abrasive pads, the grey primer invariably revealed a few imperfections here and there. I've grown used to this inevitability, and when it's expected, it doesn't feel so disappointing. Indeed, I like to treat this first primer coat as a proving stage, allowing the paint to reveal blemishes that would be almost impossible to identify on 'naked' black plastic.

Accordingly, I used a generic automotive primer (from Halfords) and concentrated on achieving even coverage, which is easier said than done on such a complex object. Very short bursts of paint, approaching the subject from every angle, will help the primer reach inside the frames with less risk of building up puddles or drips. Once the blemishes were addressed with fine abrasive sheets, lubricated with soapy water, the frames were once again cleaned and dried before a finer grade of primer was applied in a similar manner.

The red topcoats were also built up over two stages, with a light shade added first using a matt finish and applied with an airbrush. The air pressure was set fairly low (around 10psi) and the paint thinned to a degree that allowed it to flow freely through the tool – akin to the viscosity of skimmed milk. Airbrushing at a lower pressure, and with a much finer spray pattern than an aerosol, it took some time to build up the colour over the entire chassis, working it evenly within the intricate framework. Both the airbrush and chassis were moved around repeatedly, allowing the finish to be applied from all angles.

However, this approach gave me much more control over how the paint behaved, in contrast to the spray cans. Indeed, the airbrush could be employed at very close quarters to the subject with a much reduced risk of 'blowback' or puddling, provided that the paint flow was kept to a minimum. When this undercoat had hardened, the final glossy topcoat shade was applied: a mix of Tamiya X-7 Gloss Red with a hint of XF-9 Hull Red and a drop of X-5 Gloss Green mixed in. Application followed the same procedure with the airbrush, working patiently at a low air pressure and with a carefully regulated paint flow until the finish appeared smooth and consistent across the entire chassis.

The frames were then left to harden for a few days before the detail painting was undertaken by hand, picking out the mudguards, battery-box cover, rear coupling and barrier. Clear gloss coats followed, applied from an aerosol, blending the hand-brushed elements and building up a deep lustrous finish that allowed the various decals to adhere securely. After a final clear gloss coating, the chassis was set aside for a week to harden completely prior to the weathering stage.

WEATHERING

From the outset I'd planned on treating this truck to a comprehensive weathering job, with the overall aim of recreating a hardworking vehicle that had been in frontline service for a good few years. While the cab and bodywork would be kept in good order – though not totally pristine – the chassis would show more signs of wear and tear, with deposits of ingrained dirt and faded paintwork.

I began the process by applying 'fading' and 'highlight' washes, which act by giving the bright paintwork a more 'lived-in' appearance. The effect can be tailored to reflect the amount of fading desired, simply by adjusting the amount of wash employed. AK Interactive's oil-based fading paints were employed, applied neat in small blobs before a brush dipped in thinners and cotton swabs manipulated the medium. The darker grey shade produces a translucent, dulling and shading effect, while the lighter shade mimics fading, and a combination of the two can produce some lifelike results without necessarily creating a dirty outlook. Indeed, this stage is great for portraying a generally clean truck, but one whose paintwork has faded over time.

A dirty chassis, however, is what I was aiming for, so once the grey oils had dried completely, I moved on to a range of brown and black enamel weathering washes. These were mixed together to form the desired shade of generic grime and brushed liberally over the frames, working on a small area at a time. The excess wash was immediately wiped away with cotton swabs, in vertical strokes wherever possible, leaving the deposits of dirt in key areas and creating subtle streaking effects. Just like the Kenworth Aerodyne in Chapter 7, the red frames suddenly sprang into life as the surface relief received much greater definition. As the images show, this approach is particularly effective on brightly coloured frames, although similar methods can also be employed on black frames, as we'll see in later chapters.

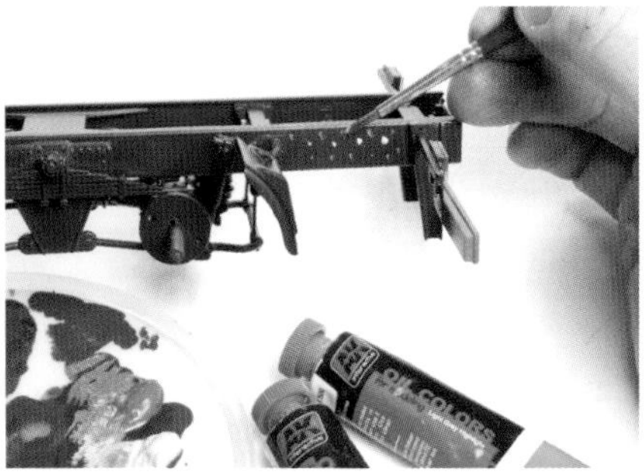

To alleviate the pristine appearance of the painted chassis, AK Interactive's fade and highlight oil paints were applied in small blobs. A mix of the lighter and darker grey shades was employed, dotting the neat paint randomly around the frames.

A soft, flat brush is dipped in thinners, and the paints were washed over the chassis, working on small areas at a time.

Most of the paint was removed with swabs, also dipped lightly into the thinners. The aim is to remove most of the paint, while leaving faint traces of the grey pigment to create a subtle faded appearance.

After an overnight rest, the frames were treated with enamel washes. A blend of brown and black washes was brushed on to the chassis before wiping much of it away, leaving the grimy pigment to add definition to the surface relief. Vertical strokes were employed wherever possible to mimic the streaking effects created by gravity.

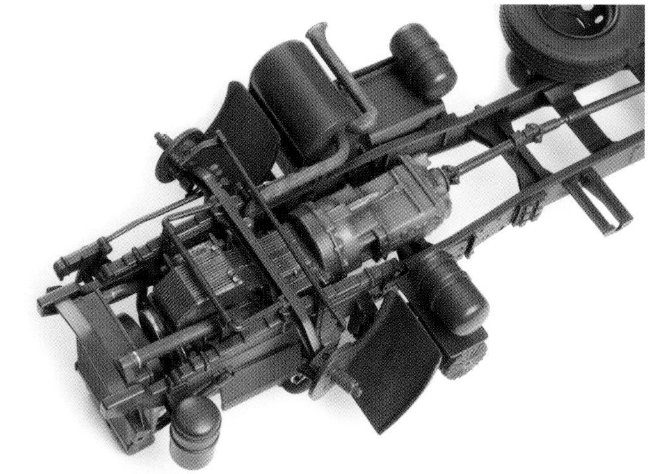

The engine and transmission could now be permanently installed and the exhaust system added, with hand-stippled Mr Surfacer giving the pipework a suitable texture, prior to the application of rust-toned acrylic paints.

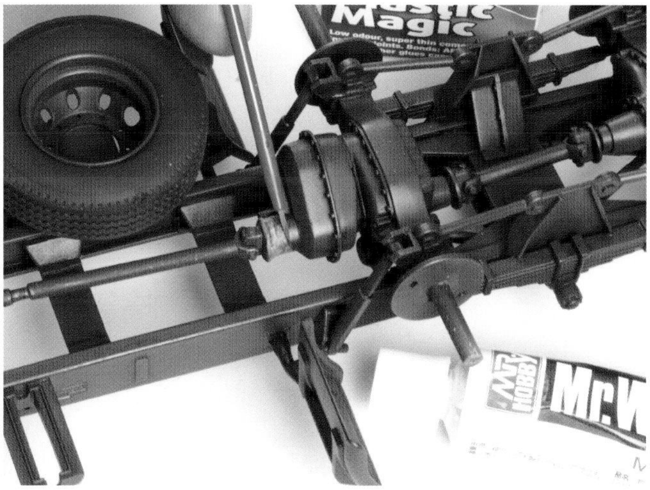

The driveshaft was found to be slightly too short, so the gap at the axle end was filled with putty and manipulated with liquid poly to reduce the need for sanding. Once cured, the fillet could be painted and weathered to blend into its surroundings.

Despite the chassis now being almost complete, the appearance of the rear fender was beginning to annoy me: the lack of any raised bolt detail seemed incongruous, so I added some punched discs and hex nuts, securing them with clear acrylic varnish, then touching them in with paint.

Heavier deposits of grime were created inside the frames and around the suspension and transmission components – those areas least likely to receive regular cleaning – by applying extra coats of the enamel washes, allowing each layer to dry in turn. The contrast between the matt sheen left behind by the washes' pigment and the glossy outlook of the original paintwork creates a very attractive finish. A little work with an airbrush and generic dirty brown/dark grey shades of Tamiya acrylic paints allowed a more diffuse misting of grime around the chassis, helping to reduce any harsh edges left behind by the wash stages and creating a softer, overall appearance. Dry weathering pigments then followed, brushed over key areas, especially to the inside of the chassis frames, providing further contrast of sheen and texture with the previous weathering stages.

Once happy with the appearance of the frames, the engine and transmission could be installed, along with the various pipework, driveshafts and exhaust system. All these elements slotted into place neatly, save for the main driveshaft, which turned out to be fractionally too short. After gluing in position, the gap was filled with Mr Hobby putty, with liquid poly-cement employed to sculpt the filler neatly to match the profile of the differential input. Once this had cured, the putty was painted and weathered to blend everything together, with similar work carried out to the joints between the other newly installed components.

A NEW SET OF WHEELS

Most 1:24-scale truck kits feature a generic set of moulded wheel rims and hubs. While they can look quite good when painted and weathered to a decent standard, the minimal relief in the studs and the lack of authentic hub detail can be disappointing. It is possible to significantly improve the kit parts with the use of a set of hex and disc punch tools, while careful reaming of the moulded circular and oval rim apertures can greatly improve their profile. However, fitting replacement wheel rims and/or hubs can seriously improve realism for minimal extra effort.

For this DAF 95 project, I set out to replace the kit's wheels, not least as I wanted some authentic DAF-branded hubs for the powered axles, but also because the plastic mouldings were of variable quality. A set of resin replacement rims and hubs was duly ordered from KFS, and these parts were cleaned up and prepared for painting. It is worth applying a gloss black undercoat before spraying on a metallic finish, so the rims were thus treated, prior to the airbrushed coats of Alclad II metallic lacquer. Meanwhile the hubs were painted gloss red to match the chassis frames.

I managed to damage one set of rear wheel rims whilst relocating my workshop, and decided to give up and see if the kit's wheels could be improved to match the realism of the KFS castings. This proved to be an interesting exercise,

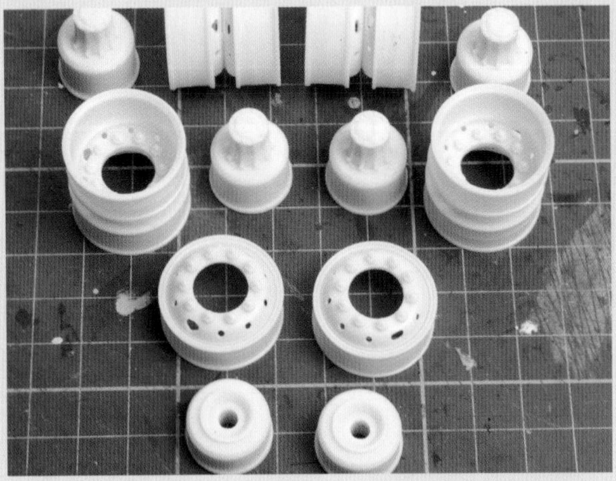

Resin wheel rims and hubs, such as these from KFS, offer a convenient upgrade option. With far greater detail and accuracy, a choice of profiles is available. Like all resin components, the wheels require gentle fettling to open up the perforations and remove excess material. Sanding needles of various abrasive grades are a great help. Remember to wash the parts thoroughly before priming.

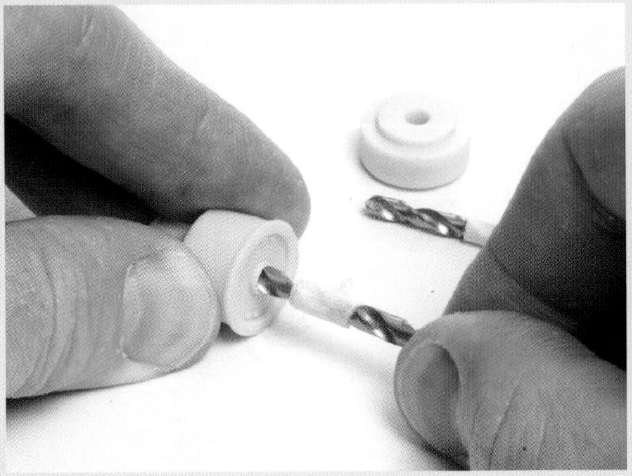

The hubs must be drilled to accept the plastic axles. Choose a bit that is fractionally larger than the axles, and add a strip of masking tape to act as a depth gauge. The soft resin can be readily cut with a hand drill, taking care to bore the hole as squarely as possible in relation to the end of the hub.

Axles may need trimming to a suitable length to allow the hubs to slot snugly against the brake drums.

After cleaning up, the resin parts are ready for priming and painting. A gloss black undercoat precedes the metallic finish. A means of holding the rims during painting was improvised from copper wire.

Alclad II Aluminium lacquer has given the rims an authentic metallic finish, while the hubs have received a glossy red to match the DAF's chassis.

Hand-painting the studs and nuts a contrasting metallic shade is a quick and easy way of boosting realism. After a sealing coat of clear gloss, a weathering wash further enhances the fine detail.

Italeri's plastic wheel rims can be improved, especially if used in combination with a set of separate hubs.

After chopping away the waste material from the moulded hub, the aperture can be reamed to the correct diameter.

A mini chisel (this tool is from the Trumpeter range) is perfect for cutting away the moulded wheel nuts.

The disc and hex punch-and-die sets come to the rescue once again, providing material to form washers, hex nuts and studs.

Combined with the KFS DAF hubs (left), the modified Italeri wheel rim looks far superior to its original form. It will look even better after painting and weathering.

The wheels are an important element of any truck, so investing a little extra time in improving the rims, hubs and tyres is always worthwhile.

and I include the results of my labours here by way of comparison. It also provided a little interest to the finished truck, with the tandem axles featuring a slightly different rim profile.

After painting the rims and hubs, they were treated to a clear gloss coating, followed by treatment with enamel weathering washes and a gentle misting with the airbrush, in the same way as the chassis frames.

The DAF's cab bodywork slotted together really well. Using the interior assembly as a former, the parts were taped together and checked, then a small amount of liquid poly added carefully into the joints with a fine brush. Once the body had cured, the interior unit was removed and a more serious attempt at bonding the joints could be attempted from inside.

The canvas bodyshell is built up as a large, rectangular box, with the sides and ends erected around the base. Check the corners with a set-square as assembly continues, and apply the adhesive from the inside for a neater joint.

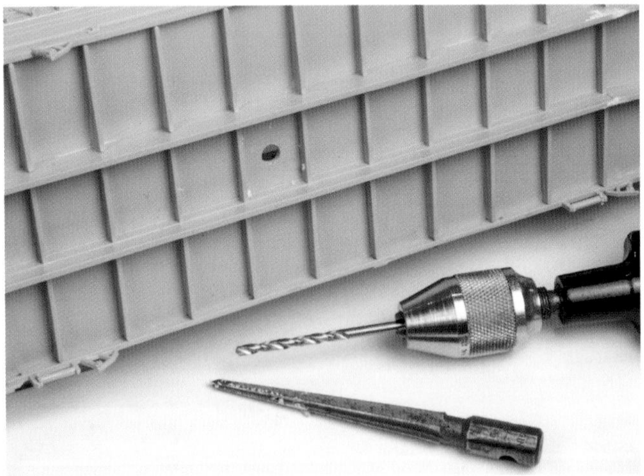

Allow the walls to dry before drilling a hole into the base in a discreet location. This will allow any trapped solvent fumes to escape when the roof is fitted. Furthermore, when we come to wash the body during preparation for painting, any trapped moisture can also escape.

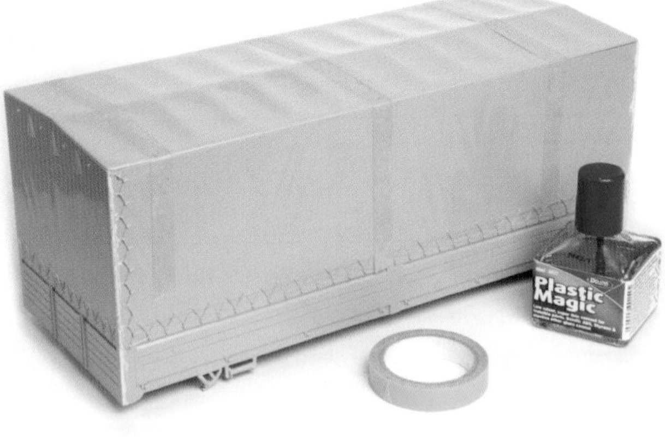

Clamp the roof securely while gluing it in position. Most of the exterior joints will ultimately require filling and tidying up.

PAINTING AND LINING THE CAB

The assembled cab exterior was treated in a similar way to the chassis: it received a proving coat of primer in the first instance, and any imperfections were duly dealt with before a final layer of high-quality primer was applied. The colour coats followed – and this is where things became a little complicated. My initial choice of green turned out to be a mistake as it wasn't quite what I was aiming for, so I had to wait for this to dry out completely before rubbing the cab down and trying again with a different, slightly lighter shade. I didn't like this either, and began to wonder why I'd chosen green in the first place. However, a little perseverance and trust in a more familiar shade eventually paid off.

British Railways Standard Locomotive Green is a colour I usually apply to steam and diesel locomotives of the 1950s and

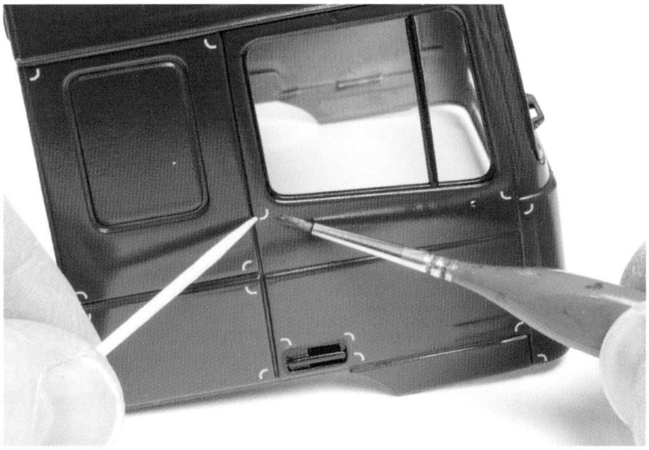

The cab was painted with a lustrous enamel finish, courtesy of Railmatch Paints. Several days were allowed for drying before the clear gloss coats were applied (using a Mr Hobby spray can). More waiting followed before the lining could begin, using a range of waterslide elements from Fox Transfers. First, the curved corners were positioned carefully within each panel.

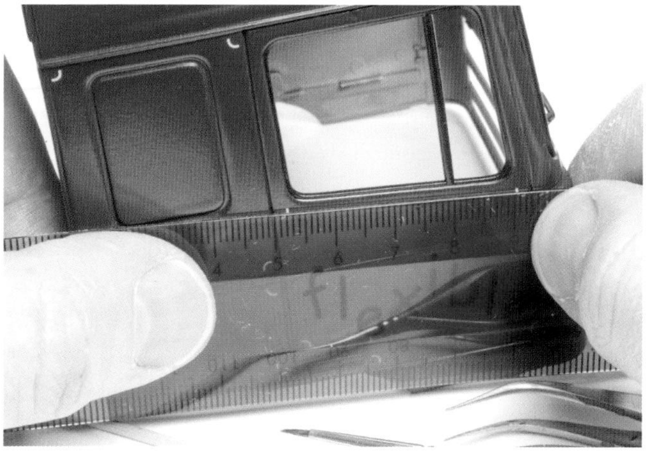

Alignment of the corner elements was checked with a straightedge, and any adjustments made before the decals dried.

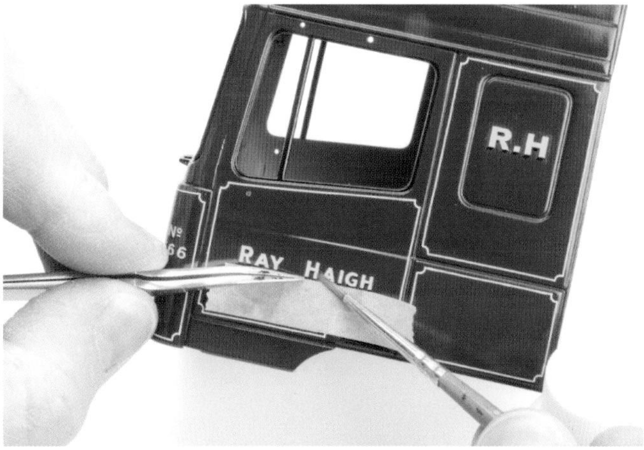

Straight sections of lining were then used to fill the gaps between each corner. The lining was sealed with further clear gloss coats, then the logos were built up from individual shaded characters, using low-tack masking tape to aid alignment.

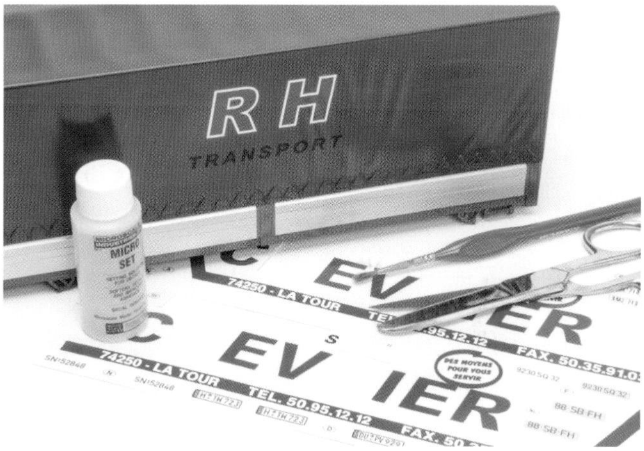

Larger logos for the canvas body were improvised with characters from the Italeri kit's decals.

1960s, so it felt rather strange adopting the shade for a larger-scale truck model. However, as things turned out, it proved to be perfectly suited to my overall plan, and contrasted well with the shade of red adopted for the chassis, bumper and wheel arches. Railmatch's enamel paint is a joy to spray through an airbrush, and many light layers can be built up gradually until a deep, lustrous finish is achieved. The paint dries to a hardwearing, satin sheen, and only requires a few coats of clear gloss to achieve a mirror-like finish.

THE LINING PROCESS

The lining process could now get underway using waterslide decals. First the corner elements were applied, positioned with the aid of a finely sharpened tailor's chalk pencil, which had marked out the locations with small dots. These chalk markings are easily removed with water as the waterslide decals are applied, and providing they are applied with minimal pressure on the surface, no trace will be left.

The yellow lining decals came from the Fox Transfers range and consisted of 1mm-thick, shallow radius curves and straight elements, intended for miniature steam locomotives. Having placed the various corners, and checking their alignment with a ruler, they were left to dry overnight before being sealed with a thin clear coat (applied by airbrush). This is important, as the clear coat will prevent the corners from being disturbed as we add the sections of straight lining. These were individually cut to length and applied carefully, aligning them perfectly with the corners and checking to ensure that each was straight and true; any deviation or waviness in the lines will be glaringly obvious.

This is a painstaking process in some respects, especially when there are many individual panels to treat, but when it's done well, lining can make a dramatic difference to even the most mundane truck. Incidentally, Fox Transfers offers a wide range of lining packs, in terms of colours (single- and multi-coloured schemes), sizes and curve radii. Once all the elements are in place, a further clear coat seals them in position before the logo decals are applied.

APPLYING OTHER DECALS

Continuing the railway influence, the fictional haulage firm's logos were created from some leftover decals that were originally designed for a Highland Railway steam locomotive. This time, the waterslide decals were cut up and the letters rejigged to create a believable haulier by the name of Ray Haigh. The various lettering and numeral sizes fitted the lined panels of the cab perfectly, with a fleet number chosen to mirror the digits on the UK licence plates.

Before application, the characters were set out on the workbench and the overall lengths of the legends were measured, including the spacing between the words. These dimensions can be transferred to the strips of masking tape with a pencil or fine marker pen, which will help with quick, accurate alignment. Work patiently and allow each letter to dry before adding the adjacent character. Once the legend is complete, leave overnight before gently peeling away the tape, and seal the decals with yet another clear gloss coat.

Further decals, featuring a telephone number and a quality-assured logo, were from another leftover OO-gauge railway decal sheet, this time aimed at modern ISO containers (an Italian shipping company). Again, the decals were cut into individual digits to create a Liverpool area telephone number. The same decal sheets provided just enough material to put on the rear of the canvas body, while Italeri's supplied decal sheet was raided for the larger R H TRANSPORT legends that were applied to the canvas sides. There's a slight discrepancy in styles, but I'm happy with the overall scheme. After all, being entirely fictional, it allowed me to adopt a degree of modeller's licence, and the improvised nature of the livery makes it even more satisfying.

WEATHERING THE CAB AND CANVAS BODY

The cab and canvas body were weathered before smaller detail fittings (and glazing) were installed, to avoid the risk of breaking any delicate components during handling. Similar processes to those used on the chassis were employed, save for the fading/highlight oil washes, which were not required. The dark/dirty wash coats were kept to a minimum on the cab, as I wanted to maintain a well-polished appearance. However, the roof and rear bulkhead were given a grubbier look. A fine, airbrushed misting of Tamiya acrylics over the roof, rear and lower edges finished the job.

The canvas body, in contrast, was treated with extra layers of airbrushed grime, aiming to enhance the subtle moulded detail in the canvas sheeting. The tensioning ropes were dry-brushed with a mix of pale grey and light green to enhance their relief, while the deposits left behind by the washes added greater definition to these areas. Various metallic shades were also dry-brushed over the ratchet strap securing points around the base of the dropside panels to mimic burnished steel.

Instead of the supplied plastic pins, which are designed to be shaped with a hot blade to form retaining flanges, I opted to fit the tilting cab to the chassis with a pair of small self-tapping screws. The holes in the brackets had to be reamed to allow the screws to fit.

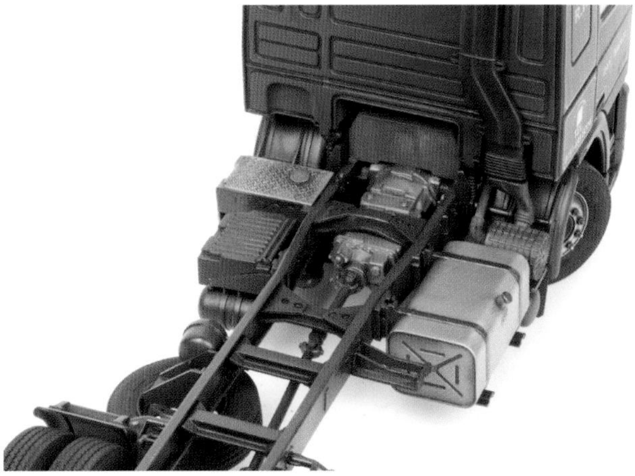

The alignment of the cab was checked, ensuring that it sat correctly on the frames and that the air-intake conduit lined up with the filter unit fixed to the chassis.

When I was 100 per cent satisfied that the cab was correctly fitted, the front fender assembly was secured to the chassis.

The canvas body was attached with Glue 'n' Glaze adhesive, applied in thin beads to the upper faces of the chassis frames and allowed to turn tacky for a few minutes before the parts were brought together. The glue allows for adjustment before it cures, while any excess can be cleaned up with a damp swab. The resulting bond is strong enough to keep the body in place, but can be broken fairly easily if necessary.

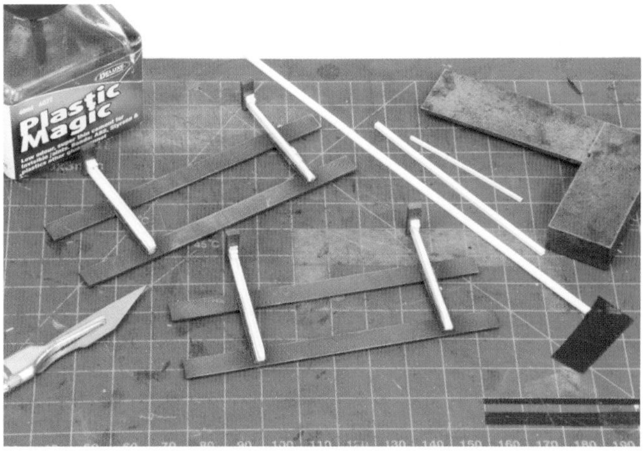

The run-under barriers proved troublesome, as the necessary length could only be gauged once the canvas body was fitted to the chassis. It transpired that the supplied brackets were too flimsy, so I strengthened them with strips of plastic angle.

ATTACHING THE CAB TO THE FRAMES

After adding the glazing, installing the interior sub-assembly (securing it to the cab with a few strategically placed blobs of Glue 'n' Glaze adhesive) and adding the finer details such as wing mirrors, horns and wipers, the cab was ready to be attached to the frames. According to the kit's instructions, cab installation involves a pair of plastic pins, the ends of which should be melted to form flanges, in the same way as the steering arm of the chassis. This method precludes future removal of the cab without physical intervention, so I employed a pair of small pan-head self-tapping screws instead. The holes in the cab's drop brackets were opened out slightly with a tapered reamer to allow the screws to pass through freely, allowing the cab to tilt easily. The chassis brackets were also reamed just enough to allow the screws to cut their own thread into the plastic.

It's important to drive the screws gradually, turning them anti-clockwise half a turn for every full turn clockwise. This takes some of the pressure off the plastic and lowers the risk of splitting the material. Happily, the cab sat squarely on the frames with no need to make any adjustments to the brackets, this being discerned before adding the screws.

LESSONS LEARNED

Despite the minor travails of the painting stage and the lost set of resin wheels, this was a project that offered few serious challenges and proved to be a useful illustration of how 1:24-scale heavy truck kits go together. Hopefully, readers can appreciate the importance of a diligent approach to parts preparation and assembly, especially when building a ladder-frame chassis. Furthermore, the DAF 95 also revealed the considerable amount of work involved in an almost-out-of-the-box build, with minimal extra detailing work undertaken. However, a serious investment in time is required in order to do justice to most 1:24 truck kits, and later chapters show how even more time and effort can be expended in the pursuit of customization and super-detailing.

The lining and lettering of the cab have turned out very well, with good use made of spare decals to create a convincing corporate identity. The leopard-print seat covers add a wonderful sense of brash vulgarity to the cab interior, contrasting with the sober livery.

A lot of work is involved with a 1:24-scale truck kit, especially if aiming for a realistically weathered finish.

CHAPTER TEN

SHOW PONY: 1:24-SCALE MERCEDES-BENZ ACTROS MP3

Modern subjects, specifically trucks from the post-2000 era, do not usually feature in my list of modelling ambitions. Indeed, prototypes from the 1970s and 1980s are my primary interest, but occasionally we all feel like doing something different. Such was my reasoning when I recently set myself the challenge of building an iconic twenty-first-century European truck, with the added dimension of portraying the vehicle in showroom condition.

As you might have gathered already, by examining the projects in earlier chapters, weathering is something I really enjoy. Alas, for this truck I would have to rein in my desire to apply a lived-in or grimy patina to the chassis and bodywork. As we'll see, modelling trucks in pristine condition demands a high degree of care and discipline in order to achieve an immaculate finish. There's no hiding behind a gentle weathering wash or a dusting of dry pigments in order to disguise any less-than-perfect joints or detailing work! Unsurprisingly, therefore, such a project can take just as long – if not longer – than one involving a multi-faceted weathering job.

Modellers are not short of 1:24-scale kits featuring post-millennial prototypes, and initially I chose Italeri's DAF XF105, having been smitten with the 'Smoky Jr' boxing that appeared in 2016. Horses are one of my great loves, and anything with an equine theme is bound to appeal to my imagination, so this striking addition to Italeri's 'Show Trucks' stable had no competition as far as I was concerned. The intricate artwork featured images of wild horses and snowy mountains, complemented by more contemporary elements and colour separations. Custom, chromed exhausts and fat tyres added extra lustre to the package.

So far, so good. Unfortunately, however, the chassis is rendered as a single moulding, with a rigid front axle, no engine or gearbox, and minimal transmission and suspension fittings to assemble and install. This is the case with a number of modern tractor unit kits, and while superb models can still be produced, I find much less joy in building them. Not everybody feels the same way, I'm sure, but I do prefer to erect my own chassis frames, and labour over the powerplant, transmission and all the myriad small fittings.

My mission to build a striking modern truck in 1:24 scale started with the purchase of this Italeri kit, featuring a souped-up DAF XF105 and amazing custom artwork.

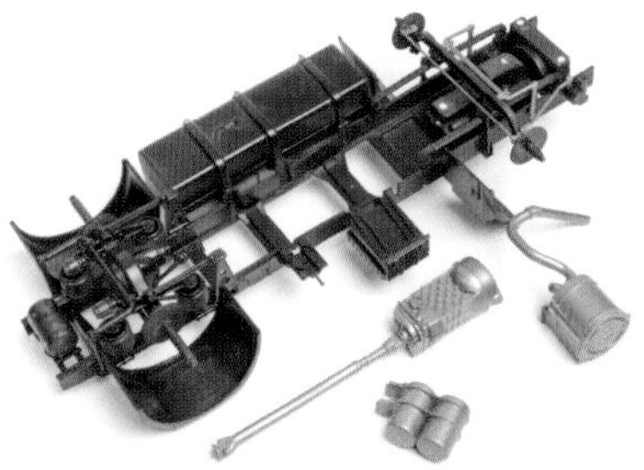

While there was much to admire within the box, Italeri's decision to render the chassis as a single moulding, with very little detail and no engine (save for a moulded sump), tempered my enthusiasm. I'll finish building it one day, but I decided to search for something more rewarding instead.

Initially unperturbed by this arrangement, I decided to forge ahead with the build. I'd recently finished the 1:32-scale Kenworth Aerodyne (Chapter 7), so I was feeling confident that the barren chassis frames could be significantly enhanced with some detailing work. My early enthusiasm waned, however, and I was soon on the hunt for a more rewarding kit to work with. It didn't take long before I came across Revell's Mercedes-Benz Actros MP3, complete with native American-themed decals (including horses). This was not an obvious subject with which to embellish a German truck, perhaps, but the decals looked superb, and the added challenge of a metallic silver finish was another enticing prospect.

THE ACTROS RANGE

Building on the success of its previous truck designs, Mercedes-Benz first launched the Actros range in 1996. Featuring an all-new chassis and cab design, various configurations were offered to suit a host of applications, with a choice of 12-litre/6-cylinder or 16-litre/V8 engines. Subsequent upgrades and redesigns followed, and the Actros remains a hugely popular truck within the European market.

This Revell kit portrays the Actros MP3, a much improved truck that made

This Revell-boxed Mercedes-Benz Actros MP3 answered my calls for a comprehensive kit with a fully detailed chassis, engine and transmission. With a much higher parts count than the DAF XF105, the Actros was still cheaper, making it a great value 1:24-scale kit.

its debut in 2008 and featured high-tech electronic engine, transmission and braking control. The kit was first released by Italeri in 2013, and subsequently re-boxed by Revell in 2015. First impressions were very positive, with the plastic components crisply moulded and an impressive array of parts, including a full engine/transmission and a ladder-frame chassis to construct in the traditional way. Different shades of grey plastic have been employed throughout, and this is a real boon to the builder, as blemishes and imperfect joints are much easier to discern prior to the application of primer. Taking into account the high parts count, the quality of the moulds and the superb decals, this Revell kit offers fantastic value.

GETTING STARTED

As well as deciding to model the Actros in pristine condition, I also set out to build the truck virtually 'out of the box', with only a handful of extra detail additions, the most notable being a set of cast resin tyres to replace the nondescript rubber originals. With most of the chassis frames hidden behind aerodynamic panels and tread plates, I didn't think it was worth the effort to install brake pipes, hydraulic lines and electrical cable, while I also resolved to keep the cab interior free of clutter. Having made these decisions at the outset, work could get underway with a clear goal in sight.

WORK ON THE CHASSIS

Work began by fettling the chassis elements making up the various multi-part sub-assemblies, such as air tanks, differentials and engine block. Once cured, any gaps were filled and the joints abraded, working through successive grades of abrasives before washing the parts to remove all traces of debris, the ultimate goal being a seamless finish to all surfaces. As each part and sub-assembly was completed, they were moved to a lidded box to keep them clean and safe before assembly began in earnest. This preparation takes a little time, and watching the pile of components grow within the box may not be as exciting as sticking everything together straightaway, but there's a certain sense of reward and heightened anticipation to be gained from this patient approach.

Curiously, the Actros' chassis frames come in two sections per side, with a joint about three-quarters of the way along the total length. Shorter components reduce the risk of any warping or twisting once the plastic is removed from the moulds, and I assume that this approach also allows the manufacturer to offer different chassis iterations without a complete re-tooling. Whatever the reasons, it's imperative for us to ensure that the frame sections are joined carefully, as

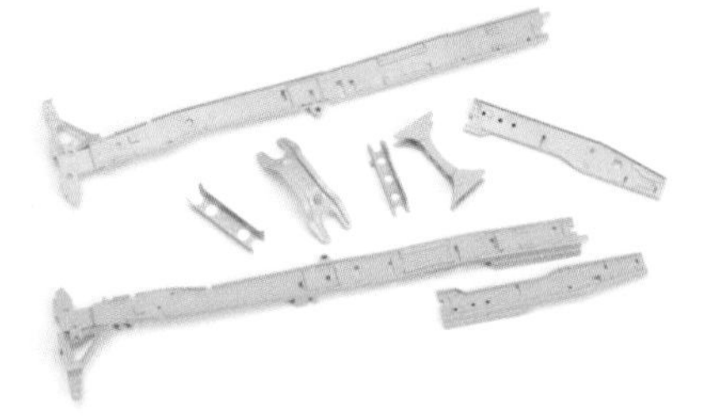

The chassis side frames are split into two sections. Shorter parts are less prone to warping than longer ones, but care is needed to achieve a perfect union.

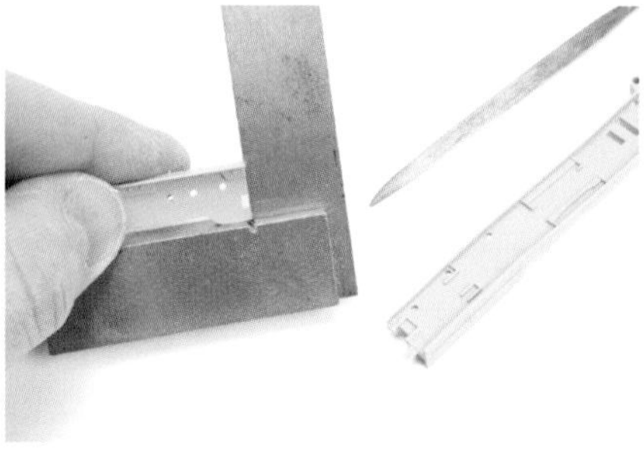

Each mating face was dressed with a flat file and checked with a set-square. It's easy to remove too much material, so go gently and keep checking that both assembled frames will be exactly the same length overall.

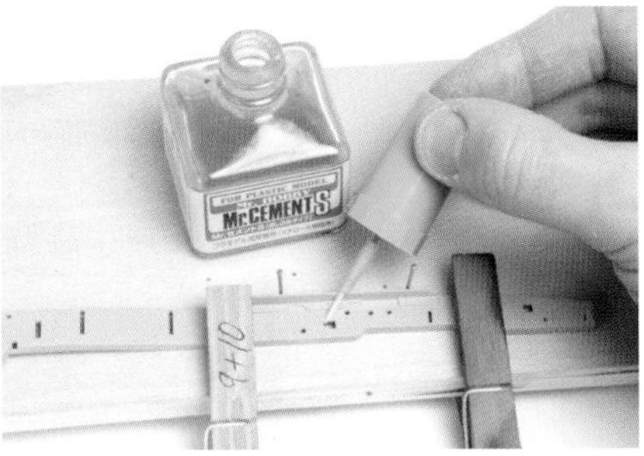

A simple assembly jig was created from an offcut of plywood, with fine panel pins acting as locating guides and clothes-pegs holding the parts in position. After checking the alignment with a straightedge, the cement was brushed into the joint and the parts left to harden for a few hours; the task was then repeated with the opposite frame.

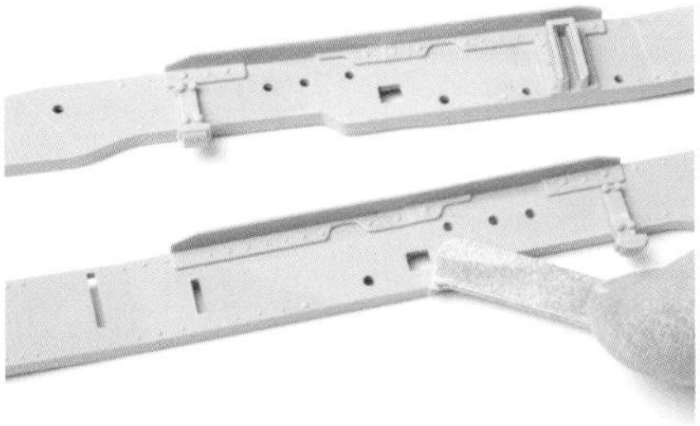

When the glue had cured, the outer surfaces were abraded flat and square, the aim being to create a seamless transition across the joint, especially for the fifth-wheel mounting flanges.

this will influence how the rest of the chassis fits together.

The mating faces were prepared with care, the aim being not to remove too much material, and test-fitting at regular intervals. Checks were made that both assembled frames would be the same length overall, which in turn would ensure that the various apertures and mounting points for the cross-members, engine, transmission and suspension were all perfectly aligned.

In fact the various raised elements didn't marry up particularly well across the joints, so I prioritized getting the vertical edges square so that the parts butt-jointed as cleanly as possible. This would ensure the maximum contact surface area for the poly-cement to act upon, and a pair of simple assembly jigs were fashioned from offcuts of plywood. Small panel pins acted as locating aids, and the two halves of the frame were clamped in position with clothes-pegs. After checking that the upper edges of the frames were aligned and straight, the cement was brushed over the joints and the parts left overnight before being removed from the jigs.

When fully cured, the joints can be tidied up with filler if necessary, before abrading the faces and edges to produce a seamless appearance. This took time to achieve, as the fifth-wheel mounting flanges didn't meet perfectly across the joint in the frames. As a result, there was plenty of work to be done with files and abrasives to get the outward profiles consistent. While the outer faces of the frames will subsequently be hidden by the various external suspension mounts, the upper edges will remain highly visible, so it's worth making the effort to get things right.

At this stage, I marked out and drilled rows of 1.5mm-diameter holes into the flanges, fore and aft of where the fifth-wheel mounting bracket will sit. This simple task improves the appearance of the chassis considerably, although it's important to get the holes equally spaced and in a straight line, so mark the locations carefully with a fine point (an embroidery needle or pin will suffice) and employ a sharp drill bit.

Assembly of the chassis frames followed the same process outlined in the previous chapter. The cross-members were test-fitted and fettled until they sat perfectly into their locating points. In contrast to the DAF 95's frames, the Actros' cross-members feature a great many stress-relieving apertures, which

Frame assembly followed the same procedure as the DAF 95 in the previous chapter, the parts being assembled without glue, with masking tape holding everything together. When sure that all was straight and true, the cement was brushed into the joints.

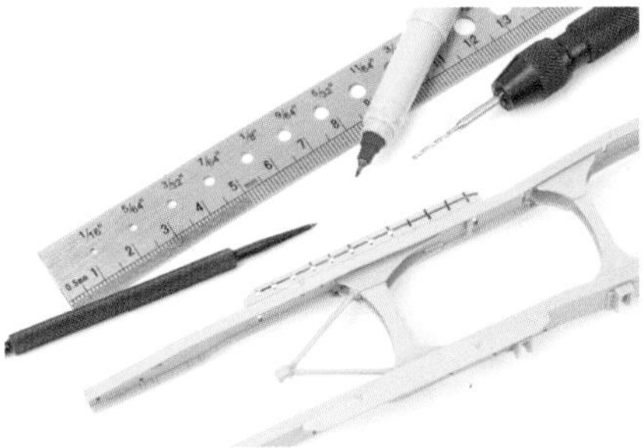

A row of 1.5mm-diameter holes was drilled along each of the fifth-wheel mounting brackets.

required the attentions of round files and sanding needles to improve their profile and remove the visible mould seams. Once fully prepared, the frames were dry-assembled and clamped with masking tape before the liquid cement was brushed into the joints, having made the usual checks for correct alignment.

THE MERCEDES ENGINE

The kit provides an impressive rendition of the Mercedes V8 OM542 engine, and this was built while the chassis frames cured. Various separate elements go together to make up the powerplant, some of which are best painted individually, such as the air manifold cover, fanbelt/pulley array, and the turbocharger assembly. The latter features pipework that is moulded hollow in parts, so these areas were filled with Milliput epoxy putty.

WHEELS AND TYRES

Attention then turned to the wheels and tyres. The kit's wheel rims were deemed good enough to retain, but the rubber tyres looked more suitable for older trucks. Instead, a set of cast resin tyres was obtained from KFS, their immaculate deep treads and raised sidewall detail making them ideal for a more recent vehicle in pristine condition. The resin components were nice and clean, with only minimal dressing needed on the tread faces to remove casting marks, before the parts were

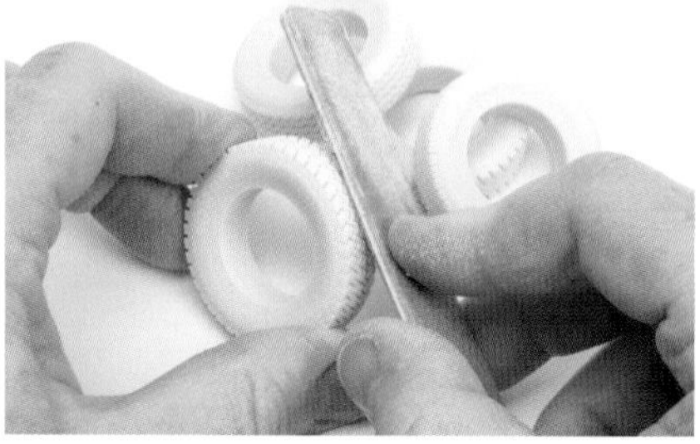

While the frames hardened, the resin tyres (from Kit Form Services) were tidied up with abrasives. Remember to wear a mask when working with resin parts.

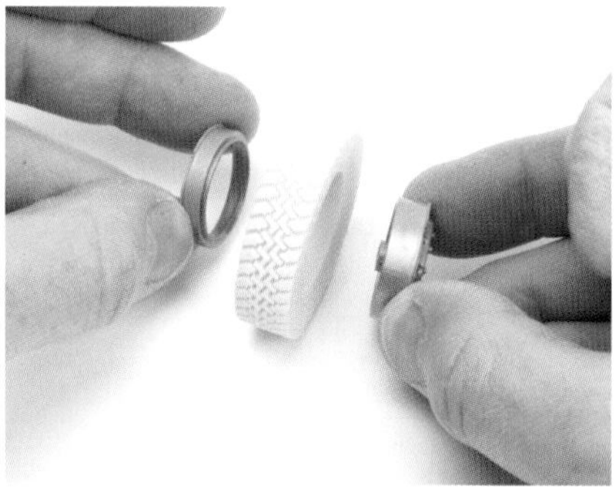

After fettling the kit's wheel rims, they were assembled around the tyres, sandwiching the resin between both halves. Slow-drying cyano secured the plastic to the resin, then liquid poly bonded the plastic sections to each other; this made for a very strong bond.

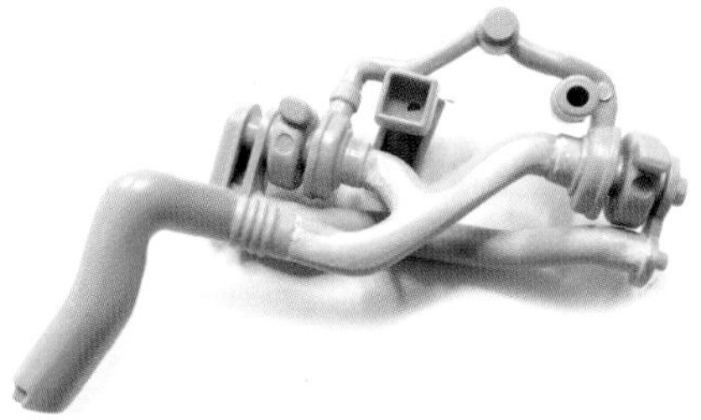

The engine block was also erected at this stage, built up in several individual sections to make painting easier. The underside of the turbocharger pipework is moulded in half relief, so the hollow sections of pipework were filled in with Milliput epoxy putty and smoothed to match the overall profile.

After fixing the suspension and axles in position, the wheels were temporarily attached to check for correct alignment. Now was a good time also to check the fit of the engine and other chassis fittings. Things were beginning to get exciting!

given a thorough wash to shift any silicone residues.

In contrast to rubber tyres, which are simply pushed on to the completed rims, the plastic wheels need to be assembled around the inflexible resin tyres. I bonded the plastic parts to the resin with slow-drying cyano glue, before running liquid poly-cement into the joints between the inner and outer plastic rims, thus sandwiching everything together securely.

The completed wheel sets can then be primed and painted as single units. Before that happens, however, they were employed to test the chassis as the suspension and axles were prepared and installed. Again, a number of chassis and transmission parts were only test-fitted at this stage, as they were to be painted separately, even though they might all be receiving the same colour. The reservoir tanks are a good example, as once installed, it would be tricky to work the paint around their entire profile, especially if spraying with an aerosol or airbrush. Remembering that any imperfections in the paint coverage couldn't be disguised with weathering, I had to accept the necessity of painting a greater number of separate chassis components than usual.

PAINTING BEGINS

Once the allotted components had been installed on the chassis, the frames and various sub-assemblies were thoroughly cleaned before Mr Surfacer Black primer coat was applied, providing the perfect base for the dark grey topcoat colour. The Tamiya paint employed – XF-63 German Grey – dries to a heavy matt finish, creating a rather uninspiring colour. However, after several coats of clear gloss, the grey paint is transformed into something far more attractive. It may not be an exact match for the dark grey shade that Mercedes employed on much of its Actros fleet, but it's close. More importantly, it

Black primer was sprayed over the chassis, the engine, and all the various sub-assemblies. This provided the perfect base for the proposed topcoat colours.

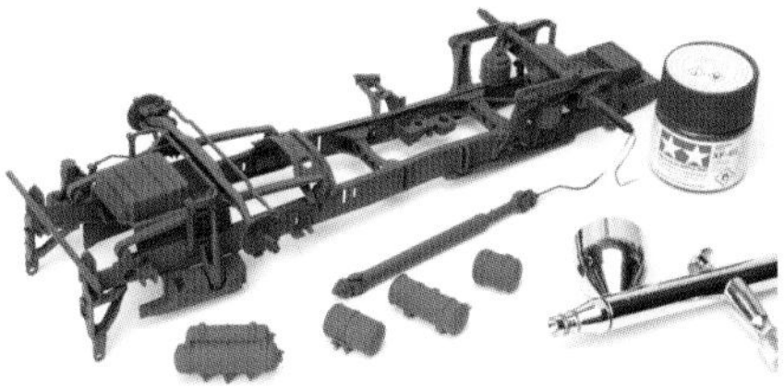

Tamiya XF-63 German Grey was airbrushed on to the chassis as well as the air tanks and driveshaft, taking care to work the paint into all the nooks and crannies.

The Tamiya grey dries to an ultra-matt finish, which is not surprising for a military paint shade. However, once a deep clear gloss finish was applied, the colour becomes much more interesting. The brake discs were painted with Alclad II Aluminium lacquer, followed by clear gloss.

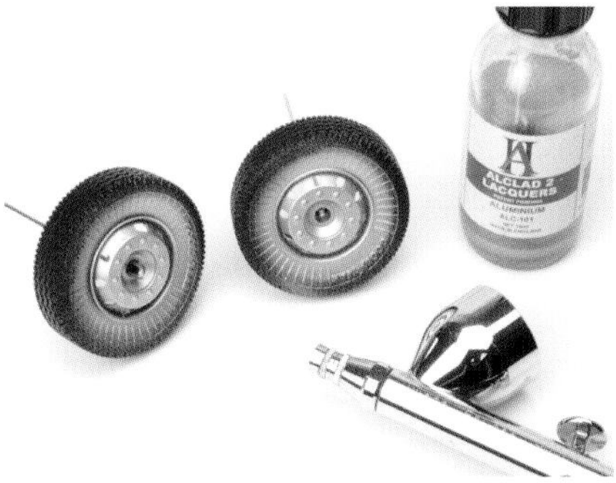

The assembled wheels also received a black primer coat, after which the rims were treated with Alclad II Aluminium. The tyres were painted by hand, then clear gloss coats were sprayed on via an airbrush.

would eventually complement the silver bodywork perfectly.

Prior to the gloss coats, certain parts were hand-painted in appropriate colours, including the rubber air-suspension bags, engine shrouds and sump guard; also the front brake discs received a bright metallic finish (the rear discs were treated remotely and fitted later).

The wheels and tyres were also treated with black aerosol primer as a prelude to Alclad II metallic lacquer. The tyres were later hand-brushed with Lifecolor's acrylic UA733 Tyre Black, building up with three coats to ensure full opacity and an even finish. The final touch consisted of an airbrushed coat of clear gloss to the metallic rims to build up a deep shine, while lighter gloss coats were also sprayed over the inner and outer tyre sidewalls, in keeping with the overall showroom finish, although the matt sheen of the tread faces was retained to provide a convincing contrast.

Part of the attraction of this project was the potential for recreating a clean, modern power unit with a metallic finish. Even though much of the engine is eventually hidden by the chassis frames, it felt like a worthwhile exercise. After a black primer coat, Alclad II Semi Matt Aluminium lacquer was airbrushed on to the main engine block and gearbox. The two cylindrical oil filters were given a slightly different metallic shade, hand-brushed with Darkstar acrylic Tarnished Steel, while the filter mounts and exhaust manifolds received further variations of acrylic metallic shades (a mix of Darkstar's Copper and Blue Steel applied over an undercoat of Lifecolor UA205 Rotbraun), again applied by hand.

After picking out the cylinder-head covers in black, the unit was given an

Alclad II Semi Matt Aluminium was airbrushed over the engine block, then details were painted by hand and an overall clear coat was sprayed on. The engine and radiator elements were treated separately, with a range of shades and sheens to create some diversity in appearance.

Upon assembly, any gaps between the parts were filled and the paintwork blended in.

The kit provides a handful of decals for the engine block, cylinder head and oil filters.

overall clear gloss coat before the kit's decals were applied. The turbocharger assembly and radiator also required multiple shades, which were applied by hand and by airbrush; this was followed by gentle dry-brushing with a metallic silver shade to draw out the relief in the cooling elements. It was also important to achieve some contrast between sheens as well as shades, so plastic hoses, rubber fanbelts and universal joints were rendered in a flatter sheen to the shiny metal elements. The exhaust outlet pipe was hand-stippled with several coats of matt acrylic paint, and later dry-brushed with traces of Darkstar Steel to accentuate this texture.

Further clear coats followed, using gloss, satin and matt where appropriate, before the parts were assembled. A few gaps presented themselves, particularly where the exhaust manifolds met the turbocharger, but these were easily filled before the paintwork was touched in. Other parts to receive metallic finishes at this stage included the brake discs, exhaust unit and fuel tank, each of which were finished in shiny Alclad II metallic lacquers, applied by airbrush; these were followed by clear gloss coats.

The fuel tank in fact required a lot of work in order to create a flawless joint between the two parts. The metallic finish would highlight even the slightest blemish, so there was a great deal of filling, abrading and test-priming until the surfaces were perfect, including the retaining straps that encircle the tank. Maintaining a square edge to these raised elements across the joint between the upper and lower halves of the tank demanded careful use of files and sanding sticks, as it's all too easy to lose definition by being a little over-eager with the abrasives.

Alclad II Aluminium was airbrushed over the black-primed tank, and when that had dried, masking was applied to allow the straps to be sprayed a slightly darker colour (Alclad II Steel). To add some visual interest, I then removed the masking and airbrushed a light misting of Pale Burnt Metal, which gave the surface a slight sepia tone – this looked very effective and offered just a hint of shading. Clear gloss coats followed, to seal the metallic lacquers and create a more lustrous finish. Incidentally, the tank was held securely during the painting process by simply pushing a wooden cocktail stick into the mounting hole for the filler cap (which was painted separately and fitted later). The cocktail stick was then mounted in a mini hand vice so I could keep both hands free.

After a coat of Alclad II Aluminium, the tank was masked to expose only the two retaining straps; these were sprayed with Alclad II Steel. After removing the masking, a very fine mist of Pale Burnt Metal was airbrushed around the edges of the tank and straps to add a little shading. This was an experiment into adding some visual interest without necessarily weathering the component.

CHASSIS ASSEMBLY

While it took several weeks to get all the individual elements finished to a high standard, final assembly of the chassis progressed fairly quickly. First, the air tanks and rear brake discs were secured to the frames with cyano glue. For other parts that were more liable to damage during handling, a more resilient bond was required. In these instances, especially when the fit of the parts is snug, liquid poly-cement is preferred, and the fuel tank, air cleaner, exhaust pod and mudguards were all fixed with Plastic Magic.

To ensure an effective bond, the mating faces of these parts – and their locations on the chassis – were cleaned back to bare plastic with the edge of

Once all the separate chassis elements had been painted, assembly could begin.

Cyano joints can be brittle and epoxy messy, so I prefer liquid poly-cement for structural joints wherever possible. To facilitate this, the joint faces were scraped back to the bare plastic with a sharp blade.

Strips of 10thou' styrene were employed as shims where necessary, to ensure that the parts fitted snugly into their slots. Liquid poly was then run into the joint with a fine brush.

The air tanks had to be treated differently, due to the diminutive size of their mounting lugs, so cyano glue was applied with a cocktail stick.

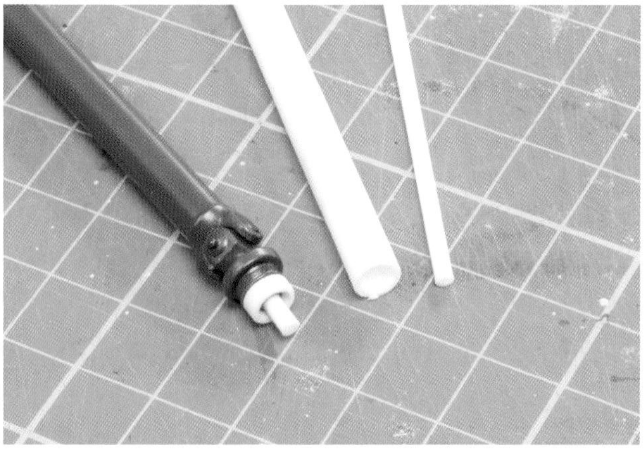

The driveshaft was found to be slightly short, so a new spigot was formed from plastic rod, fixed into a hole drilled into the end of the shaft. A sleeve was also cut from styrene tube to bridge the gap between the differential casing and the yoke.

a fresh scalpel blade. If the joints felt loose, the Plastic Magic would struggle to create a reliable bond, so ultra-thin strips of styrene were inserted wherever necessary to act as shims. Minimal liquid cement was applied with a fine brush, to avoid damaging the surrounding paintwork, and the parts were aligned carefully before the chassis was put to one side to allow the glue to cure.

Later, the frames were examined to identify any areas where the paintwork needed repairing. Unpainted mounting lugs and shims for the recently fitted items, protruding through the frames, were touched in with a fine paintbrush, using the same Tamiya German Grey, followed by an airbrushed coat of clear gloss, to maintain a consistent sheen with the rest of the chassis.

The wheels could then be permanently installed, following the kit's instructions; this always feels like a momentous occasion with any truck kit. During test-fitting of the engine and transmission I realized that the driveshaft was slightly too short, leading to a very sloppy and insecure fit between the gearbox and the differential casing. This is something that I've had to address on virtually every 1:24 truck kit I've built, so I don't know why I didn't notice the problem when trial-fitting the parts prior to painting.

I effected a simple remedy by cutting off the protruding plastic pin at the axle end of the shaft and drilling a hole to accept a length of styrene rod. However, while this would bridge the gulf between the shaft and the differential, there would still be an unsightly gap between the casing and the driveshaft yoke, so a short section of plastic tube was also cut and fixed in position. This 'sleeve' of tubing had to be chamfered slightly on its outer edge to compensate for the angle at which the driveshaft leaves the differential, so repeated test-fitting and fettling was necessary until the fit was perfect.

All the new glue bonds between the chassis components were touched in with paint and clear gloss to ensure a flawless finish.

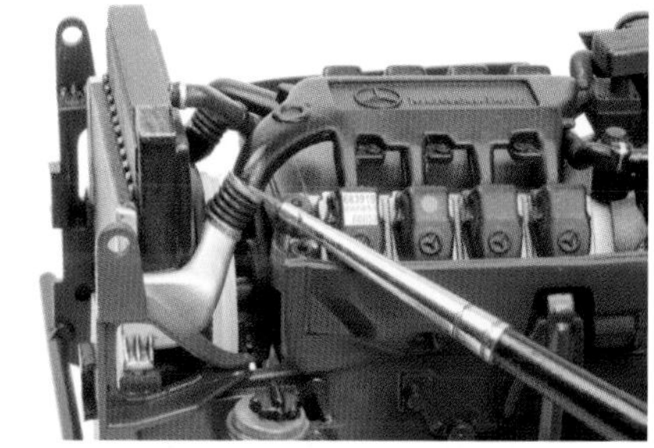

After installing the engine and associated pipework, a set of jubilee clips was fashioned from strips of masking tape, secured with cyano glue. Metallic paint gave them the finishing touch.

These new bits of plastic then had to be painted to match the chassis before the driveshaft could be installed permanently, so there was an element of frustration as progress stalled. Momentum was soon regained, however, and it felt exciting to finally fix the engine to the frames, followed by the cooling system and pipework.

A little finesse was added to the pipe joints in the form of improvised jubilee clips, formed from thin strips of masking tape cut with a sharp scalpel blade. After trimming them *in situ* and securing the ends with a drop of cyano glue (applied with the sharpened tip of a toothpick), they were painted with metallic silver paint. As well as looking nice, these clips

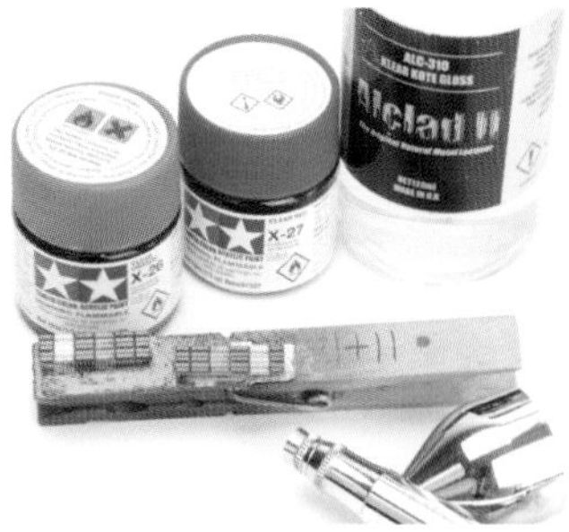

The clear plastic tail-light units were primed with an airbrushed coat of clear gloss, which helps the Tamiya Clear Orange and Clear Red paints adhere more effectively. Silver paint was applied to the underside of the parts to create a reflective effect.

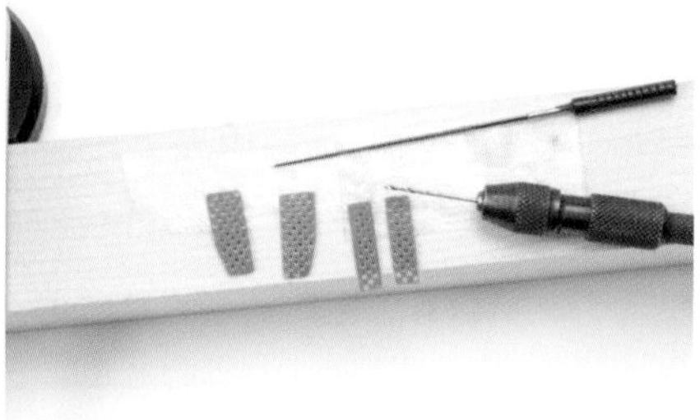

The small step treads for the cab and side skirts were greatly enhanced by drilling and reaming out the moulded perforations, prior to priming and painting with a metallic finish.

The air-smoothed side skirts acted as a testbed for the proposed paint finish for the cab.

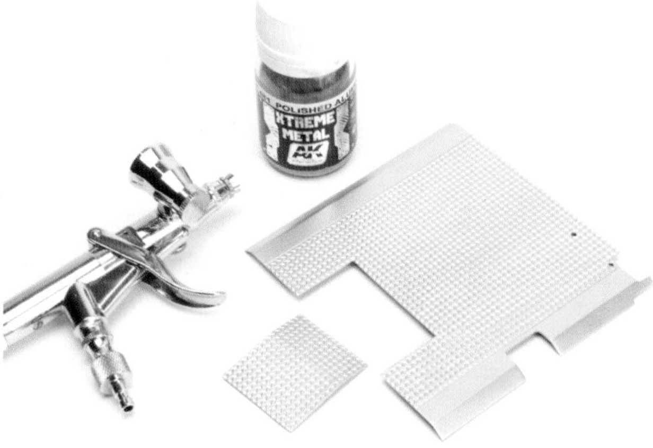

Sheets of chequer-plate decking were taken from Italeri's Truck Accessories pack (Set 2 No. 3854). However, I didn't like the thick chrome finish, so I rubbed down the surface and sprayed on a coat of black primer. AKI's Extreme Metal Polished Aluminium was then applied, followed by a gloss clear coat.

The decking plates finish off the chassis nicely, as it awaits the arrival of the cab. Incidentally, the plastic mudguards were finished with a few coats of Alclad II's Light Sheen clear coat, which offers a subtle contrast with the glossy appearance of the chassis.

also serve to hide any gaps between the pipe joints. This is a technique that will be shown in more detail in Chapter 12.

THE CAB INTERIOR

My quest for a clean new truck meant that I had to restrain myself from filling the cab interior with my usual array of designs and clutter. Instead, I poured my energy into enhancing the impressive moulded components provided in the kit. The luxurious seats were painted carefully by hand, with subtle washes applied to bring out the ribbed upholstery without making it appear dirty. Mid-grey washes were useful in this respect, run into the seams with a fine brush. A combination of matt and satin clear coats followed the application of the Mercedes-Benz logos to the headrests (supplied on the kit's decals sheet), to balance the look of the contrasting fabrics.

The actual interior shell, consisting of the floor, inner walls and roof, were airbrushed with subtle shading effects to augment the various panel and seam relief in the mouldings, and to avoid a one-dimensional appearance. Furthermore, the highlights and shading, achieved through the use of various greys, effectively captured the look of

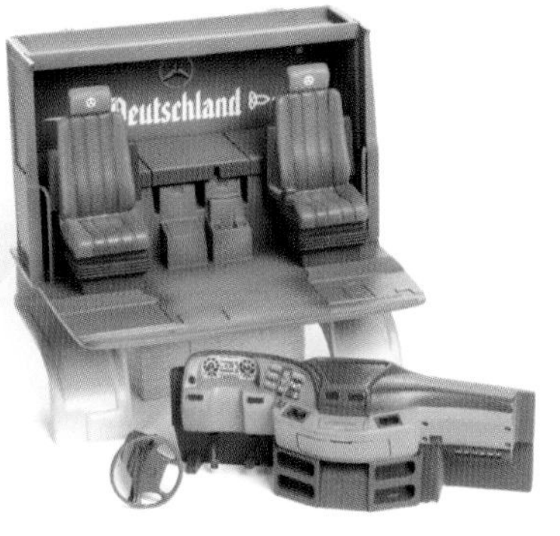

The cab interior parts are excellent, and I spent several happy hours picking out all the detail with appropriate colours. A dark enamel wash was run into the seams of the upholstery, and some gentle shading was applied with an airbrush. The kit provides decals for the dashboard, but I added some extra logos to the rear bulkhead, courtesy of the Italeri Accessory Pack.

The door inner cards were modified to fit on to the completed interior unit, allowing the whole thing to slide inside the outer cab shell.

the interior's trim. The dashboard unit is impressive, with various decals provided to recreate the electronic displays and control consoles. A little customization involved the use of extra decals from Italeri's Truck Accessories Set 2 (No. 3854), adding a patriotic touch for the German owner.

The interior was treated in several separate sub-assemblies, which were eventually brought together. As will be explained, I deviated from the kit's instructions at this point, making up the interior into a substantial self-contained unit that would act as a forming aid for the erection of the exterior shell. As part of this plan, I had to modify the door inner trim panels so as to fix them directly to the interior unit rather than the outer shell.

Like any interior, it's important to achieve strong bonds between the various components: seats, bunk, dashboard, door panels and inner roof section. The last thing we want is for parts to work loose over time, and in general I prefer to fuse the parts together with liquid poly wherever possible, scraping the mating faces back to bare plastic to ensure a satisfactory joint. Where this isn't possible, a strong but flexible adhesive is employed, such as epoxy or Deluxe Materials' Glue 'n' Glaze.

THE EXTERIOR BODYWORK

The first part of the outer bodywork to be treated was the side skirts. Indeed, they would be the 'guinea pigs' for my choice of metallic finish, because if things didn't work out, they'd be easier to strip than the cab. Preparation involved an initial aerosol primer coat of grey Mr Surfacer 1000, subsequently rubbed down with Micro-Mesh abrasive sheets, used wet, and working from 4,000grit down to 12,000grit until the surface was super smooth and blemish free. Another primer coat followed, this time using Mr Surfacer Black 1500, followed by a further light abrading with the higher grades of Micro-Mesh (8,000–12,000grit). When clean and dry, it was time to add the topcoat colour.

After weighing up various paint options, I decided to try Tamiya's AS12 Bare Metal Silver spray can; the metallic colour was built up lightly over a few even coats, with several hours allowed between coats so each could dry properly. When fully cured, the surfaces were checked and a few slight blemishes were discovered, due to tiny dust particles. This entailed yet another session of wet-sanding with the finer Micro-Mesh grades until the surfaces were perfectly smooth, taking care not to rub through the silver paint to reveal the primer beneath.

After painting the orange reflectors by hand, the skirts were then treated to a high-gloss clear coat, courtesy of Mr Hobby's Premium Topcoat, again in aerosol form and applied over a few individual layers. This dries to a superb, ultra-hardwearing finish, and it gave the metallic silver a wonderful lustre. Suitably impressed by the results, I felt ready to proceed with the cab.

The kit instructions may recommend building the cab around the interior sub-assembly, having painted, glazed and finished each section beforehand, but that approach really didn't appeal to me. How would any gaps be addressed, and would the bonds be strong enough to hold everything together? To my mind a much more attractive prospect was to assemble the cab as a separate shell, and slide the interior unit into it at the end of the build.

After the individual cab parts had been tidied of excess material, they were placed around the interior unit and held together tightly with masking tape. The fit of the parts was universally good, with just a few hairline gaps that would be addressed later. After double-checking that everything was correctly aligned, small amounts of liquid poly-cement were applied at key points to tack the panels together. The cement would only need to hold the parts securely enough to allow the interior to be removed in due course, so it was applied with restraint and a fine brush.

Once the cement had cured, the interior was gently extracted, and then the inside of the shell was examined. It was

Using the interior as a former, the exterior panels were clamped together with tape. After checking that everything was aligned correctly, a small amount of liquid poly was run into the joints.

Once the cement had cured for a couple of hours, the interior unit was removed. The panel joints could then be reinforced with thin styrene strip and more liquid poly-cement, thus creating a super-strong outer shell. Any gaps were filled, and the shell was wet sanded until it was perfectly smooth.

A grey primer was applied in the first instance, to help identify any blemishes. Once these were treated and the shell gently abraded, a black primer was applied. This, too, was wet sanded with fine grades of Micro-Mesh abrasives until the surface was absolutely flat and smooth.

Tamiya AS-12 Bare Metal Silver, in aerosol format, was sprayed over the cab in light coats. Again, patient abrading work was necessary to flatten the surface. The window seals were picked out by hand, then the clear gloss coats were applied.

The side panels of the spoiler featured pronounced ejector-pin craters on their inner faces, so these were filled with punched plastic discs. When the cement had cured, the surfaces were abraded flat.

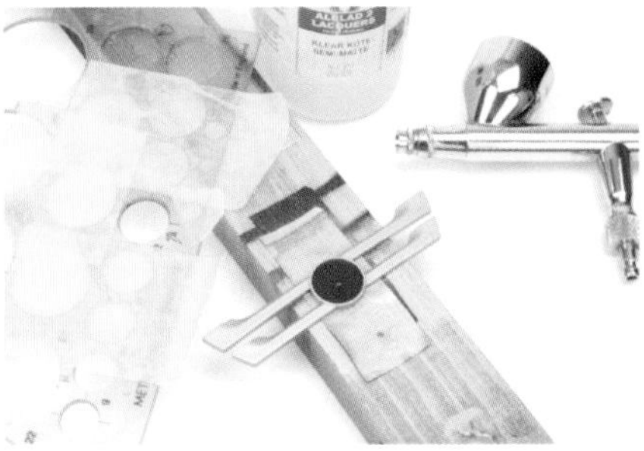

After the front grille overlay had been given a coat of Tamiya Bare Metal Silver, the base for the Mercedes logo was painted black. A quick way of masking the surrounding area was to employ a circle stencil of the correct diameter.

clear that there was minimal surface area with which to create truly secure bonds, so 20thou' strips of styrene were glued to the inside of the joints to 'beef' them up a bit. The styrene strip also acted as a base against which filler could be forced into the narrow gaps, giving the material a firmer footing. After working all the way round the interior, treating each panel joint carefully, the shell was allowed to cure for twenty-four hours; by this time it had taken on a very rugged feel.

The few gaps between panels could then be addressed with putty, and when these had been made good, preparation for the painting stages could begin. The process followed the same pattern as the side skirts, alternately abrading, priming, testing and abrading again, until the final black primer layer was added. The swirly plastic employed by Revell for the cab parts proved somewhat distracting, as it was difficult to discern how smooth the surface was until the first grey primer coat had been sprayed. The Tamiya Bare Metal Silver aerosol provided the silver topcoat, built up over three layers, with each light coat wet-sanded when dry, before the next was applied. Building up the topcoat gradually has a far greater chance of a successful finish than attempting to get it done in one go.

When happy with the final topcoat, the surface was once again abraded with Micro-Mesh, to flatten the surface ready for the gloss clear coats. However, before they were sprayed, the window frames and air-stream strips were hand-painted. After glossing, the silver paintwork looked fabulous, with a deep metallic shine. At this point I really couldn't wait to make a start with applying the decals; however, I managed to restrain myself, and allowed the paint to harden for a few days. Incidentally, the front fender assembly was treated at the same time, following exactly the same procedure.

ADDING THE DECALS

The Native American-themed decals are certainly impressive when viewed on their backing paper prior to application, and I did wonder how well they would perform. Close scrutiny revealed that some of the outer limits of the clear carrier film would have to be dispensed with to fit within the various side panels, so a degree of planning was necessary before making a start. Also, I should have waited before fixing the cab door handles in position, as the decals had to be cut to fit around them. It would have been much easier to fit the handles afterwards.

Furthermore the raised Mercedes-Benz legends moulded into the base of the cab doors impeded the application of the decals. The kit actually provides decals to replace the moulded versions, although this had escaped my notice at the outset, but by then it was too late to make any physical corrections. Instead, the decals had to be trimmed, and the bleeding effect reinstated using an airbrush. But we're getting ahead of ourselves a little…

Having cut the main decals into separate sections with a pair of sharp, fine scissors (avoid using a knife as there's a chance you'll damage the edge of the carrier film), I began by adding one of the head-and-shoulder figure portraits. While the decal soaked in a bowl of warm water, the cab's surface was brushed with Micro Set solution. After sliding the decal into position, the excess moisture was carefully brushed away and absorbed with tissue. This was the easy bit; coping with the recessed panel lines would be more difficult.

For this, Micro Sol was used, the companion decal setting solution to Micro Set; this is a stronger formula that

Care was taken to gently slide each decal into position, as the carrier film is rather thin and fragile.

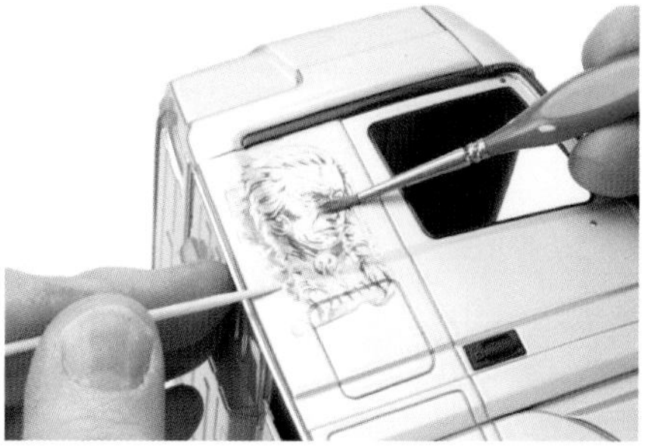

A soft brush helped to position the decal, with a blunt cocktail stick used as an anchor. Avoid using metal tweezers as they are more likely to damage the film. Excess moisture was gradually absorbed with cotton swabs.

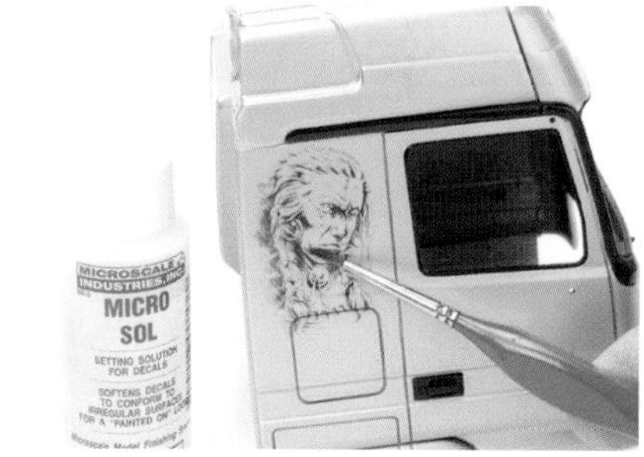

Once the decal was in position and settled on the surface, Micro Sol was applied and left for a few minutes to work to its full effect.

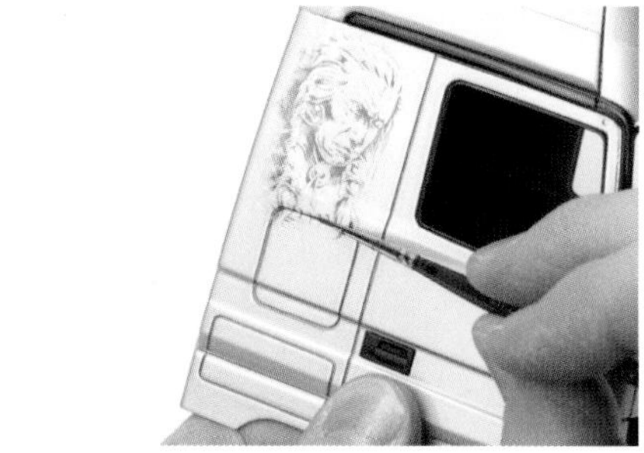

As the Micro Sol softened the decal film, it could be manipulated into the recessed panel seams with a fine brush.

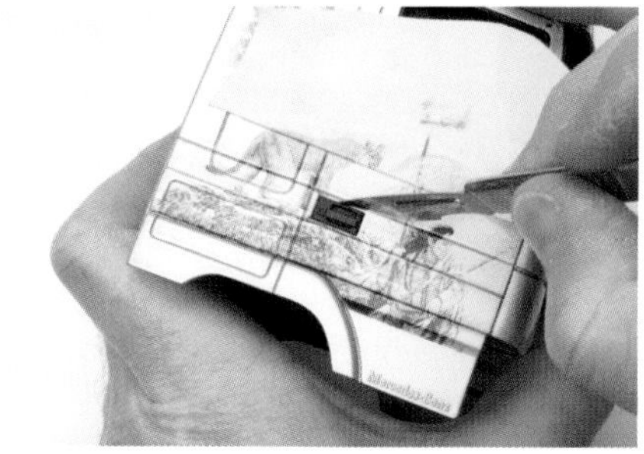

The impressive decals were applied one by one, taking the time to gently persuade them to conform to the undulating surfaces. I fitted the door handles too soon, so had to trim the decals to fit around them, using a fresh scalpel blade.

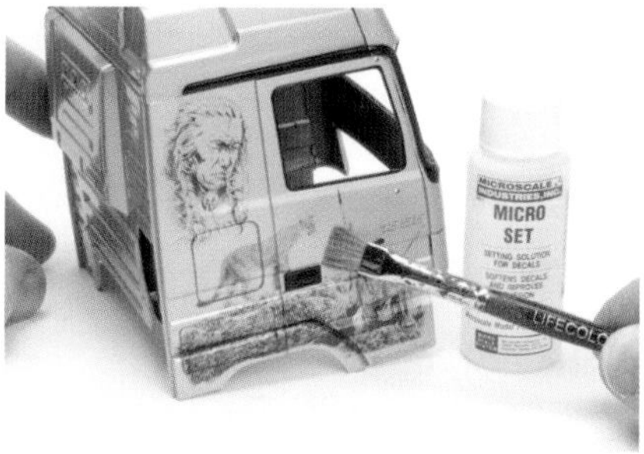

Once each decal is sited and settled, a little more Micro Set can be applied; the model can then be put to one side to dry naturally, prior to adding the next element. The process is laborious, but a patient approach is essential.

actively softens the decal and renders it flexible enough to be manipulated over undulating surfaces. The process takes time, however, and can't be rushed, so we must be patient and wait for the fluid to take full effect, helping the film into the recesses with a soft brush, and adding more Micro Sol at intervals to prevent the surface drying out too soon. Once the decal is sitting correctly, we can move on to the next element, following the same procedure.

It took a whole day to get the artwork applied to both sides of the cab, working methodically with the Micro Sol to persuade the decal film to conform to the surface profiles. With a very sharp scalpel blade, the decals were cut to fit round the door handles; the larger elements – especially the team of horses and riders – had to be slid from the backing with great care to avoid damaging the delicate film. The task was certainly laborious, but the rewards were great, as the decals looked superb on the silver paintwork.

With all the decals in position, the cab was left to dry out for twenty-four hours; then a clear gloss coat (Mr Hobby's Premium Topcoat) was sprayed over the entire shell, thus sealing the artwork permanently in place.

Next I attempted to reinstate the bleeding effect to the artwork at the lower edges of the cab doors by airbrushing a tiny amount of Alclad II Aluminium (a very close match to the Tamiya silver paint). A steady hand and an airbrush with a fine nozzle are required (I used a 0.3mm-diameter nozzle-equipped Iwata airbrush), and subtlety is essential. The end results aren't perfect due to the hard edge of the trimmed decal film, but overall it looks acceptable at most viewing angles and distances. I am probably more likely to notice any imperfections because I know they're there!

After sealing the decals with a further clear coat, the lower edges of the artwork were given a graduated effect with a misted coat of metallic paint to match the underlying silver shade. Yet another clear gloss coat followed.

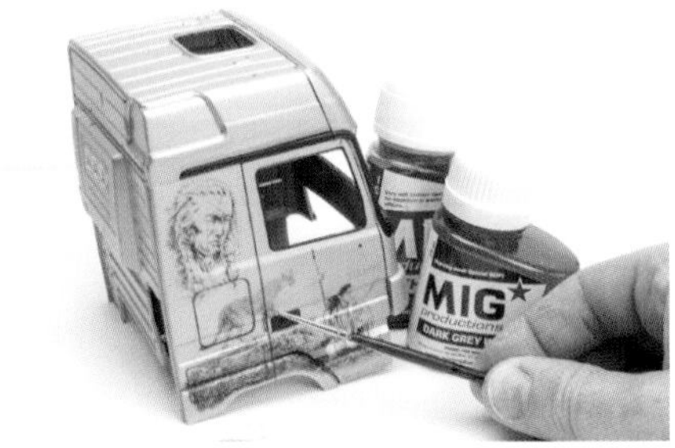

To add greater definition to the panel seams, a dark grey shade of enamel weathering wash was brushed into the recesses.

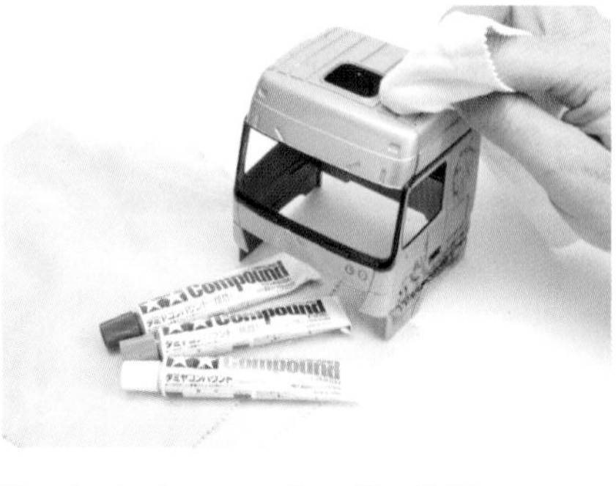

Tamiya's three grades of polishing compound, together with their matching cloths, are highly effective for creating a shiny, showroom gleam to the finished paintwork.

After adding the smaller logo and character decals, another clear gloss coat was applied; this was allowed to harden for a week, then extra definition was added to the door and panel seams with a dark grey shade of enamel weathering wash. This also served to separate the decals, which unrealistically stretched across the panels. When this had dried, the cab was ready for the polishing stage.

This is another facet of modelling that I rarely undertake, but it's a worthwhile step towards creating a truly flawless paint finish. Successive grades of Micro-Mesh abrasives, from 8,000–24,000grit, were employed once again, used with plenty of warm soapy water; afterwards the cab shell was rinsed thoroughly. The dry surface was then buffed with Tamiya's polishing compounds, working through the three separate grades (coarse, fine and finish). Tamiya's special buffing cloths were employed, the colour-coded fabrics matching each cloth to the relevant compound. These pastes contain micro-abrasive particles that remove any remaining scratches from the Micro-Mesh, while also imparting a highly polished clear coating – just the thing for a showroom finish.

FINAL ASSEMBLY

In between jobs on the cab exterior, I resolved to get the chassis complete by installing the side skirts and the extra upper decking plates, which came from one of Italeri's Truck Accessory kits. A few modifications were required to provide an aperture for the fuel-filler cap and to clear the air-intake ducting, as well as mounting holes for the access handrail. The decking was pre-finished with a rather garish 'chrome'-effect paint, but I wasn't too keen on its appearance. Instead, I rubbed it down with abrasives, just enough to give an aerosol primer a suitable 'key' and allow the paint to adhere correctly. The black primer was followed by airbrushed coats of AK Interactive's Extreme Metal Polished Aluminium, which in turn was followed by a deep clear gloss coat.

A set of susie cables was created, again using material from Italeri's accessory set, wrapping the coloured cable around the shaft of a screwdriver. The outer ends were enhanced with short lengths of styrene tube, fixed on to the cables so that a few millimetres of wire protruded through. These ends were then painted with a tarnished brass finish (Darkstar acrylics), creating a passing resemblance to a set of cable plugs. The susie-cable mounting bracket was drilled to accept the cables, and was then mounted to the rear of the cab.

When fitting the cab glazing, disaster struck. The windscreen provided with my kit was incredibly thin and split in two as I tried slotting it into the cab. Luckily I'd recently bought a second kit to build at some point in the future, so the spare glazing was pilfered in order to keep this truck moving. This time, the component looked to be moulded correctly, and I had no problems fixing it into position with Deluxe's Glue 'n' Glaze. The level of transparency was impressive, so all I had to do was clean away any fingerprints once the glue had set. For this, I used a small screen wipe of the type intended for cleaning smartphones, after testing

After glazing the cab and fitting the front grille, the interior was slotted inside the shell and secured with a few blobs of Glue 'n' Glaze adhesive.

To avoid using the heated screwdriver method of securing the cab hinge pins, I punched a hole in the centre of a couple of styrene discs. The holes must be large enough to slot readily over the hinge pins without being too sloppy.

Working in such a confined space is rather fiddly, but I managed to push the rings on to the tails of the pins. With a fine brush, a small amount of liquid poly was then applied to the outside faces of the rings, securing them to the pins without interfering with the operation of the hinges.

The front bumper assembly was secured with a slow-setting, thicker poly-cement, having stripped the mating faces back to bare plastic. This allows plenty of time for adjustment. The part was supported with Blu-Tack while the cement cured.

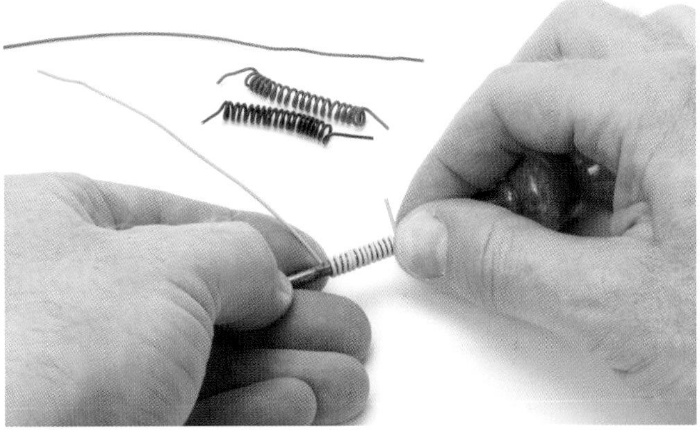

A set of susie cables was created from coloured cable, wrapped around the shaft of a screwdriver.

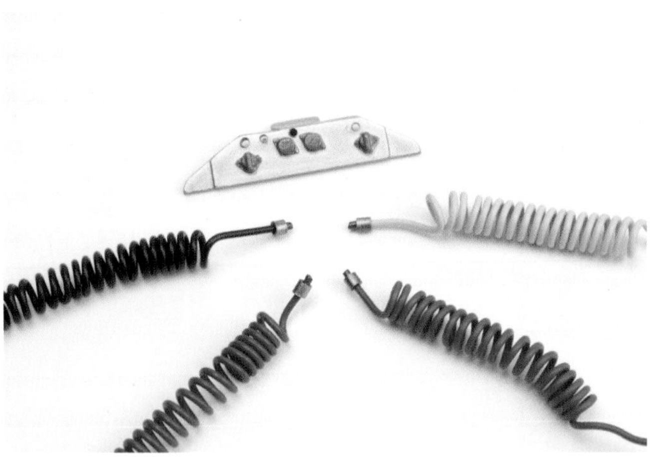

Plugs were fashioned from styrene tube, slotted over the cable and painted with a faded metallic brass shade.

it on the broken windscreen to check whether the alcohol-based fluid would be safe on the clear plastic.

After fitting the front grille, the cab interior unit could be slid inside the cab's shell and secured with a few blobs of Glue 'n' Glaze. The spoiler and streamline panels were then installed, and the cab was ready for its 'wedding' to the chassis. As with the DAF 95 in the previous chapter, I eschewed the use of a hot screwdriver tip to secure the cab to the hinges, preferring to employ a pair of plastic rings and the kit's locating pins instead. This doesn't give the option of easy removal, as would the screws fixed to the DAF 95's cab, but it does remove the risks involved with wielding a hot metal tool in a confined space, surrounded by delicate plastic components.

With the cab installed, the front fender could be attached to the frames, followed by the various smaller fittings: wipers, side mirrors, aerials, horns and the susie cables.

A WORTHY ADDITION TO THE TRUCK FLEET

After countless hours, weeks and months of toil, the finished truck has surpassed my expectations. The combination of the metallic paintwork, superb decals and the pristine finish has created a dramatic addition to my model truck fleet. All that time spent abrading, painting and polishing the paintwork, not to mention the labour involved with the decals, has definitely paid off.

I certainly learned a lot during the assembly and finishing stages, and it has left me eager to build the second kit I have in my possession. Indeed, next time

The susie cables were the final details to be installed, following the mirrors, aerials and horns.

round I am tempted to remedy the lack of an Adblue tank; this would involve either obtaining a resin casting or scratch-building my own, while having to make a few alterations to the equipment layout on the frames in order to accommodate it. Furthermore, I'd be tempted to put more effort into detailing the chassis frames, and would omit the decking plates to allow the extra details to be admired. But all that is for the future. First I will need to get hold of a replacement windscreen…

The Actros MP3 kit proved to be a challenging but highly rewarding exercise.

Aiming for a flawless showroom finish meant that I had to alter my usual approach to truck modelling, but it was worth the extra effort.

CHAPTER ELEVEN

LOCKDOWN MODELLING: 1:24-SCALE MERCEDES-BENZ 2238

Italeri's kit might date back to the 1980s, but this 2019 boxing proves that it's still an excellent package in terms of detail and value.

By now, readers may be thinking that I'm a Mercedes-Benz obsessive, but I hadn't originally set out to build this truck. My initial goal was to construct an Italeri Volvo F16, and I'd obtained various aftermarket detailing accessories from KFS and Czech Truck Models (CTM), covering everything from new wheels, tyres, headlamps and a full etched metal upgrade set. Alas, the Covid-19 pandemic of 2020 and the consequent lockdown to control its spread, kept me at home and forbade travel to my city-centre modelling studio, which also contained many of my tools, kits and equipment, for three long months. What could I do during that time of confinement? Luckily I did have a skeleton toolkit at home, along with a handful of paints. Furthermore, many model traders were still operating an impressive mail-order service, so after shopping around for a likely kit at a reasonable price, I landed upon this Italeri boxing of the iconic Mercedes-Benz 2238.

A CHALLENGING TIME

I'd originally chosen the Volvo F16 because I wanted to demonstrate the various methods involved in adding extra detail to a 1:24-scale tractor unit, especially items such as brake pipes, valves and electrical cables. Although the choice of kit subsequently changed, my original plan remained, albeit with a few necessary alterations. The national lockdown of 2020 forced me to improvise much of the detailing work, making use of scrap materials and whatever plastic strip or rod I had in the bottom of my toolbox, although a few things were bought in for specific tasks, especially copper and brass jewellery wire, plus various aerosol paints.

Indeed, a degree of inventiveness was required during the assembly and painting stages, as I reverted to working at a table in the front parlour, with the ever-present fear of ruining the carpet and creating a general nuisance. Thankfully, the weather remained fine for the duration of the lockdown, allowing the smelliest and dirtiest jobs to be undertaken outdoors. This was not without its own hazards, however, and the local bird population did its best to precision bomb my newly painted components. Living at altitude also led to a running battle with the wind, which can seriously hamper the application of aerosol-based paints. But more of that later.

Despite the challenges, I ended up thankful for the experience of building this truck during that unprecedented period of confinement. Unsurprisingly, the project helped keep me in a positive frame of mind, and the need to concoct different ways of working, making the most of what I had to hand, brought me back to my modelling roots. In fact, I'd forgotten how rewarding this kind of modelling approach can be.

Furthermore, by keeping the onus firmly on the enjoyment factor, I also decided to take a more relaxed approach to certain aspects, injecting a little fun into the cab interior and finishing the truck in a generic, fictional livery scheme. As a result, this turned out to be one of the most gratifying modelling projects I've undertaken in years. Also, having built a Mercedes 2238 in 1:72 scale (Chapter 2) a few months before, it was interesting to create a much larger version of the same prototype.

ASSEMBLING THE ENGINE

Work began with the erection of the powerplant, and the kit provides a pleasing representation of the OM422 V8 engine, consisting of several individual components. However, the two halves of the main block did not meet up particularly well, and after cutting away the locating pins, the parts were aligned more accurately by eye; masking

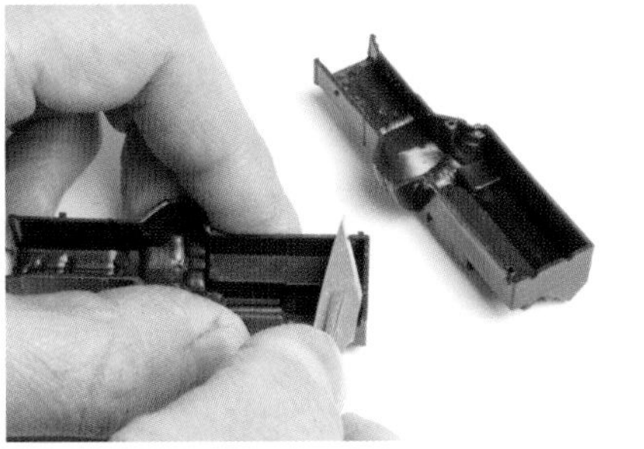

The engine block refused to marry up correctly, so I cut the locating pips away and flattened the mating faces with a broad file.

One of the drivebelt pullies lacked any form of mounting, so I fashioned a simple piece of apparatus from plastic rod and strip. The assembled engine block had first been primed with Mr Surfacer 500, stippled by hand brush, before the green acrylic coats were applied.

tape held them together while the glue cured. The common situation of a drive-belt's pulley wheel sitting in mid-air is present here, so I crafted a simple shaft of plastic rod to make it look a little more authentic.

Most of the engine was assembled before painting, in contrast to the Actros' prime mover, and this allowed me to add some welcome texture to the surfaces – and seal any gaps – with a stippled coat of Mr Surfacer 500. A hand-painted and weathered finish followed, using a mix of acrylics and Tensocrom washes. A dry-brushed coating of metallic silver really brought the engine, gearbox and cooling system to life, allowing the fine detail relief in the mouldings to be appreciated.

When the painting and weathering were almost complete, the fuel-injector pipework was installed, using nickel-silver rod from Albion Alloys, fixed into holes drilled into the injector rail and cylinder heads. Short lengths of Tamiya's flexible black 'Detail Up' cable were also added to various parts of the engine and gearbox casing, which was a good way of using up offcuts from previous projects. These new additions were then blended into their surroundings with a little extra weathering, using paints and washes. This completed this first stage of proceedings.

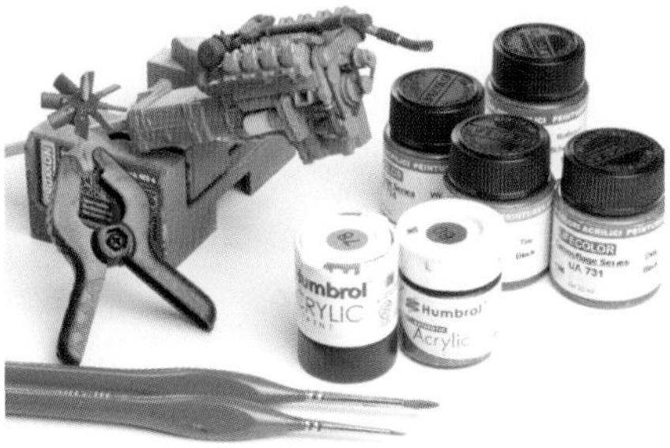

It took a few coats to build up the Humbrol acrylic green to full opacity; the details were then picked out in the relevant colours.

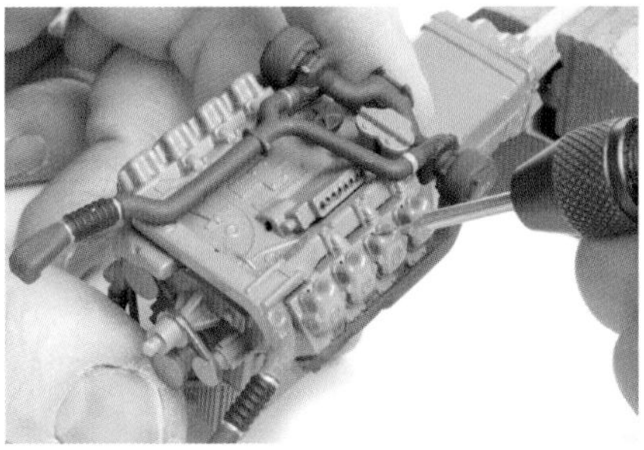

Holes were drilled into the injector rail and cylinder heads to accommodate the pipework, along with larger holes in the gearbox and alternator for hoses and cables, all of which will be fitted later.

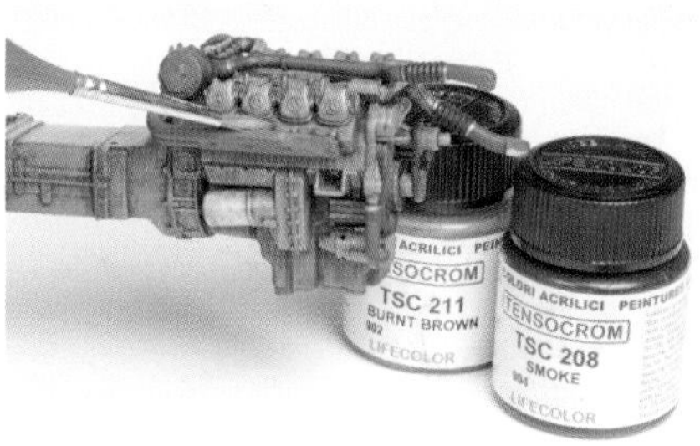

Weathering began with coats of Lifecolor's Tensocrom washes, brushed over the surface and manipulated with cotton swabs.

The exhaust manifolds gained a rusty patina thanks to stippled coats of Lifecolor's various rust shades, ranging from dark red-brown to orange-yellow.

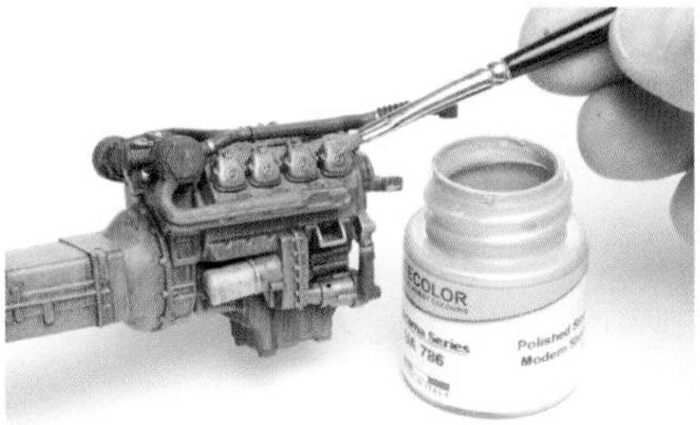

The impressive surface relief was accentuated by dry-brushing with a flat brush and faint traces of Lifecolor's Polished Steel.

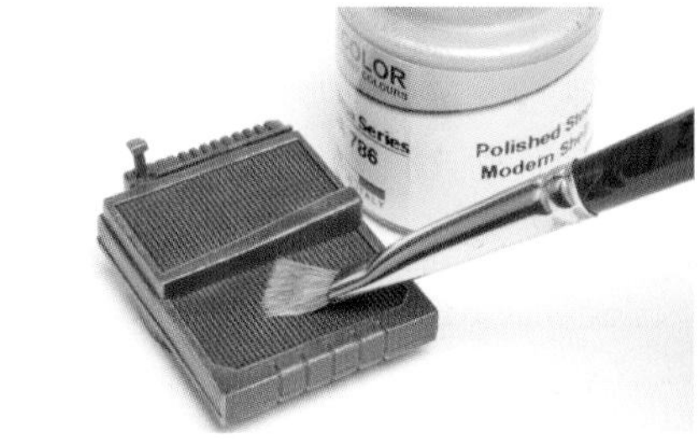

The same metallic paint was also dry-brushed over the radiator, highlighting the mesh detail and giving a realistic burnished appearance.

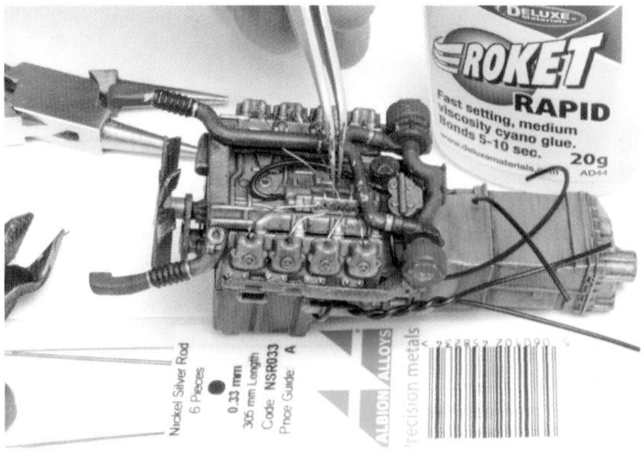

Once the engine was fully assembled and weathered, the injector pipework was installed, using 0.33mm-diameter nickel-silver rod from Albion Alloys. Scraps of Tamiya's 1mm flexible hose were also installed to represent the fuel lines and electrical cable.

ASSEMBLING THE FRAMES AND DRIVESHAFTS

The frames feature a number of cross-members, each of a different pattern and length, so it took some time to get them all fettled, checked and ready for installation. I struggled to hold the parts together squarely with tape before gluing: I was missing my absolutely flat workbench surface, so a different approach was taken. The cross-members were attached to one side frame, checking their position carefully with a set-square and straightedge to ensure they were all aligned correctly. When satisfied, they were allowed to harden for half an hour or so, then the other side frame was installed, with tape employed to clamp it all together. Further checks were made while the parts could still be manipulated, then it was set aside overnight.

Next the axles and suspension components were prepared, including the front axle, which had its steering rod attached using the hot screwdriver method. The locating pins were nice and long, leaving plenty of protruding material to work with, so the heat-formed

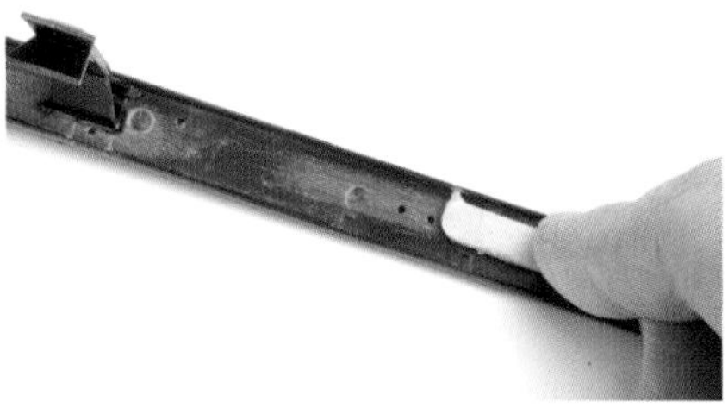

With an eye on fixing pipework and valves to the chassis, the inside faces of the frames were abraded flat, removing any unwanted moulding marks.

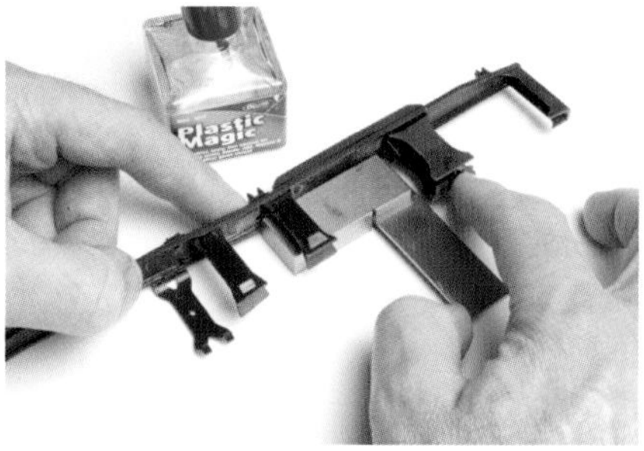

Having fettled the frames and cross-members carefully, assembly began. Each cross-member was installed to one of the side frames, checking for correct alignment.

The second side frame was then installed, and the assembly clamped together while the cement cured. All the angles were checked carefully while the parts could still be adjusted, ensuring that the frames showed no signs of twisting.

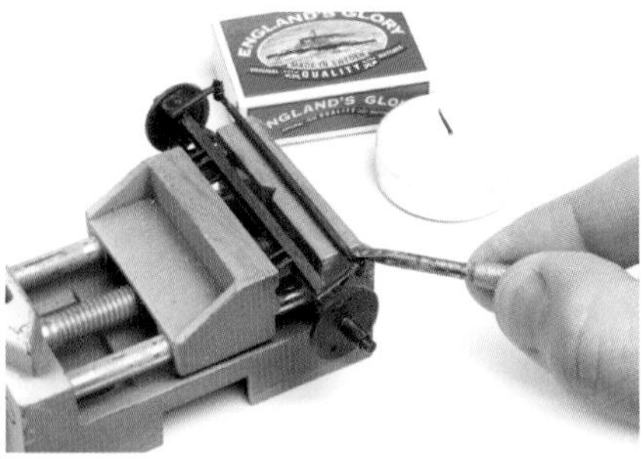

While the frames cured, the front axle was assembled, the steering-arm spigots being secured with a hot screwdriver blade.

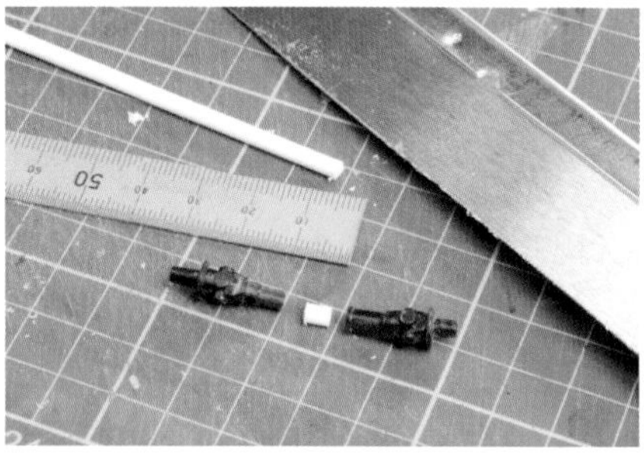

The rear driveshaft was too short, so it was cut and a fillet of plastic rod inserted to bridge the gap. Luckily I had a length of Evergreen styrene rod of virtually the same diameter.

The fillet was secured to the shaft in situ, and when cured, flexible abrasive strips smoothed the shaft and created a seamless finish.

A cast-metal texture was achieved by stippling Mr Surfacer 500 over the differential casings and driveshaft.

flanges have proven reliable so far. Assembly followed the same pattern as the previous 1:24-scale projects, with just a few eventful happenings, including the discovery that the driveshafts were woefully too short. Thankfully this was anticipated, so I was able to implement a satisfactory solution.

Beginning with the rear driveshaft, I measured the shortfall and cut the existing shaft in two. Plastic rod of a similar diameter was cut to the required length and this extension piece was inserted into the gap after the shaft ends had been fixed to the differentials. The aim was to achieve a snug fit for the extension piece, so that the assembly would support itself securely while the glue set, without sagging. Later, flexible strips of abrasive were used to tidy up the joints, and a couple of stippled applications of Mr Surfacer 500 ensured there was no trace of this intervention. The main driveshaft would be treated in a similar manner, later in the project, when installing the powerplant.

CREATING A VARIETY OF FITTINGS

Without my hex and disc punch-and-die tools, I created my own styrene bolt heads, rods and washers, with varying degrees of success. Cutting hex bolts of a consistent shape and size from scraps of plastic strip was not as easy as I imagined. But I'm glad I persevered, as the fifth wheel mounting brackets look much better for their inclusion, along with the circular washers that were sliced in thin sections from styrene rod with a sharp blade.

As will be seen in the following chapter, it is possible to purchase a variety of valves, regulators and connectors as resin or metal castings for the purpose of adding detail to the chassis frames. I'd stockpiled a few sets of these items, but thanks to Covid-19, I was unable to access them. As an alternative, I settled down to creating my own approximations of these fittings using scraps of plastic sheet, strip and rod. They looked somewhat rough and ready to begin with, but after shaping the plastic with needle files, and drilling them to accept the pipework, they began to look fit for purpose.

I had to take a fairly uneducated guess at where to site many of these fittings, as online research failed to produce any useful images. Linking the brake reservoir tanks to the axle-hung chambers and thence to the brake drums was straightforward enough, so the scratch-built valves were inserted into these lines to mimic the presence of

A variety of valves and regulators were improvised from scraps of plastic sheet, rod and section. I also found a few green plastic cones at the bottom of my toolbox, which, I seem to remember, came from a Plastruct factory kit. Bolt-head detail was created with small pieces of rod, and once the main assemblies had cured, needle files helped to refine their profile and holes were drilled to accommodate the hoses and cable.

Multiple strips of fine, black-coated nickel wire were held in a pin vice, and while the other end was held between the fingers, the wire was twisted to bind it together.

After fixing the plastic valves to the frames, they were linked together with lengths of Tamiya's flexible hose, which was also fixed into holes drilled into the brake chambers and drums.

The plumbing and cables heading towards the engine compartment were terminated by fixing beneath a shallow styrene channel section. These will be hidden when the engine and transmission are installed.

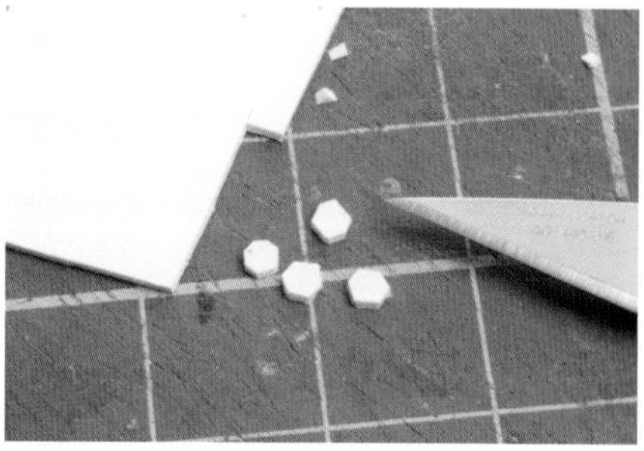

Hex bolts were cut from plastic sheet. They were not perfect, but only the side profile will be glimpsed.

After a row of holes was drilled into each mounting flange, the improvised hex bolts and small lengths of round rod were fitted beneath to match the position of the fifth wheel's base.

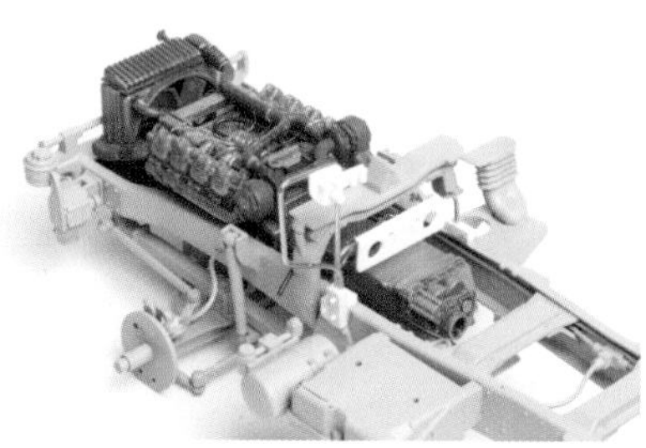

An initial primer coat was sprayed over the chassis to test the surface. After tidying up a few areas, I crafted a susie cable mounting stage and integral handrail from brass wire and scraps of styrene. The powerplant was temporarily installed to check for clearance.

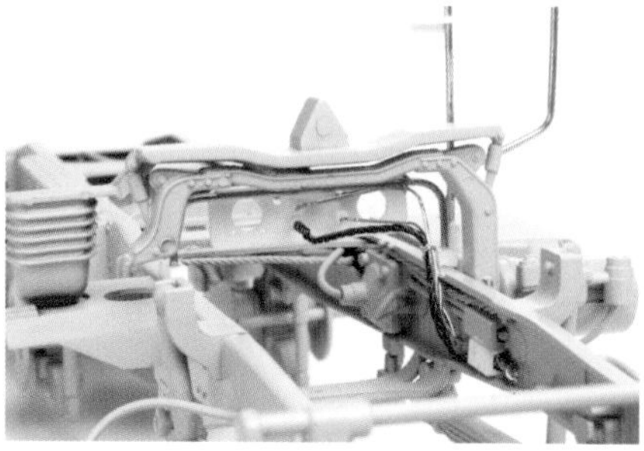

The rear of the faceplate was adorned with wires leading to the susie cable sockets.

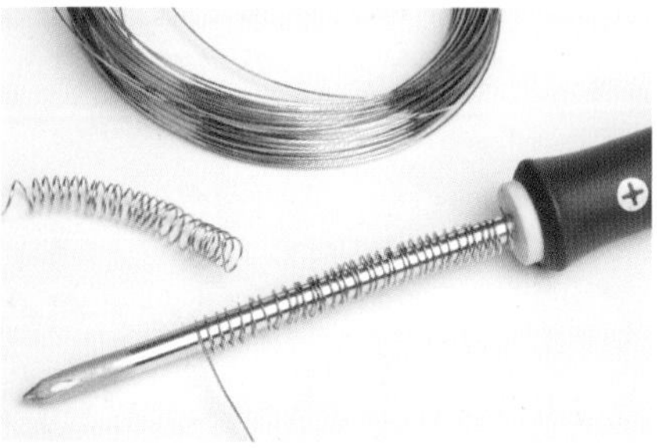

Lengths of 28-gauge copper wire were wrapped around a screwdriver shaft to form the susie cables. These were then sprayed with Mr Surfacer black primer.

regulators, connectors and air-cleaning apparatus. I really should have drilled the mounting holes for the pipework into the individual kit parts before assembly, but I was too eager to get the chassis assembled. As it transpired, the holes could be drilled in situ without too much trouble.

A mix of Tamiya's flexible hoses and super-fine electrical cable was employed for the plumbing (mostly offcuts from previous projects), while several lengths of thin copper jewellery wire were twisted together to mimic electrical harnesses.

A susie cable mounting bracket was also created from scratch, based around a thick brass wire frame with a styrene sheet faceplate. The assembly was inspired by a photograph I found of a Scania truck of a similar vintage, and the slightly home-made appearance of the real thing had appealed to me. Piping and cables were attached to the rear of the faceplate to coincide with the locations of the susie cables, which were also created from copper jewellery wire.

PAINTING THE CHASSIS

After the detailing work was complete, the chassis was primed and painted using aerosols. To hold the chassis, I drilled a hole into the end of one of the rear axles (about 10mm deep) and fixed a length of stiff wire into the aperture with cyano glue. Once the

Tamiya's TS-15 Blue was sprayed over the chassis in several light coats. The air and fuel tanks and fifth-wheel bracket were treated separately to ensure even paint coverage over all surfaces.

painting was complete, the wire was cut and trimmed flush with the axle end. Spraying the primer and paint had to be done outside on a still day, with a repurposed cardboard box acting as a booth to collect the overspray. More cardboard was laid flat over the patio flags, preventing them from acquiring a painted finish, and a facemask was worn at all times while spraying. If even a light breeze blew up, it would send the paint off course, so I attempted to work in as sheltered a spot as possible.

Gaining an even coating of the whole chassis took a patient approach, taking care not to overload the surface with excess paint. Working it into the frames and around the extra pipework is difficult enough when working in a spray booth with plenty of light, so it was doubly challenging in a shaded corner of the garden. With this in mind, I resolved to build up the colour in at least three sittings, aiming to get the paint applied as evenly as possible during each session. When dry, I studied the paintwork in bright light to identify any 'underdone' areas, which were duly addressed with the following coat.

Aside from the extra time and effort required, this approach served me well, and I'm very happy with the paint finish on this model, especially given the circumstances. Later the cab would be treated in exactly the same way, albeit with a lighter shade of blue. The Tamiya paints dried to a pleasing, deep gloss finish, and after hand-brushing certain areas with appropriate colours, the chassis was ready for the weathering stage.

WEATHERING

Heavy wash coats came first, using a mix of Lifecolor acrylics (UA205 Rotbraun, UA733 Tyre Black, UA734 Worn Black and LC02 Matt Black). The exact colours aren't too important, as any mix of matt red-brown, dark grey and black will do. Having mixed the colours on a scrap of plastic, the paint was brushed liberally on to the chassis, working it into all the surface relief. A couple of square inches of chassis was treated at a time, as much of the paint had to be removed with swabs before it dried.

This brush-on, wipe-off form of weathering has been explained already, but when using acrylics rather than enamel washes, it's possible to achieve a much grubbier finish very quickly. The main drawback is the speed with which the paint dries. Working on a glossy surface helps, and dipping the swabs in Tamiya's acrylic thinners allows stubborn deposits to be loosened and manipulated (or removed altogether). Feeling rushed when modelling, especially if trying a new technique for the first time, is rarely a good thing, so I'd recommend trialling this practice on a less precious model until a degree of confidence is gained.

Heavy deposits of the grimy paint mix were left inside the frames and around the assorted valves, connectors and pipework. Severe build-up of dirt and grease can be achieved by layering the acrylic paint treatment, perhaps adding a small amount of talcum powder or dry weathering pigments to the paint mix to provide a grittier texture. Using finer swabs (from Tamiya) to reach into the frames and around the axles and suspension allows more of the paintwork

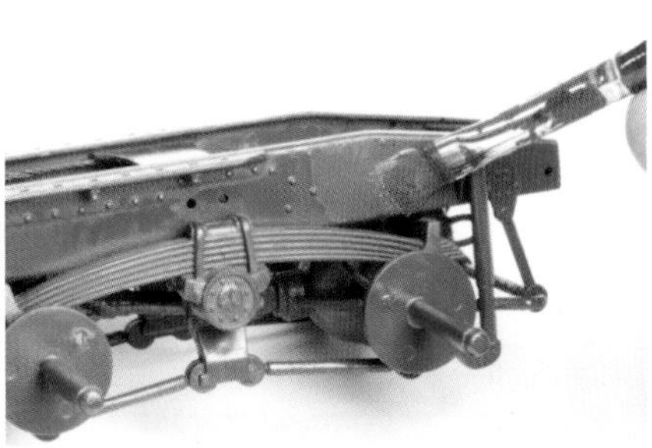

Weathering began with a heavy coating of Lifecolor acrylics, mixed from various dark brown and grey shades. The paint was brushed on to a small area at a time, working it around the surface detail.

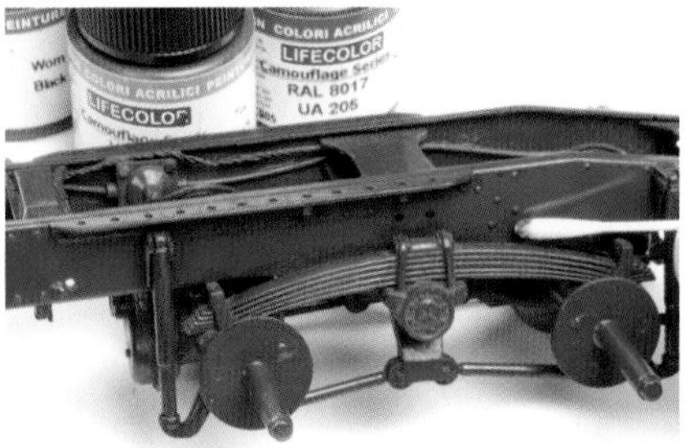

Cotton swabs then quickly removed most of the paint, leaving behind deposits and streaks.

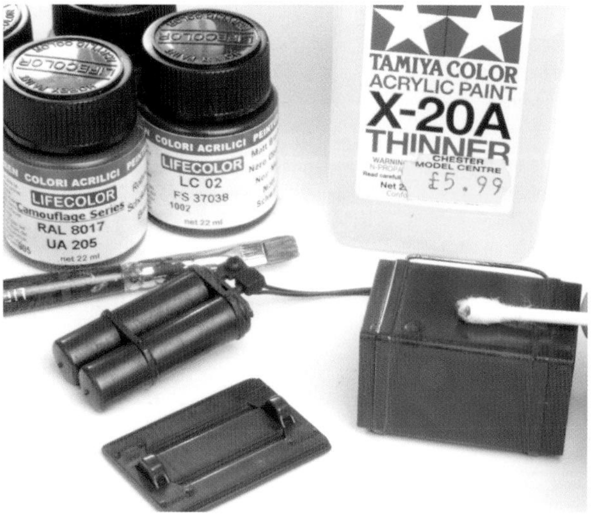

The extra chassis components, including the wheel hubs, were treated in the same way. Dipping the swab in Tamiya acrylic thinners helped to shift any stubborn traces of paint and create more pronounced streaking effects.

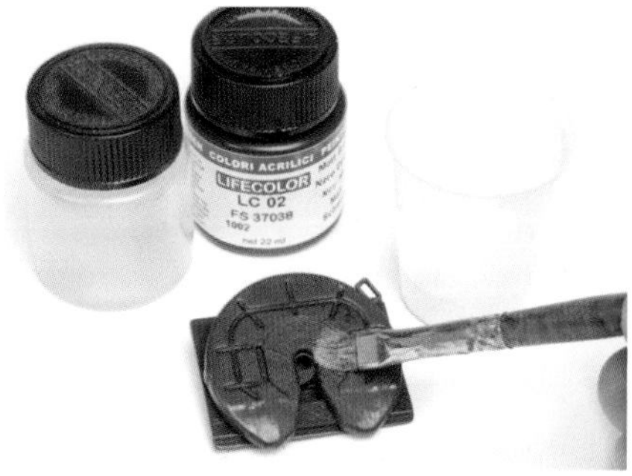

Heavier deposits of grime were achieved by mixing talcum powder with the paint to create a heavier texture. A little clear gloss was added to the mix also, to replicate oil and grease; this was especially useful for the fifth wheel.

Dry pigments followed, adding a dusty contrast with the initial weathering stage and the underlying glossy paintwork. A mix of dark earth, red-brown and dark grey shades were lightly brushed around the underframe and suspension.

Before completing the weathering stage, more assembly work was undertaken, adding the various tanks and walkways, each having been pre-weathered in the same way. The susie cables were also installed at this point, after they'd been given a dusting with dry pigments.

to be revealed, while vertical strokes tell the story of rain-soaked dirt running down the frames. The contrast between the matt paint deposits and the glossy blue paint proved to be very attractive.

The paint treatment alone can look good, but inevitably it creates hard edges to the dirt; this can be improved with a light coating of similarly coloured dry pigments. These will naturally cling to the matt paint deposits more readily than the glossy paintwork, while imparting a dustier sheen.

RESOLVING SHORT PARTS

With the chassis and the associated sub-assemblies weathered, they could be gradually fixed together, and the wheels installed permanently. After fitting the power unit, the air intake pipe linking the cleaner and the turbocharger was found to be a few millimetres too short. Just like the rear driveshaft, I cut the pipe and inserted a short length of plastic tube of a similar diameter. The main driveshaft also required an extension, following the same process to the rear shaft described earlier.

Yet another similar issue arose with the twin exhaust outlets, which were shorter by an even greater amount. These were not so easy to cure, as the pipes are curved and angled to meet up with the silencer assembly, and due to their exposed position beneath the truck, I wanted to be sure that they would be resilient enough to withstand handling.

When the engine had been fixed into the frames, the shortfall in the main driveshaft's length was measured, and a length of plastic rod spliced into place. Any gaps were filled before the shaft was primed and painted by hand, matching the shade of blue as closely as possible with a blend of Lifecolor paints. Weathering would hide any minor discrepancy.

The air-inlet pipe was also found to be too short, and again, the original part was cut and new material inserted.

Having completed the chassis, thoughts could turn to the cab.

Therefore, I made a cut into the outlet pipes beneath the lower of the two raised sleeves, thus disguising the joint with the fillet pieces. The styrene rod, which was slightly undersized, was the closest match I could find; it was immersed in hot water and shaped to the desired profile, then cut to length and grafted into position. Filler was required to create a seamless bond, followed by a stippled coating

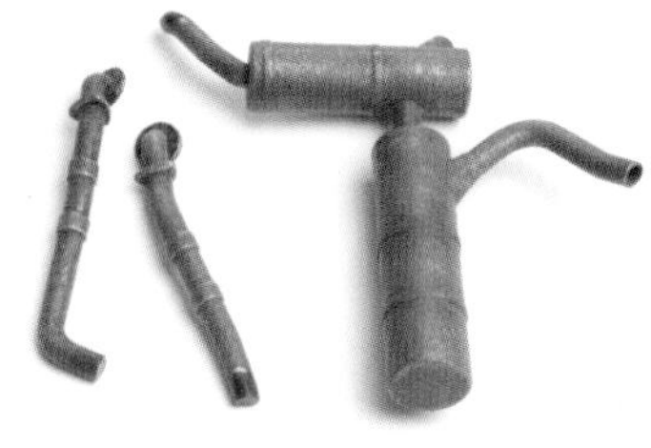

The exhaust pipes and silencers were given a textured, metallic finish, thanks to Mr Surfacer 500 primer, followed by various shades of Lifecolor acrylic, all applied by hand with a stippling action. Dry-brushing with a metallic steel shade added the final touch.

of Mr Surfacer 500 to act as a texturizing primer coat; this had already been applied to the separate exhaust components prior to painting and weathering.

Earlier, during initial assembly of the exhaust outlets, I'd drilled out the nozzle to a depth of around 6mm, having marked the centre of the solid plastic moulding as accurately as possible with a fine scriber tool. This helped to guide a sharp 2.3mm-diameter drill bit as it bored steadily into the material. Enough plastic needs to remain around the circumference of the nozzle aperture to maintain integrity, but the open end looks far more convincing than the solid

Once installation of the exhaust elements began, these were also found to be undersized, so sections of plastic rod had to be shaped and fixed into position, with plenty of filler needed to effect a seamless transition before the parts were painted and weathered.

plastic of the original part, especially after the painting and weathering stage.

CONVERTING TO RIGHT-HAND DRIVE

In Chapter 9, I described the conversion of a cab from left- to right-hand drive, using a drop-in resin casting. Here I decided to try doing the work myself, chopping out certain sections from the interior base and swapping them round. The task wasn't too onerous, but the dashboard proved much more demanding. Having pondered my options, I elected to cut the dashboard into five

In an effort to improve the seats, the hollow backs were filled in with plastic sheet. Once the glue had cured, the sheet was carved flush with the seats' profile.

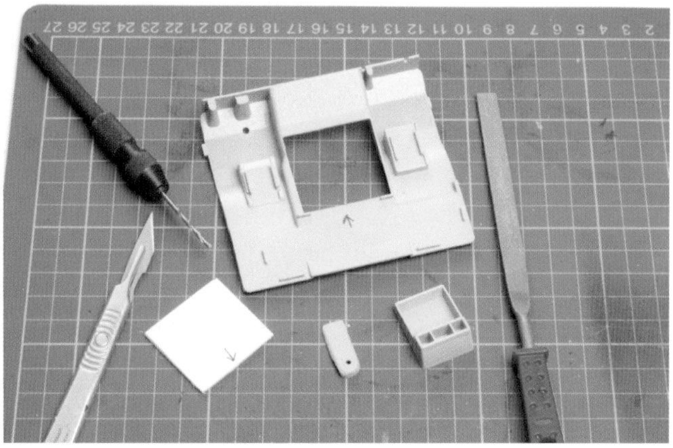

To convert the cab to right-hand drive, a square section was cut out of the interior floor: a series of holes were drilled around the perimeter and then cut through with a blade. A file tidied up the floor and the salvaged console and gearshift base.

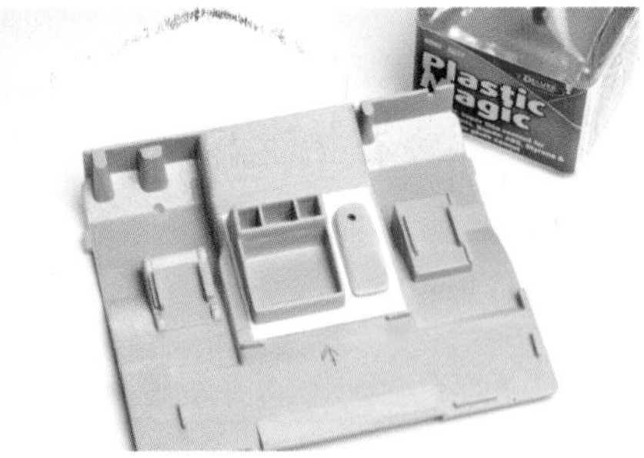

A piece of thick plastic card was cut and fettled to fill the hole in the floor, and once secured, the console and gearshift mount were installed in their new positions. Mr Surfacer 500 was stippled around the parts to reinstate the texture of the floor covering.

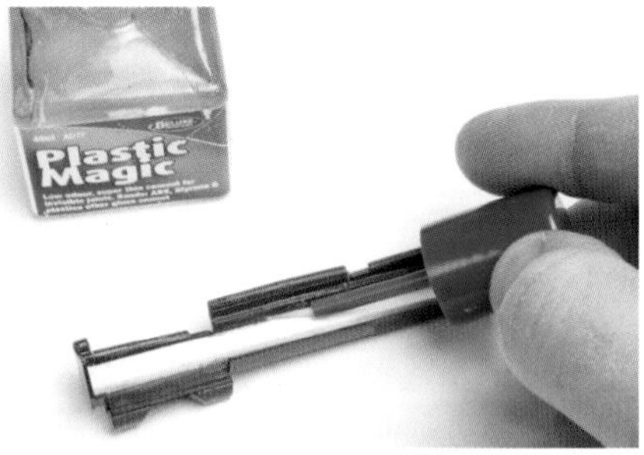

The dashboard was cut into five pieces and reassembled around a length of thick plastic strip.

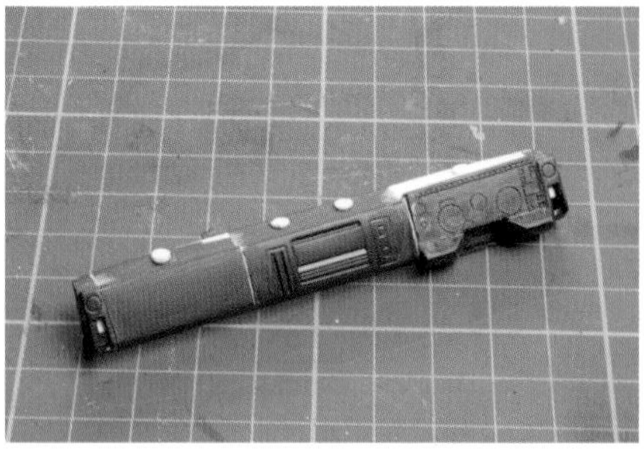

The gaps were filled and the rear profile was recreated by inserting fillets of plastic that were shaped with files and sanding pads.

pieces, using the moulded seam lines as cutting guides for a fine razor saw. The edges were cleaned up as neatly and squarely as possible before the parts were rebuilt, using a strip of thick rectangular plastic rod as a former.

The overall length of the original component had been noted, and the five sections were fixed to the rod, spacing and aligning them carefully to match the dashboard's original footprint. Inevitably, gaps existed between the sections, but these were filled with slithers of plastic strip and putty. So far, so fairly simple. However, regaining the necessary profile on the rear section, to match the curvature of the cab and windscreen, was more difficult. Sections of over-sized plastic strip were fixed to the rear, and when the cement had cured, the curving profile was recreated tentatively with files and abrasives, checking the fit against the inside of the cab at regular intervals. Once the profile looked correct, the plastic was abraded with successively fine abrasives to create a smooth finish.

Without my trusty disc-punching tools, I tried in vain to cut uniformly thin slices of solid plastic rod to create the raised ventilating pods. Once securely bonded to the dashboard, however, they were gently filed to ensure they each stood at a uniform height. Instead of the approach I adopted on both the DAF 95 and Unimog, which was the creation of a thin overlay for the dashboard console, here I simply painted the dial and switch detail on to the raised moulded relief, and this looked perfectly satisfactory.

INDOOR FUN

During the period of domestic confinement, I decided I would add a driver figure to the cab. This is something I seldom do, usually due to the amount of extra work involved, but I ended up having a great deal of fun in this instance.

The handsome figure came as one of a pair of male characters (one seated, one standing) from the Italeri Truck Shop Accessories kit (No.764). Consisting of a separate torso (made up of two halves), legs, arms and head, there is plenty of scope for customizing the seated pose to suit a variety of vehicles. In truth the parts are not brilliant, fitting together poorly, lacking definition in some areas, and featuring a great deal of flash, so there was plenty of filling and fettling involved. Indeed, the feet had to be cut off and reattached, after removing a few millimetres of material at the ankle to provide clearance for the pedals. In addition, a large fillet of epoxy putty was required to fill the gap between the lower back and fundament, as well as the armpits.

Once the figure was assembled (apart from the head) and the filler carved to match the body contours and undulating fabric, he was ready for priming and painting. Acrylics were employed throughout, utilizing Lifecolor's range of flesh tones. The head was treated separately in order to allow the neck and upturned jacket collar to be painted more easily, while it also allowed me to fine-tune its position once the body had been installed permanently into the seat. I prefer to treat the skin first, building up several layers of paint and working shadow and highlight tones in strategic areas to improve realism.

The body of the Italeri driver figure was tacked together while sitting in the driver's seat in order to gauge the correct posture and position of the limbs.

The figure's posture resulted in a large gap at the rear of the torso, which was filled with epoxy putty. The material was shaped and contoured before it cured, using water to help create a smooth finish.

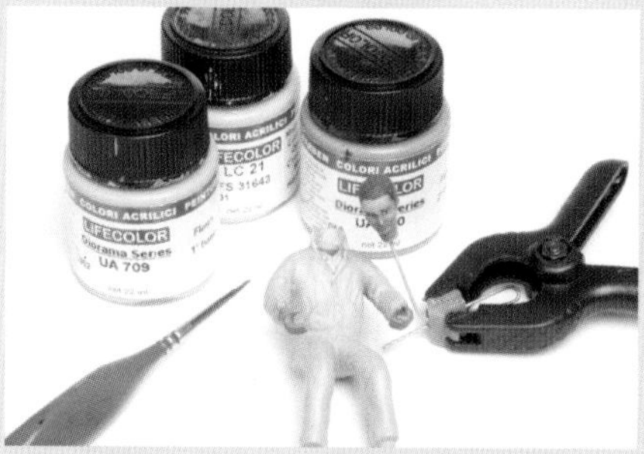

After priming, the head and hands were painted first, using a range of skin tones to achieve a degree of shading and highlights.

Once this stage is complete, an ultra-fine brush can add the lips and the whites of the eyes, followed by eyebrows and any facial hair. The pupils were touched in with a fine black ink pen, and then the hair was treated, once again employing several similar shades to avoid an overly flat appearance. Only when the skin and hair are complete do I move on to the clothing, following a base layer of colour with shading and highlights, following the contours moulded into the plastic as a guide.

This approach does take time, but it's a worthwhile endeavour and can be an enjoyable pastime in itself. In addition to the Italeri figures, there are plenty of others to choose from – the Master Box Miniatures range, in particular, offers some interesting truck drivers and passengers in 1:24 scale.

To complement the driver, a great deal of other interior detail was sculpted from epoxy putty, including bedding, cushions, curtains, gloves, baseball cap, holdall, flask, sandwich, apple and even a cuddly toy mascot. Deluxe Materials' Eze Putty was employed, kneaded and rolled out like pastry, then shaped with the aid of talcum powder (to prevent it sticking to the work surface, tools and fingers), while water was employed to help smooth out the putty and remove fingerprints. The putty cures rapidly, so it could be painted later the same day.

Fun was had painting the jazzy 1980s-style bedding, recreating the blue and orange colours of my childhood duvet – a vivid pattern that I can still recall forty years later! Printed designs was also prepared, including road maps, newspapers and magazines, along with a couple of Liverpool FC banners to enliven the bunk area, the driver clearly wanting to compensate for driving a blue truck.

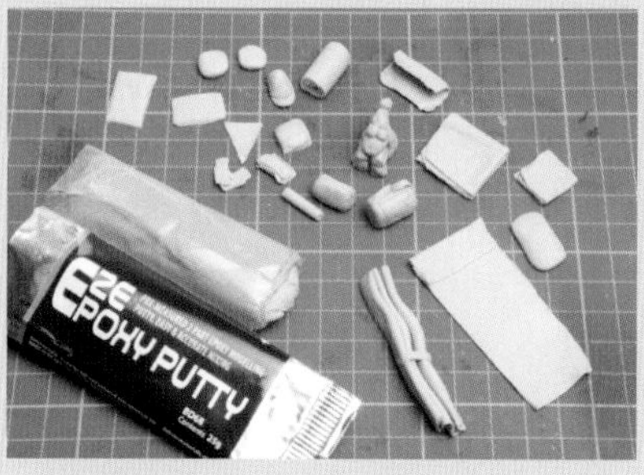

Epoxy putty was also used to sculpt a variety of interior fittings, from bedding and curtains to baggage and a cuddly toy.

An attempt was made to recreate the snazzy upholstery pattern favoured by Mercedes-Benz during the 1980s by dabbing the surfaces with a variety of brown, orange and grey colours.

The driver was fixed to the seat with epoxy adhesive, while the various smaller details were installed with either PVA or cyano glue. A seatbelt was fashioned from thin strips of black electrical insulation tape, and secured with cyano for a more reliable bond.

CAB AND FINAL ASSEMBLY

Assembly of the outer cab shell was easy thanks to the separate sides, ends and roof being cleanly moulded, and the joints slotting together positively. The instructions suggested building the shell around the interior, but like previous projects, I deviated and made a couple of modifications to allow the interior unit to slot inside freely. This entailed cutting away the small locating pins on the inside of the rear, along with the two inwardly curving sections at the base, which ostensibly act as a shelf on which the interior can sit. However, I found the interior fitted just as well without them, with a pair of locating clips in the inside of the front corners acting as retaining aids.

At an early stage of assembly, the outer cab shell was placed over the interior unit to gauge the position of the hinge brackets, checking that the cab was sitting squarely on the chassis.

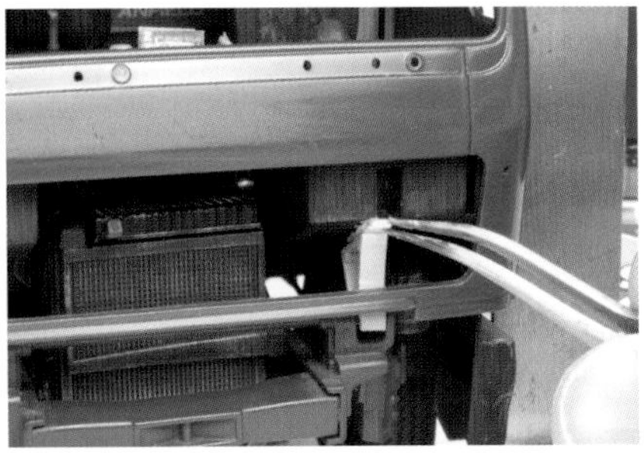

The brackets required shims of a different thickness on each side to enable the cab to sit correctly.

Before progressing with the outer shell, the finished interior unit was temporarily slotted inside and the whole cab was employed to check the fit of the hinging brackets. Some alignment issues were duly encountered, and thin plastic shims were required to get the cab sitting squarely on the chassis. These minor alterations had the knock-on effect of influencing the fit of the front bumper to the chassis, which also required the use of shims to allow it to protrude an extra couple of millimetres from the frames, thus providing space for the cab to hinge forwards.

Making these checks at this early stage, when modifications can be effected easily, is highly recommended. Interestingly, this kit doesn't feature any means of fixing the cab to the chassis permanently. Instead, the hinge brackets simply rest on the rocking bar on the frames, allowing the cab to tilt realistically, but also permitting it to be lifted off completely.

Priming and painting of the cab then followed, using my improvised garden spray booth, and building the Tamiya spray paint into a deep, lustrous finish over several thin coats. After picking out the window seals by hand, a few coats of clear gloss (also from a Tamiya aerosol) followed before the decals were applied. As well as the decals supplied with the Mercedes 2238 kit, I made use of logos from another Italeri Truck Accessory kit (No.720), which fitted well enough. That same accessory kit also provided a pair of mud-flaps and reflectors to enhance the front wheel arches.

The heavy deposits of dirt on the chassis were effectively rendered with acrylic paints, but I wanted the cab to look a little less filthy. MIG enamel washes were employed instead, with a mixture of brown and neutral shades applied by brush, while the dark wash

After thorough preparation, the cab shell entered the painting stage. Another Tamiya spray can provided the pleasing shade of blue (TS-10), while the window seals were painted by hand; then the cab was given a clear gloss coat, and finally the decals were applied.

The cab was weathered with a mix of MIG enamel washes, applied in thin layers and manipulated with swabs. A much more subtle effect was desired, in contrast to the grubby chassis.

Glue 'n' Glaze effectively secured the glazing and interior roof and door panels.

The wiper blades, before they were glued in place, were used to mark out a card masking stencil. Held in place with a small blob of Blu-Tack, a semi-matt clear coat was then airbrushed over the exposed areas of windscreen.

The reconfigured dashboard and the radiator grille were installed with Glue 'n' Glaze adhesive; this was left to cure overnight, before the interior was slotted into place.

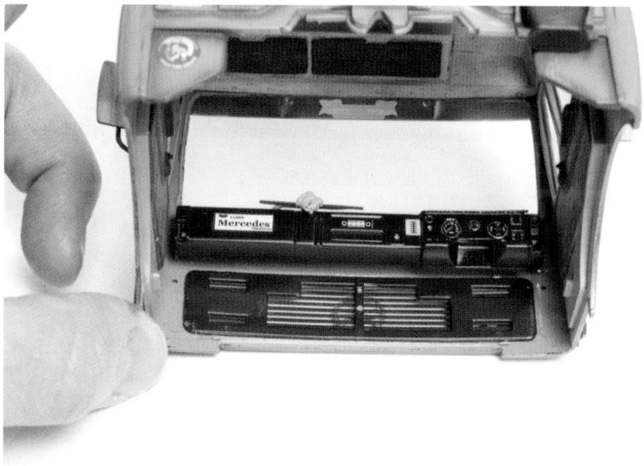

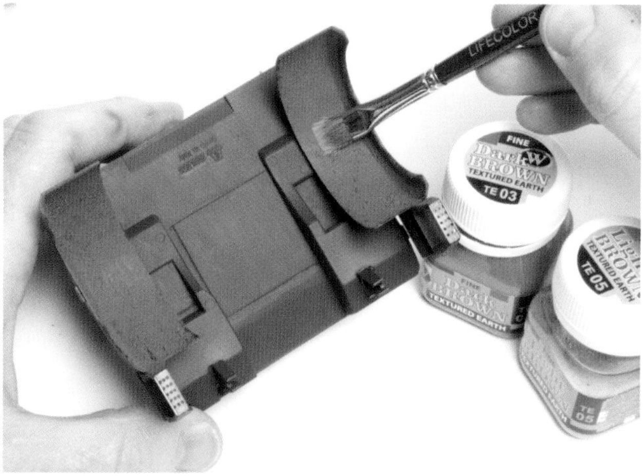

Wilder's Textured Earth acrylic paints were roughly stippled on to the underside of the front and rear wheel arches. A few different shades were employed for variety. The coarse appearance was then softened by misting the underframe with similarly dirty brown shades via an airbrush.

In my workshop I could make use of my airbrush to add a little finesse to the weathering job.

shade was brushed directly into the door seams to improve definition. A restrained approach, using thinners to remove excess wash pigment, allowed the glossy blue paintwork to be retained, while giving it a slightly aged, work-worn appearance.

After three months, the truck neared completion, and a relaxation of Coronavirus restrictions meant that I could access my workshop again: so I made use of an airbrush to add a little finesse to the chassis and cab weathering. Layers of textured acrylic paints had been stippled on to the undersides of the wheel arches, so these areas were also greatly improved with the airbrush. Misted coats of Tamiya acrylics softened any hard edges and created subtle shading effects to the bodywork.

AN INTERESTING CHALLENGE

Despite being built during a difficult time, I'm very pleased with how this truck turned out. It certainly provided a welcome distraction from the dismal reality of living through a global pandemic, and the need to improvise and employ what materials and tools I had to hand provided an interesting challenge. Indeed, the improvisation and 'make-it-up-as-I-go-along' attitude felt liberating in a way, allowing one to concentrate on modelling purely as a pleasurable leisure exercise.

The quality of the kit really helped, with no annoying elements to wrestle with, apart from the short driveshafts and exhaust pipes. I'm particularly proud of the right-hand-drive conversion, which turned out better than I'd envisaged, as well as the detail additions to the chassis, especially when I think about how it was virtually all created from scrap, vindicating my propensity to retain leftover plastic, wire and other detailing materials.

There's no doubt that I had been looking forward to building the Volvo F16, but as things turned out, this Mercedes-Benz 2238 provided ample compensation.

Italeri's kit provides the basis for a realistic model, but also offers the modeller plenty of enjoyment and great value.

The addition of the various pipes, cables and valves to the chassis has greatly enhanced the kit.

The hand-crafted susie cables and bracket were deceptively easy to create. The spot lamp on the rear of the cab is a resin casting from the KFS range.

Given the challenging circumstances in which this truck was created, the project proved to be highly rewarding, highlighting the positive impact that hobbies can have on our wellbeing.

CHAPTER TWELVE

PRIDE OF LOUISVILLE: 1:24-SCALE FORD LTL9000

The artwork adorning the box of this model is captivating, conjuring up misty-eyed visions of New Mexico, as a heavy breakdown truck rumbles through a small town, kicking up dust in its wake. The Santa Fe logos and hook-shaped stripes give the truck a sense of style and purpose, while the allure of something a little different to a regular tractor unit is always hard to resist.

Having got the kit home and rifled through the parts, I began to wonder about making a few changes to the truck's function. The components for the wrecker unit have been offered with a variety of other Italeri kits over the years, featuring both US and European prototypes, so I was sure that the parts wouldn't go to waste. Indeed, I have a few MAN, Scania and Volvo kits put aside that might benefit from conversion to a breakdown truck. But what could I do with the Ford's empty frames, which would create some visual interest? After some head scratching and rummaging through my collection of kits, I found the solution.

IDENTIFYING THE TRUCK MODEL

My knowledge of North American trucks is limited, but I did guess that the truck depicted on the box was a Ford, due mostly to the blue lozenge adorning the front grille. There's a vagueness to the artwork and branding of this kit, presumably due to licensing issues, but the truck in question is a Ford LTL9000. The heavy-duty L Series was introduced in 1970 and built at Ford's Louisville, Kentucky plant. The 9000 model was designed for long-haul work and first appeared in 1976, but the kit depicts a post-1978 version, with the distinctive numerals cast into the grille. The LTL9000 featured a choice of diesel-power units from Cummins or Caterpillar, and apparently these trucks were the first vehicles in the USA to carry Ford's iconic blue lozenge logo.

It might not say it on the box, but Italeri's ambiguous 'US Wrecker Truck' is actually a tandem-axled Ford LTL9000. Despite being drawn to the breakdown truck, I decided to take the kit in a slightly different direction.

After a few hours of trawling the internet for images, quite a motley selection of LTL9000s took my fancy, especially those that had clearly enjoyed long careers over a number of different roles. One or two did not have the sleeper cab, and I found their appearance far more attractive. With just a day cab, however, the long chassis would look a little odd, so something would have to take up some of the space. Another of Italeri's Truck Accessories packs (No. 3854) includes a pivoting crane, complete with a three-part extendable boom, control unit and stabilizing legs, and this looked to be just what was wanted. While it is arguably more European in nature, nevertheless I decided to install it, creating a fictional truck that would be suited to hauling a flatbed trailer that could be loaded with plant, heavy equipment, or perhaps even a logging trailer, although the crane would need to be converted into more of a grabber. But I resolved to worry about that later and to just get on with the kit, as I'd been keen to tackle a large-scale American 'Big Rig' for some time.

With a plan in place, I began to consider what elements of the kit I could improve, through detailing work or replacement. The fifth wheel and turntable immediately sprang to mind: although a complement of parts is provided with the wrecker kit, they are rather bland in appearance. A heavy-duty Jost sliding fifth-wheel bed and turntable was obtained from KFS instead, along with a set of valves and regulators for the chassis' pipework. New resin wheel rims and hubs were also ordered from KFS, as again, the kit's original parts are rather bland. A set of replacement exhaust stacks was also ordered. However, I ended up keeping the kit's original exhausts, as they turned out nicely after some improvement work.

BUILDING THE ENGINE

Punched hex nuts were fitted to the cylinder heads, and when the cement had cured, they were drilled carefully to accept brass wire injector pipes.

After priming, I painted the engine in an approximation of Caterpillar's distinctive mustard-yellow shade. Prior stippling with Mr Surfacer 500 gave the powerplant a distinctive cast-metal texture, which was greatly enhanced by the weathering washes.

The engine builds into quite a substantial unit, and although it may not resemble the prototype's power unit exactly, a few extra bits and pieces made it look more convincing. The most obvious omissions were an injector unit and fuel pump, so approximations of each were created from plastic section. Mounting bolts and compression fittings were produced with my RP Toolz punch-and-die sets, while the pipework was formed from brass wire and Tamiya's flexible cable. Various filters and mounting racks were also added to the engine block, which all combined to greatly enhance the 'heart' of the truck.

Following a coat of aerosol primer, Mr Surfacer 500 was stippled over most of the engine and gearbox with an old brush, taking care not to cover the nice new details. The texture that this imparts can be very realistic, and it proved its worth after the powerplant had been painted and weathered. I mixed my own version of Caterpillar's distinctive mustard-yellow shade (yellow and brown Tamiya acrylics), while the gearbox received a coat of mid-grey. Various details were picked out in contrasting colours, such as the different filters, alternator and exhaust manifold, and a set of KFS decals added markings and an engine serial numberplate for even greater fidelity. Layers of enamel washes and dry-brushing helped give the unit a work-stained appearance, and also highlighted the wealth of detail that now regaled the engine and transmission.

The kit's powerplant lacks several important elements, such as an injector rail, fuel pump and various filters, which were all fabricated from offcuts of styrene strip and rod. The hollow tube forming the filters had the open ends filled with epoxy putty. Punched hex nuts and washers were also added.

THE CHASSIS

Erection of the chassis followed a similar path to the 1:24-scale trucks already discussed, especially the long-wheelbase DAF 95 in Chapter 9. The main longitudinal members were carefully fettled to remove a number of flaws, including the inner faces, to allow for the fitting of the cables, pipes and valves. The frames were assembled on a marble block designed for model engineers, which is something I usually employ when building etched-metal, steam-locomotive chassis. The ultra-flat surface makes it easy to ensure that the frames are concentric, while a set-square helps to check the various angles in relation to the surface. This may be considered a luxury addition to the workshop, especially for building plastic kits, but it does give the modeller confidence in the integrity of a chassis.

Once the main suspension elements were in place, but before the axles were fitted, the pipework was added to the inside of the frames while access was relatively easy. The KFS cast-metal valves were improved with careful fettling and the addition of styrene hex nuts, which had been drilled before being punched out. This was a time-consuming exercise, but the rewards justified the effort.

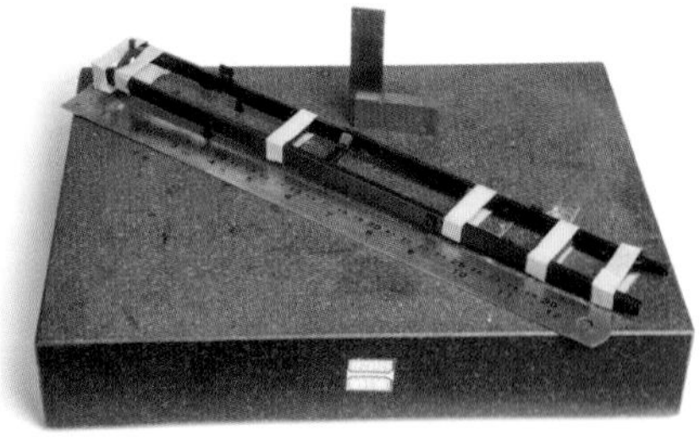

The long chassis frames benefited from being assembled on a reliably flat surface.

KFS' cast-metal valves were fettled with needle files, then punched styrene hex nuts, with holes pre-drilled through their centre, were fixed with cyano glue.

Before the axles were fitted to the chassis, some of the valves were fixed within the frames. Tamiya's flexible cable was fixed into the outlets and threaded through the gaps in the cross-members.

The styrene hex nuts resemble compression fittings, adding an extra touch of class. It's much easier to add the main runs of cable before the chassis gets too cluttered.

When fitting the axles, their alignment was checked on the flat marble block with the kit's original plastic wheels and tyres temporarily fitted. Later, the Tamiya cable was threaded into holes bored into the brake drums and air chambers. Note the punched hex nuts and washers fitted to the differential casing and the driveshaft yokes.

CTM's etched cable ties kept the pipework neat and tidy.

Cable was also run towards electrical items, such as the rear lights and battery boxes.

A superior fifth-wheel turntable and frame was installed, using resin parts from KFS. The sliding bed and turntable would be treated as separate sub-assemblies.

The resin brackets were enhanced with extra washers and hex nuts, tallying with those cast into the upper surface.

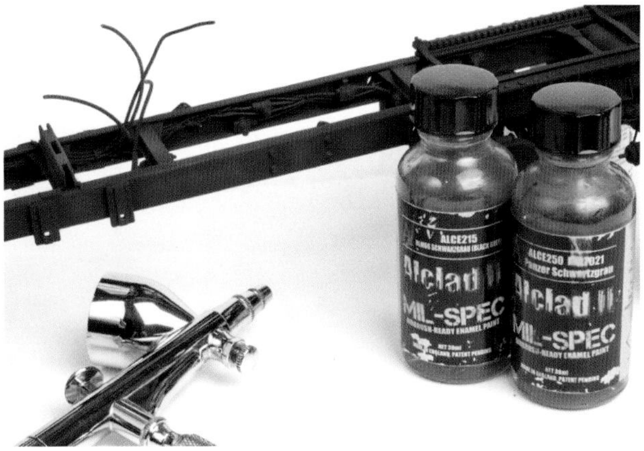

The frames were airbrushed with multiple shades of dark grey Alclad II Mil-Spec enamels, with a touch of Matt Black added for shading purposes.

The paints were built up over several layers, patiently targeting the flow into the recesses and between the frames. Shading and highlights were created by strategically targeting the different tones. This took some time, but the chassis looked good afterwards. Clear gloss coats followed.

Various diameters of Tamiya's flexible cable were employed, and without being wholly slavish to reality, the valves and pipework were arranged within the frames in a hopefully convincing pattern. Some of the valves were mounted on improvised styrene brackets, and I also added some punched hex nuts and washers to the outside of the frames to suggest through mounting bolts.

With the main runs of cable added, the axles could be installed, and these were also adorned with pipework between the brake drums and chambers, leading back up to the frames and connecting into the cast distributor valves. The frames can become congested quite quickly, so I tidied the pipework with CTM's etched cable ties. Indeed, it's important to consider that real trucks wouldn't have important cabling or air hoses dangling freely from the chassis – these are more likely to be kept well out of harm's way. The KFS fifth wheel's base frame could now be installed. Extra bolt-head and washer details were added, tallying with the fasteners on the upper edge of the side beams for greater interest.

After a thorough clean, the chassis was ready for priming and painting. A grey primer was sprayed initially, but instead of simply painting a black topcoat, I employed a handful of different shades of dark grey, from the Alclad II Mil-Spec range of pre-thinned enamels. These paints require a thorough shake before use, but they can then be loaded directly into the airbrush. The greys were a variety of military camouflage tones, with a matt black formula also kept on hand to add the darkest shades. Working the paint into the many recesses takes a surprisingly long time and demands plenty of patience. The frames and the airbrush are kept moving, to allow the tool to direct the paint from every possible angle, while helping to avoid building up excess paint in any one area.

The paints were applied strategically to create areas of highlights and shading to complement the profile of the chassis frames and the various components. Darker shades were concentrated into the deeper recesses, with lighter tones in more exposed areas, where natural highlights would occur, or where the paint would be more prone to fading. A little to-ing and fro-ing may be required, taking the time to assess how the chassis appears in natural light (where possible), while also checking that the paint has reached into all areas of the frames.

This approach, as well as offering potentially impressive results, also gives us a head start in the weathering process, as much of the shading work will have been achieved at the outset. Experience helps when deciding whether the shading and highlights are acceptable. A more exaggerated approach can often be beneficial at this stage, as the tonal shifts will be toned down by subsequent layers of weathering. Furthermore, the clear gloss coats that followed also softened the shading effect slightly, with the gloss being confined mostly to the outer edges of the frames and the axles, retaining a flat, matt sheen to the inner faces of the chassis to encourage the adhesion of weathering powders later.

Oil washes followed, with small blobs of grey and earthy brown shades decanted on to a card palette and then dabbed randomly over the frames with a dry brush. Thinners was then employed to work the pigment into the frames, removing the excess with cotton swabs. The oil paint remains workable for hours, so there is no need to rush, and gentle streaking effects can be achieved with a flat brush. Abteilung 502 oils were employed throughout, along with the matching matt-effect thinners. The process is similar to the use of enamel weathering washes, although I find that oil washes afford the modeller more control, allowing greater nuances to be achieved in the weathering effects.

Using a flat brush dipped in matt-effect thinners, the oils were diluted and manipulated over the surface, with the excess wiped away with swabs. The process is repeated over several layers, shifting to shades of brown, and allowing each to dry in between.

Lifecolor's Reflecting Agent was brushed over the fifth wheel's sliding mechanism for a more pronounced, burnished patina.

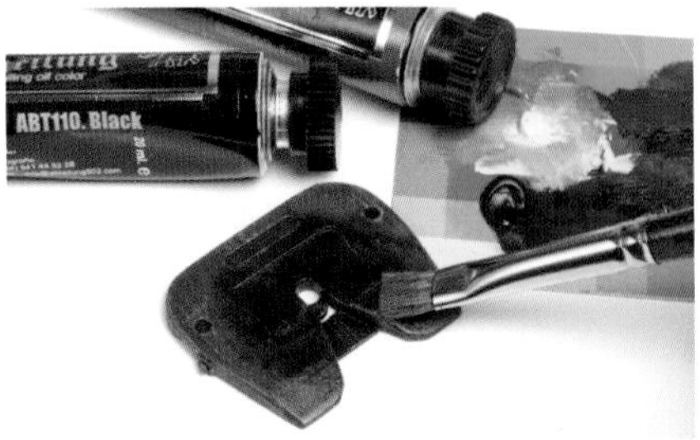

Weathering began with the use of Abteilung 502 oils, mostly brown and grey shades, plus black. The fifth-wheel turntable was treated to thick layers of paint to mimic heavy deposits of grease.

It can be a slow process, but the results can be more subtle and nuanced compared to other techniques.

Installing and plumbing-in the engine is always a high point. After painting the hoses with slightly different shades of dark grey, jubilee clips were fashioned from thin strips of insulation tape, secured with a little cyano glue.

The frames were given a grey oil wash to begin with, which ages the paintwork slightly, presenting a slightly washed-out look. Small blobs of neat oil paint were initially stippled on to the surface.

The final coat of oil wash was left for a couple of weeks to allow the thinners to evaporate completely before continuing. Dry pigments came next, with earthy brown and rusty red shades dusted into the frames. An old toothbrush removed the excess and imparted a burnished effect to the surface.

The tape was then picked out with metallic paint, in this case Darkstar's Tarnished Steel.

The fit of the exhaust sections wasn't brilliant, so instead of simply adding filler to the joints, I crafted some simple flanges from plastic sheet, which filled the gaps and looked great, too.

Painting and weathering followed my usual method of stippling the surface with Mr Surfacer 500, followed by layers of Lifecolor's various shades of rust, again stippled by hand. The random tones and textures are then enhanced with dry-brushed metallic paint. AK Interactive's True Metal Iron was employed, brushed very lightly over the parts.

When dry, the True Metal paints can be burnished effectively with a fingertip.

Oils demand a few days' drying time before painting continues, and the frames will have to be handled carefully to avoid leaving fingerprints on the damp surfaces. Next it was time for dry pigments to be applied to the frames, with dark rust and earth-brown shades worked into the inner faces initially, and the excess brushed away with an old toothbrush. By this stage the chassis had taken on a more lifelike appearance, and assembly could recommence with the fitting of the engine and transmission, and plumbing in the various pipes and hoses. Jubilee clips were fashioned from thin strips of electrical insulation tape secured with a drop of cyano glue and painted with a metallic silver shade.

The lower sections of the exhaust pipework also gained a more realistic appearance with the addition of styrene flanges and a textured, corroded patina, finished off with dry-brushed metallic highlights. The outlet pipes from the silencers would be treated later, along with the stacks.

Despite joining the fuel tank halves as carefully as possible, there were still pronounced joint lines along the barrels and at the ends. The chromed parts had been stripped back to bare plastic with abrasives before assembly, and after filling and abrading the joints, the tanks were rubbed down again. Coats of grey primer tested the surfaces in between bouts of wet-sanding with Micro-Mesh, and only when the surfaces were deemed to be immaculate were a black primer coat and Alclad II Aluminium lacquer applied. This gave the tanks a more convincing metallic appearance, with a darker Steel shade applied to the straps for contrast. Clear gloss coats sealed the metallic paintwork, and the tanks were ready for weathering.

A dark brown acrylic wash was applied: regular Lifecolor paints were brushed over one section of each tank at a time, then most of it was wiped away with a swab, leaving behind vertical streaks and deposits of 'dirt' around the raised straps. Tamiya acrylic thinner helped shift any stubborn, unwanted deposits, but the aim was to leave behind greater concentrations of pigment on the rear and lower faces of each tank. Tamiya acrylics were then airbrushed over the tanks, to soften any hard edges to the wash coat.

When installing the tanks, holes were drilled to accept the flexible fuel lines fitted to the frames earlier. Each tank received a pair of hoses, with small scraps of styrene rod acting as feed and return valves. As more items were attached to the chassis, including the mudguards and battery-box covers (which had also been de-chromed and the tops filed flat), plus the new resin wheels, the model was beginning to resemble a truck at last.

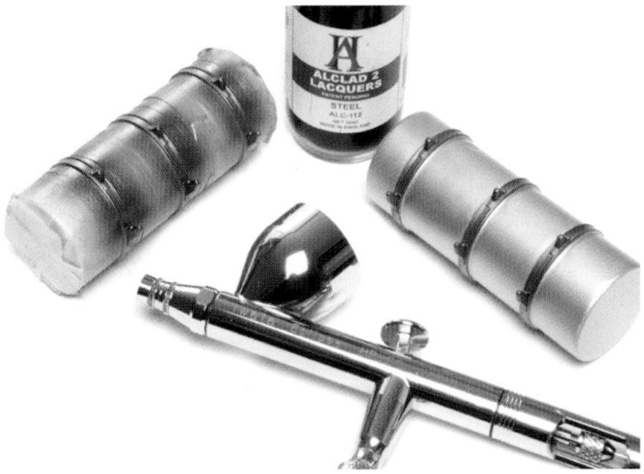

Hours were spent priming and abrading the fuel tanks until the barrels were super smooth and blemish free. Black primer preceded the Alclad II Aluminium lacquer. When this was dry, the tanks were masked so that the straps could be sprayed with Alclad II's Steel.

The shiny, chromed rear mudguards were toned down with fine abrasives, taking care not to remove too much of the coating, and avoiding too smooth a finish. Acrylic paints were brushed on and wiped away, leaving the pigment deposited around the surface relief, but also ingrained in the texture left by the abrasives. Dry pigments added a dusty sheen and further tonal variation.

The inside faces of the mudguards gained heavier deposits of muck, courtesy of a stippled mix of acrylic paint and dry pigment, which created a grainy texture. When dry, this was enhanced further with a dusting of dry pigments.

Resin wheel rims and hubs replaced the mediocre kit parts, and were weathered with a combination of enamel washes and dry pigments; the latter were also brushed over the tyres and into the treads.

With the wheels fitted permanently, the fuel tanks were also installed. Save for some touching up of the paintwork and weathering, the chassis was now complete and ready to be married with the bodywork.

BODYWORK

The cab shell was built around the interior unit, using the latter as a forming aid. The cab panels were taped together while the glue was applied precisely into the joints with a fine brush. In common with previous projects, the shell was only tacked together at this stage, the bonds being made comprehensively from the inside once the interior unit had been removed.

Not using the sleeper cab meant that a large opening was left in the rear of the cab, which needed filling. A piece of 60thou' plastic card was cut fractionally oversize with a piercing saw, then it was patiently filed and test-fitted until it made a good, close fit that required minimal filling and sanding, on the outside at least. The inside of the cab has a raised beading around the aperture, making it difficult to create a neat joint, so a whole new inner bulkhead was cut from another sheet of styrene and installed.

Adding a rear window was contemplated, but I felt it would have looked incongruous with the crane sited immediately behind the cab. Also, I couldn't face the extra labour, especially when the initial grey primer coats revealed a visible seam around the former aperture that couldn't be seen against the bare white plastic. It took a few attempts at filling, sanding and priming before the cab's bodywork looked perfect.

The bonnet, or hood, was bonded to the chromed radiator grille and any gaps were filled and abraded, taking away as much of the shiny coating as possible, prior to priming the unit as a

Without the sleeper unit, the rear aperture of the day cab needs filling. A piece of 60thou' plastic card was cut and fettled until it fitted as snugly as possible. Still, plenty of filling and sanding was required until the surface was free of any visible seam.

The hood and grille were assembled before priming and painting, allowing any gaps to be filled. The grille's chrome finish was rubbed back to bare plastic wherever possible. After a grey primer, the vibrant red shade was applied, with a slightly darker tone aimed into the recessed areas to represent a little shading.

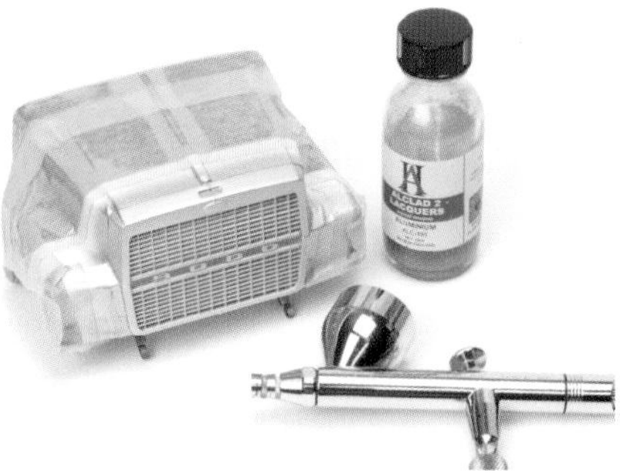

The grille was masked cautiously, before the Alclad II Aluminium was applied. With the masking removed, the whole hood gained a few layers of clear gloss.

The cab was painted in a similar way, with a gentle shading effect targeted in key areas. When the clear coats had cured, the decals were applied. A Gofer Racing sheet provided the Associated Transport emblems, while the Illinois legends were cut from a different logo.

Instead of painting the headlight units in a single metallic shade, the Aluminium base colour was overlaid with a targeted spray of Steel into the recessed areas. Pale Burnt Metal was then misted over the whole unit to provide a sepia-tinged filter. The same approach was employed with the air horns.

whole. I spent a while trying to find the perfect shade of red, to match the logos I'd obtained from a Gofer Racing decal sheet. Eventually I settled on Railmatch enamel Buffer Beam Red – the shade that British Railways used to paint on to the front valances of steam locomotives. It's quite a vibrant, orangey red, and the Railmatch paint can be built into a lustrous, hardwearing finish. A little tonal manipulation was employed, with a slightly darkened shade mixed and airbrushed around the door and panel seams. The tonal shift was very subtle, and it doesn't really show up in the photographs, but when viewing the model in person, the extra shading is rather effective.

The red paint was allowed a full week to harden, before it was lightly abraded; it was then masked to allow the front grille to be given a metallic finish. Alclad II Aluminium lacquer was airbrushed directly on to the red background and built up over several light coats, carefully working the paint into the grille's vanes. Good quality, flexible masking tape (Tamiya) was employed, pressed firmly into position at the edges to reduce the risk of paint seepage. Thankfully, when the masking was removed, the demarcation was almost perfect. After cleaning up, both the hood and the cab could receive their clear gloss coats, prior to adding the decals.

The Gofer Racing decal sheet (ref. 11052) may have supplied the main logos, but I also employed various Italeri decal sheets for other elements, such as the large US flag and the interior adornments. Being a fictional truck, I cut out the 'Illinois' element from a different logo to add beneath the Associated Transport emblems. That meant that I needed Illinois licence plates, and more online searching revealed a set of truck plates; the image was manipulated slightly in Photoshop to correct the perspective, and they were then scaled and printed out, ready for fitting at the very end of the project. Meanwhile I needed a blue Ford lozenge for the hood, and was lucky enough to find one on a decal sheet for a Belkits Ford Escort MkI that I've yet to build. Surprisingly, it was a perfect fit.

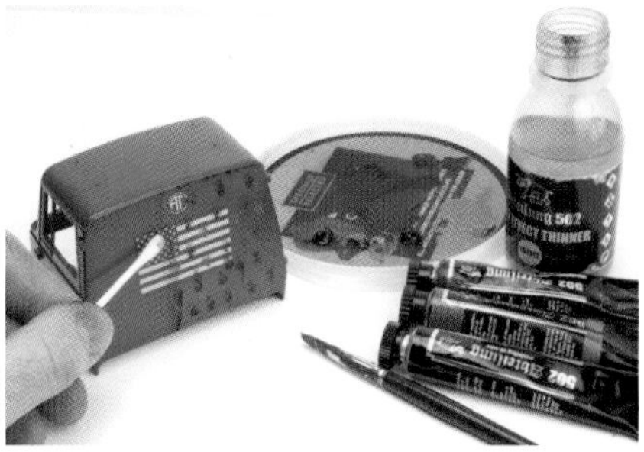

Weathering of the cab and hood followed a similar course to the chassis, with layers of oil washes applied.

The darker oil washes brought greater relief to the door seams.

Airbrushed Tamiya acrylics added some finesse to the weathering, with misted shading applied around the mounting points for the air horns and exhaust stacks, as well as general road dirt around the wheel arches and lower edges.

Like the chassis, the bodywork was weathered initially with a mix of grey, brown and black Abteilung 502 oils. The combination of colours and a layered approach resulted in a slightly faded appearance, with greater definition to the various seams and recesses, while maintaining a deep lustre to the paintwork. Working on a smooth, glossy base helps, so putting the effort into the preparation and application of the colour and clear coats is always worthwhile, regardless of whether you're aiming for a showroom sparkle or a grimy workhorse finish.

When the oil wash coats had dried, a semi-gloss clear coat followed, using a Mr Hobby Premium Topcoat aerosol, which softened the weathering effects slightly and left a more resilient surface finish that will withstand handling. The weathering was then refined slightly with the airbrush and a mix of Tamiya acrylics, adding a light misting along the lower edges, but also around the mounting points for the air horns and exhausts. The interior of the hood gained a textured coating, using a mix of Lifecolor acrylic paint and dry pigment. The grimy, dark brown/rusty red shades were stippled randomly over the inside; when dry, the airbrush refined the finish, and the treatment created a welcome contrast with the shiny paintwork on the outside.

Fitting the assembled cab to the chassis wasn't as easy as I'd imagined, with the small mounting brackets refusing to co-operate. After some fettling work and countless test-fits, I was finally satisfied that the cab was sitting squarely. Glue 'n' Glaze adhesive was applied to the joint, allowing time for adjustment and for easy removal in the future, should it be required. Once the bond had cured, the exhaust stacks and link pipes could be installed.

Scaled-down, printed designs were generated from images found online, including a topical newspaper and magazines for 1980, as well as Illinois state maps.

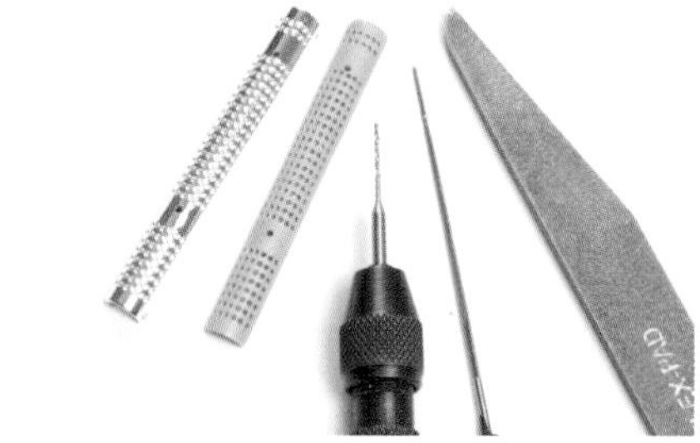

The kit's exhaust stacks looked cumbersome at first glance, but after being shorn of the heavy chrome coating and refined with files and abrasives, they appeared far more acceptable. The moulded perforations in the heat shields were drilled out individually and the holes tidied with a miniature reamer. The task was extremely tedious, but the parts benefited greatly from the hard work.

When the cab had been fixed to the chassis, the exhaust could be installed. The curved link pipes were a surprisingly good fit between the stacks and the silencers beneath the frames, with just a little filler required at the joints. The parts were blended by hand, using Lifecolor and Darkstar acrylics.

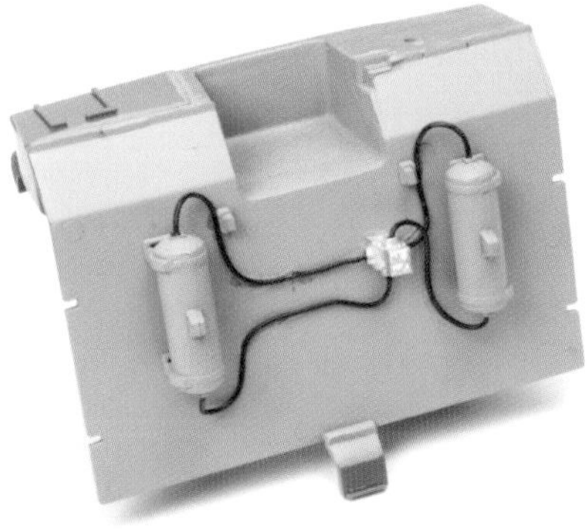

The twin reservoir tanks beneath the cab gained some generic pipework and a cast-metal valve.

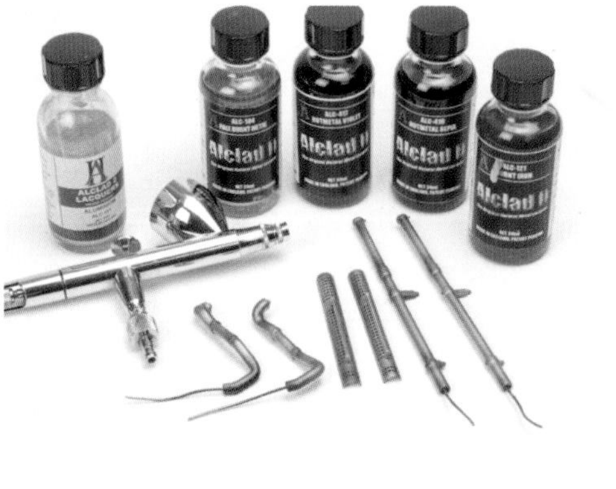

The pipes and shields gained a far more effective metallic coating, thanks to Alclad II's Aluminium lacquer. A number of Pale Burnt Metal shades, plus Burnt Iron, were misted over the pipes to add shading and heat staining. Clear coats should always be sprayed over metallic lacquers, and I used Alclad II's Light Sheen formula.

As mentioned earlier, I'd planned on replacing the stacks with superior metal and resin units from KFS, but the pack had vanished after I moved workshops. Could the kit parts – which looked rather second rate – be improved? I had nothing to lose in trying, so I rubbed away the heavy chrome-effect finish and bonded the bare plastic halves together. After more fettling of the pipes, they began to look much more refined, while the heatshields benefited greatly from drilling out the moulded perforations (168 per shield!). When the Alclad II lacquers had been applied, enhanced with various 'hot metal' effect tinting shades, the exhaust elements looked great, especially once fitted to the cab. The curved link pipes required a little filler at the joints and the paintwork blended by hand, creating a gentle transition from polished metal to corrosion at the inboard ends.

FURTHER ENGINE DETAILING

Now that the cab was fixed in place, the air cleaner and duct could be fitted to the front bulkhead. Furthermore, due to the kit's tilting hood, I decided to add more scratch-built detail in the knowledge that it could be viewed easily in the future. Brass, copper and nickel jewellery wire, of varying gauges, was installed, running from improvised junction boxes and brackets on the bulkhead to the alternator, wiper motor and elsewhere. Some cable was coiled together in a pin vice, as demonstrated in Chapter 11, and some was picked out in red, yellow and green paint.

The bulkhead also gained an array of decals from a KFS sheet, featuring warning legends and a serial number-plate. A washer-fluid reservoir and a coolant tank were also created, fabricated from scraps of styrene, complete with flexible hoses and filling caps. Mounting bolts for all these extra fittings were punched from styrene, and after everything had been painted and weathered to blend with the surroundings, the overall effect was very pleasing.

Fitting the hood turned into something of an ordeal, as it would not align with the cab without the addition of large plastic fillets between the hinges and the base of the grille. Perhaps this was due to the positioning of the cab earlier, which hadn't been an easy task either. Repeated test-fitting, with ever-increasing shims, eventually sorted the

Extra detail was added to the engine compartment, using scraps of styrene and flexible wire.

Another tank was improvised and added to the bulkhead, along with warning and serial number decals from KFS.

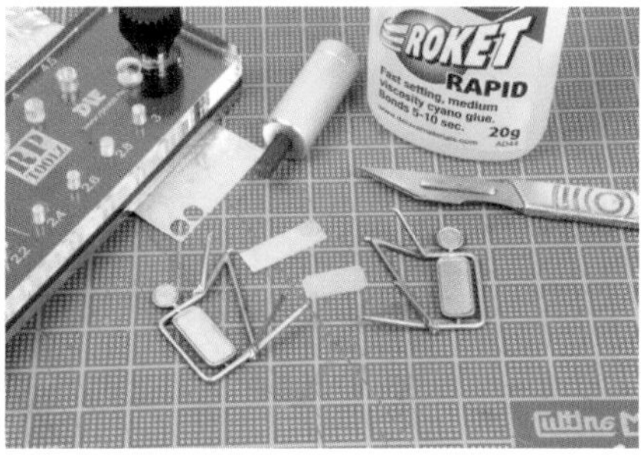

Thin, flexible metal foil was cut and punched to form reflective panels for the wing mirrors.

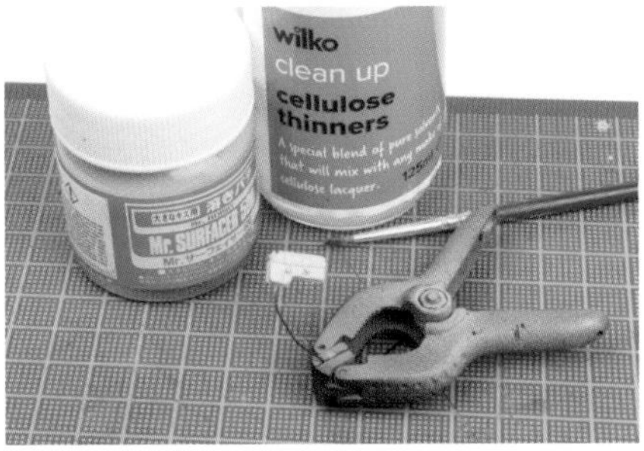

A fluid reservoir tank was created from styrene sheet and strip, then primed and painted before installation.

Most of the new components were primed and painted in situ, with the electrical cable picked out in different colours.

Trouble was encountered with the hood's hinge brackets, and plenty of styrene was required to shim the large gaps. When a perfect fit was eventually achieved, the haphazard shim layers were filled and shaped to a neater profile, and painted. To effect a reliable bond, the underside of the grille was abraded back to bare plastic and the shims secured with liquid poly-cement.

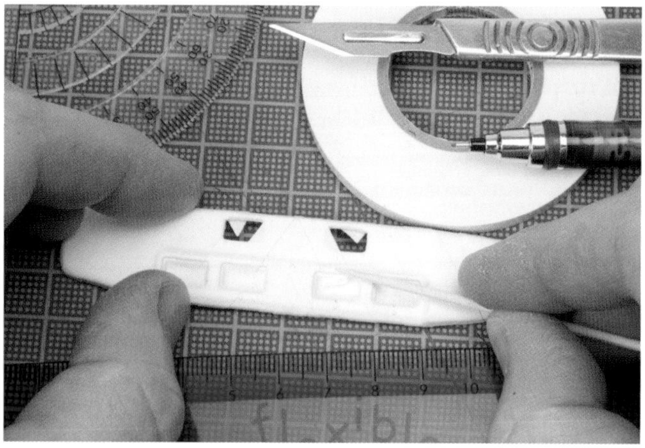

The stripe pattern was marked on to the fender with a fine pencil, and Tamiya flexible masking tape applied. The tape can be persuaded to conform to the surface profile with the edge of a cocktail stick.

A further coat of white paint was sprayed initially, to seal any gaps in the tape, before the red was applied.

Inevitably, small ridges of paint will form against the edges of the tape, so the surface will benefit from a rub down with fine abrasives, lubricated with plenty of soapy water. Clear gloss will then restore the sheen. The fender was then ready for weathering.

A set of Illinois licence plates was created from an online image and printed on to good quality paper. My ink cartridge was running low, so the red elements came out a little faded. The ink was sealed with a clear coat of gloss.

Having cut out the licence plates, the edges were touched in with a red marker pen before they were installed. A light dusting with dry pigments modified the pristine appearance.

problem, but the shims then had to be merged into the curved hinge brackets by filling and shaping, as they would be visible above the front fender.

The front fender gained a series of red and white hazard stripes, after carefully marking out their position and applying flexible masking tape. With the tape in position on the white paintwork, another coat of white was sprayed initially, thus sealing any gaps that may have been lurking under the tape. The red paint was then airbrushed, and when the masking was removed, the edges of the stripes were nice and crisp, albeit with the inevitable raised ridges where the paint had built up against the tape. Once the surface was completely dry, it was wet-sanded with fine abrasives to flatten everything; then the sheen was restored with a few light coats of clear gloss.

The truck's frames lacked enough projecting material at the front end to allow the fender to fit properly, so extra packing pieces of styrene were cut and installed until it sat correctly and allowed the hood brackets to hinge forwards. A degree of compromise had to be employed, with the hood not opening as much as I would have liked due to clearance issues over the fender. Without increasing the gap between fender and hood, there didn't seem to be a realistic alternative at this stage.

What I really should have done was alter the shape of the hood's hinge brackets rather than simply add shims, or craft a new pair from scratch, so that the hood could be lifted slightly before pivoting forwards, clear of the fender's top edge. One day I'll revisit this area of the model, and with this in mind, the hood was fixed to the chassis with a set of nylon nuts and bolts, which will ease removal in future.

BUILDING THE PIVOTING CRANE

Italeri's pivoting crane is an impressive kit in its own right, featuring a channel girder base that will sit on the parallel frames of many 1:24 trucks. I modified the base with an extra cross-member at the rear and a chequer-plate storage platform, the latter cut from an etched sheet of nickel silver from the KFS range. The crane's instructions are presented in an exploded diagram, rather than separate step-by-step instructions, so working out the order of assembly takes a little extra mental effort and a great deal of dry test-fitting.

The three-section hoist, telescopic boom and hydraulic rams are all designed to move, so the individual sections need to be assembled and fettled judiciously. There are small tabs moulded within the hoist parts that, in theory, should allow the crane to be posed in various positions, but I struggled to get these to work satisfactorily after the unit had

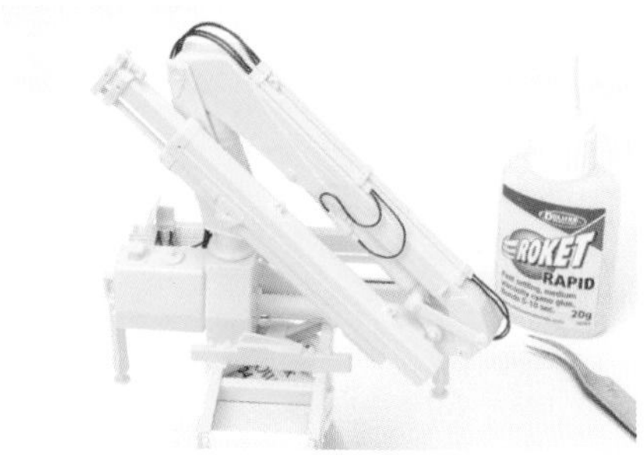

Italeri's pivoting crane can be assembled quickly, although the various sections benefit from being filled and abraded to remove traces of the glue joints, especially the telescopic boom and hydraulic rams. Hydraulic hoses were added, using Tamiya's flexible cable.

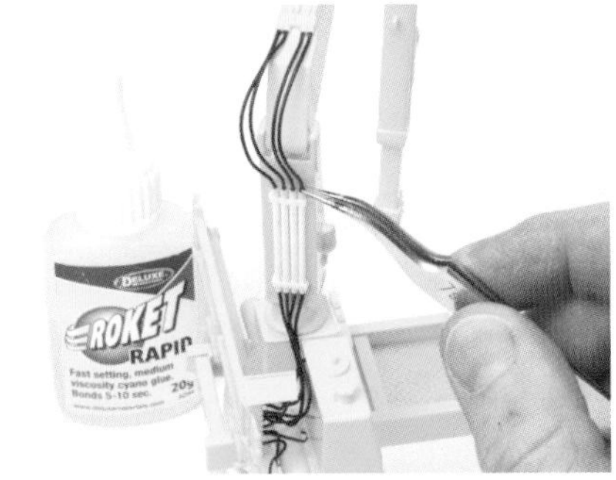

Styrene rod and strip provided material for the hose connections. Adding the hoses after the painting and weathering stages might have been a better idea.

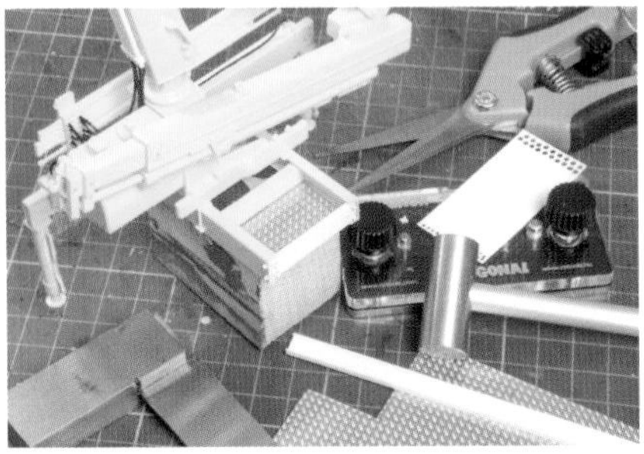

The framework at the base gained an extra cross-member and a treadplate storage platform.

been painted. Indeed, the priming and painting stage caused a few headaches, and these were not down to the paint vapours!

My plan was to install flexible hydraulic hoses, but should these be added before or after the crane was painted and weathered? And should the whole crane be painted as a single object, or treated in sub-assemblies? In the end I just went ahead with the building and detailing work, resolving to worry about the painting when the time came. Sometimes you just need to press ahead and face the challenges head on, rather than prevaricate and leave a model unfinished in a box.

As it transpired, the painting stage proved a little unorthodox, but not overly complicated. The main issue was how to handle the model while the paint was being sprayed, but this was overcome by creating a stiff wire hoop that was fixed into holes drilled discreetly into the base of the frame. This also allowed the crane to be hung upside down while drying. The shade of red was mixed ad hoc, using Tamiya acrylics (X-7 Red, XF-9 Hull Red and a drop of XF-26 Deep Green), and built up gradually with the airbrush, working it into all the nooks and crannies and around the various moving parts; it took a few sittings to get the paint layers even and consistent. Once the hydraulic hoses had been touched in by hand, a few clear coats followed to achieve a nice glossy sheen, prior to masking and spraying the telescopic rams with Alclad II Aluminium lacquer.

Once again, weathering was achieved with a preliminary treatment of Abteilung 502 oils, concentrating the darker staining around the pivot points and recesses to mimic heavy deposits of grease. The crane started to look really impressive as the weathering progressed, and it began to feel as if the project was nearing completion. A KFS susie-cable bracket was enhanced with copper wire cabling, and painted and weathered before it was installed on the crane's base, while a set of susie cables was also created from copper wire coiled around a screwdriver.

The crane kit posed a few challenges, but the extra details and the modified base have added character, and the unit looked instantly at home on the Ford's long chassis

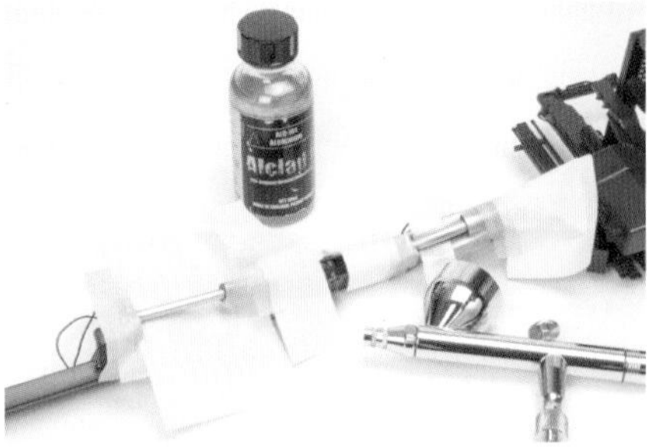

After priming and painting the crane, masking was applied and the bare steel sections of the hydraulic rams sprayed with metallic lacquer.

For consistency, the same blend of Abteilung 502 oils took care of most of the weathering.

Layers of MIG's Oil and Grease Stain Mixture enhanced the pivoting sections, with extra streaks added, in line with gravity, using a fine brush.

The telescopic boom section also gained a layer of dirty grease.

The shiny appearance of the crane was tempered in places with dry pigments, while Lifecolor's Reflecting Agent was also applied in key areas.

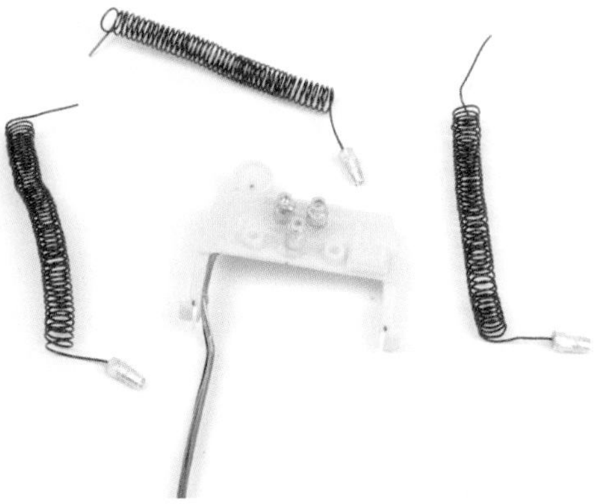

A cast susie-cable bracket and valves, from KFS, was enhanced with wire cables, while a trio of coiled cables was created from copper wire wrapped around a screwdriver shaft. These were then primed and painted.

The susie-cable bracket, with integral spotlight, finishes off the crane's platform nicely.

frames. Another panel of etched tread-plate filled the gap between the crane and fifth wheel, and a foot-step was added on the driver's side to make access easier (it was taken from the unused sleeper-cab components). Chain and a variety of tools were stowed within the crane's platform well, adding even more visual interest.

READY FOR THE ROAD

Aside from the small number of extra detailing parts and a variety of 'stock' materials, it is gratifying to think that the truck and crane were built predominantly from the kit's original parts, many of which have been enhanced considerably. As well as the detailing work, plenty of time was invested in the painting and weathering stages. I haven't attempted to count up the total number of hours spent on this truck, because work was spread over a three-year period, it did feel like a modelling odyssey in some respects. Indeed, of all the projects featured in this book, the Ford LTL9000 trumps them all in terms of time and effort. It was worth it, though, as I consider this 'Louisville Line' truck to be one of my finest models to date.

I always gain great satisfaction from improving a kit's existing components. In this case, only a modest additional outlay was required to replace a small number of parts, with the resin wheels being a vast improvement over the originals. But I'm particularly pleased with how the original exhaust stacks turned out; drilling a few hundred individual holes seemed like madness at the time, but perseverance paid off.

The well of the crane platform provided a good place to store a variety of tools and a length of chain. The KFS susie-cable bracket, plugs and sockets complement the homemade coils nicely.

In tandem with the crane, the replacement fifth wheel and mounting bracket bring plenty of compelling detail to the chassis.

A set of KFS resin spot-lamps was fitted to the rear of the cab to illuminate the crane's operating platform. The lady figures on the rear mud-flaps were from an etched detailing set I commissioned from PH Designs.

The finished Ford LTL9000 is one of my favourite models. It also accounts for the most time I've ever spent on one kit, but I enjoyed it from start to finish.

CHAPTER THIRTEEN

BRINGING UP THE REAR: A DUMPER TRAILER IN 1:24 SCALE

After building a number of tractor units, it seems logical that a trailer or two would also figure in a truck modeller's plans. Italeri and AMT offer a variety of options in 1:24 scale, ranging from reefers to canvas- and curtain-sided boxes, along with timber trailers, ISO container carriers and oil tanks. As well as building these kits straight from the box, there's also plenty of scope for customizing and conversion work, making use of a kit's underframe to create something a little different. Indeed, custom-built flatbed or beavertail trailers, not widely available as plastic kits, would allow for interesting loads to be modelled, such as heavy plant or a collection of vintage tractors.

The possibilities are endless, and I have a long list of trailers that I'd like to assemble in the future. Here, though, I'll describe how I built an Italeri dumper trailer, which is an impressive kit that builds into a very attractive model. The prototype is designed for carrying heavy loads of aggregate or earth and features a hydraulic tipping hoist, powerful brakes and a retractable canvas cover. Until recently, I lived near the limestone quarries of Derbyshire, so similar trailers would be an everyday sight and it was a feeling of homesickness that drew me to this kit. Rather than depict a local haulier's trailer, however, I rendered it in the manufacturer's livery and kept it pristine, in order to complement my showroom-condition Actros MP3, from Chapter 10.

Assembly followed the same principles that we've covered already, with attention paid to getting the chassis components prepared and assembled correctly. With long frames, it's easy to introduce a degree of twist, which will have knock-on effects when installing the bucket and platform, so it's important to get things right first time. Furthermore, the six-wheel arrangement makes it important to get all three axles aligned accurately, so that each tyre sits firmly on the ground.

Because of the open nature of the chassis and the inclusion of reservoir tanks and regulator equipment, it was decided to adorn the framework with an array of hoses and pipework, linking the various components to the brake chambers and drums. Rolls of flexible copper and brass jewellery wire were employed, in varying diameters, with

Italeri offers a great range of 1:24-scale trailers in varying formats, including this attractive aggregate end dumper, complete with hydraulic hoist.

the longer runs along the side frames kept as neat and tidy as possible. Some of this 'plumbing' work was completed before the frames were assembled, to ease access to the axles in particular. Other pipework was added after the chassis had been painted, using Tamiya's detailing cable, providing a nice contrast between the fixed wire runs and the black flexible hoses. Shiny etched cable ties added a finishing touch and confirmed the pristine nature of this trailer.

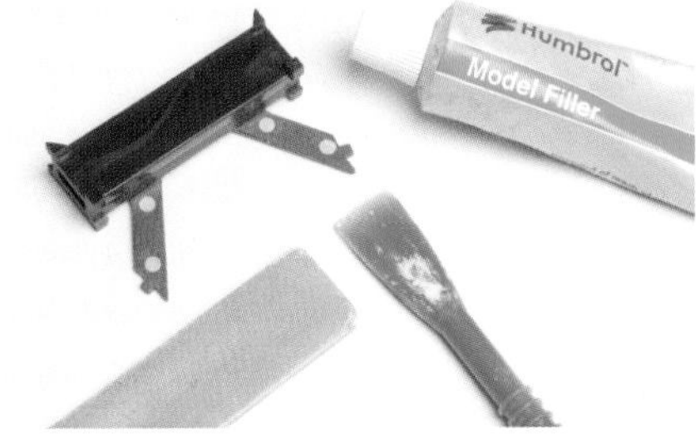

The dumper kit's chassis cross-members required some preparatory work to remove certain imperfections, including unsightly ejector-pin marks.

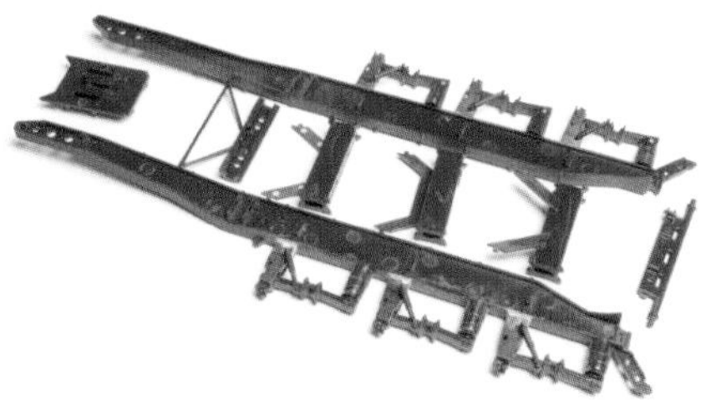

The inside faces of the side frames were also littered with moulding flaws, but these would be less visible. Once all the parts had been tidied up, assembly could commence.

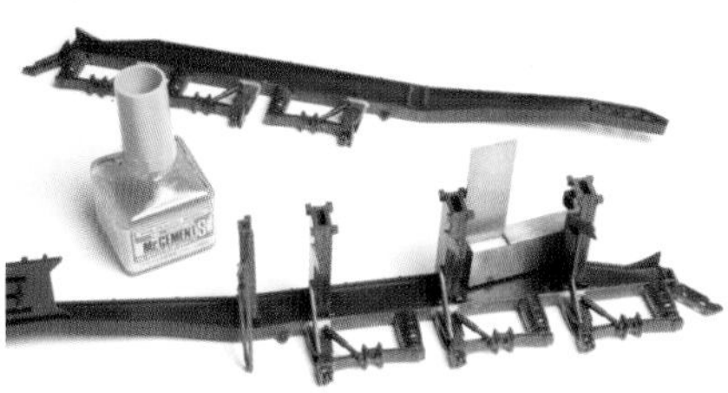

The cross-members were fixed to one side initially, checking the angle of each joint carefully.

Mini sash clamps, under gentle compression, held the other side in position. After more checks with the set-square and a straightedge, the glue bonds were made and the assembly left to cure overnight.

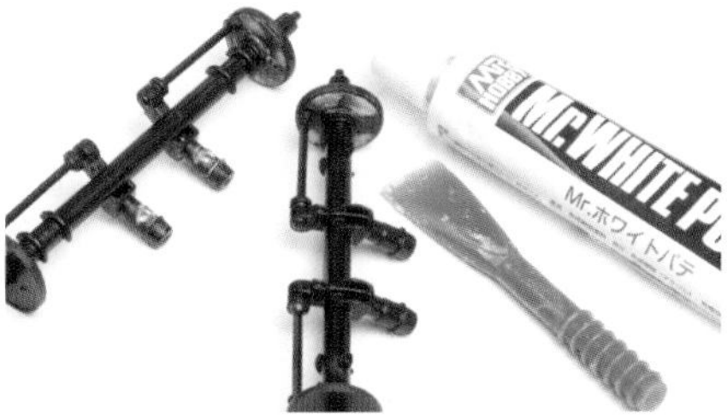

The axle units and brake drums also needed the attentions of filler and abrasives.

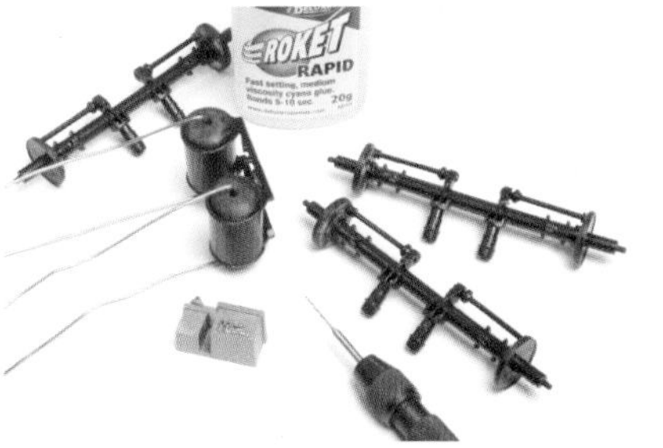

The main reservoir tanks were built up from several components and abraded to remove any visible seams. Once the parts were ready, holes were drilled and pipework installed, using flexible copper and brass jewellery wire.

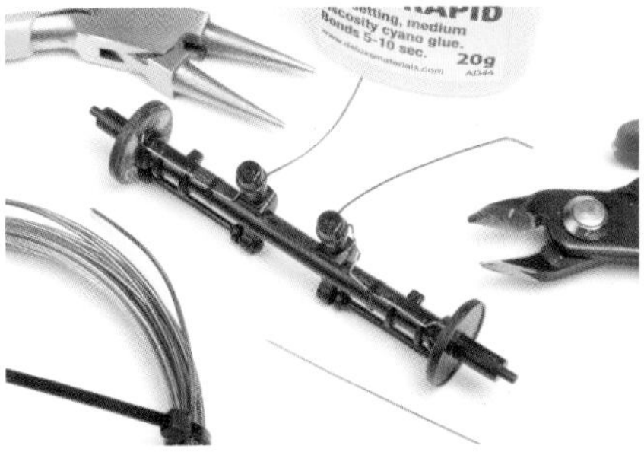

Large-gauge wire formed the main supply pipes, while thinner material was fed to the brake chambers and drums.

Thin strips of electrical insulation tape were cut and wrapped around the axles to retain the wire, aiming for a tidy and consistent appearance to each axle.

The three axles were test-fitted and checked to ensure they were correctly aligned with each other and with the main chassis frames. It may be necessary to add shims from plastic strip if there are any inconsistencies.

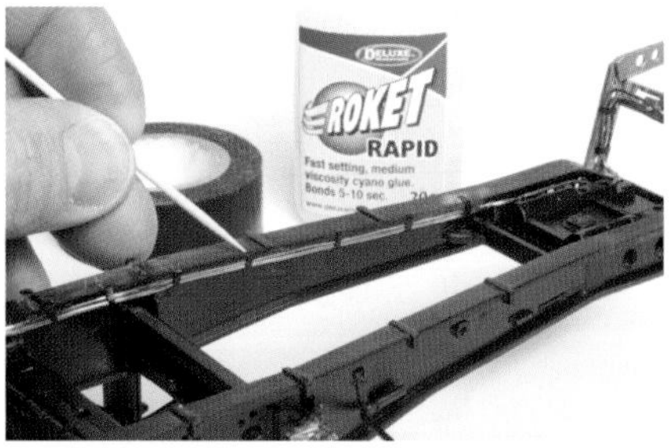

More pipework and cabling was added to the inside of the frames, linking the tanks and equipment amidships with the susie-cable sockets. Again, thin strips of insulation tape acted as retaining straps, secured with cyano glue.

Holes were drilled in line with the cable sockets, and the wire was installed.

When the detailing work was complete, the rest of the chassis components could be installed and the wheels test-fitted.

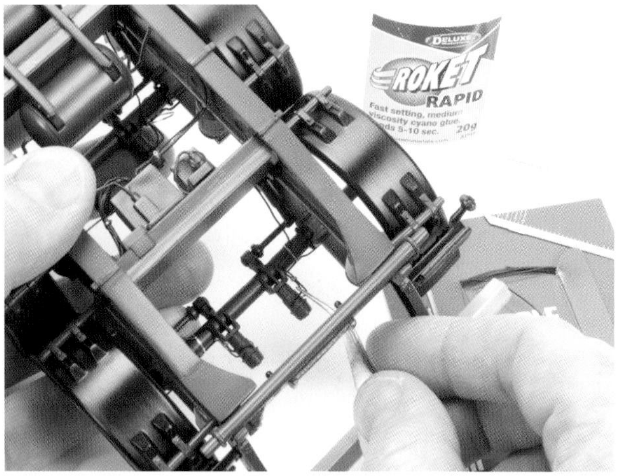

The chassis frames were sprayed with Tamiya XF-63 German Grey, and after hand-painting the wheel arches and other details, the whole assembly was treated to a few coats of clear gloss. The outstanding hoses were then installed, using Tamiya's fine black cable, and retained with CTM's shiny, etched cable ties.

The mix of painted wire pipework and Tamiya flexible hose provided some visual interest to the chassis. I've no idea how accurate this is, prototypically, but only glimpses of this area will be afforded once the body has been installed.

Apart from the need to tidy up various moulding flaws on the frames and cross-members, the chassis didn't really pose any significant problems. The telescopic hoist has to be assembled into a single unit, with each section being held captive by its neighbour. As each element is made up of two halves, much effort was expended in smoothing the glue joints and polishing the plastic to produce flawless surfaces prior to priming and painting with Alclad II metallic lacquer. The paint was applied in light coats, via the airbrush, which improved the prospect of the parts sliding easily within each other, allowing the bucket to be raised or lowered.

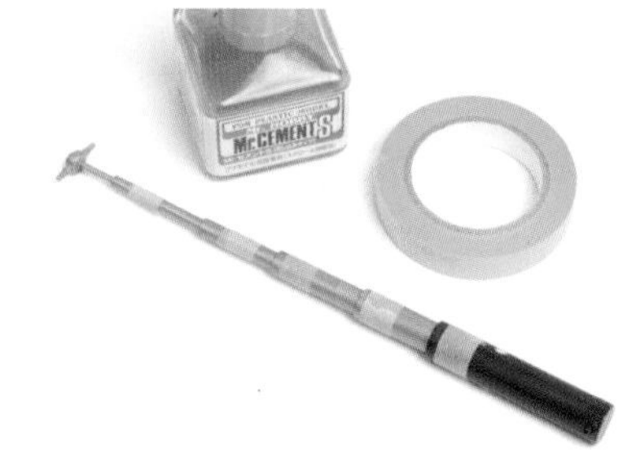

The telescopic hoist consists of several sections, each comprising two halves. The joints need to be flawless, so plenty of time was spent filling and sanding the plastic to get it as smooth as possible.

Alclad II's Aluminium lacquer gave the hoist a believable metallic finish, sealed with several clear gloss coats. Care was taken to ensure that the telescopic parts could still move freely.

With the hoist and front platform in position, the chassis was complete and ready to receive the dumper bucket.

Unexpectedly, the dumper's bucket provided the biggest challenge. My original plan was to model the cover in the open position, allowing the interior to be loaded with stone chippings. However, I soon realized that the large moulded body had become constricted, with the sides bowing inwards by a not insignificant margin. This adversely

Because of the inward bowing of the body's sides, internal braces were cut from rectangular box-section styrene. The braces needed to be a precise length to work effectively, so measurements were taken with digital calipers and the styrene section cut with a razor saw in a mitre box.

The braces were positioned carefully, checking the shape of the outer bodywork before fixing them in place. A thin shim was needed in one area to finally achieve a straight external profile.

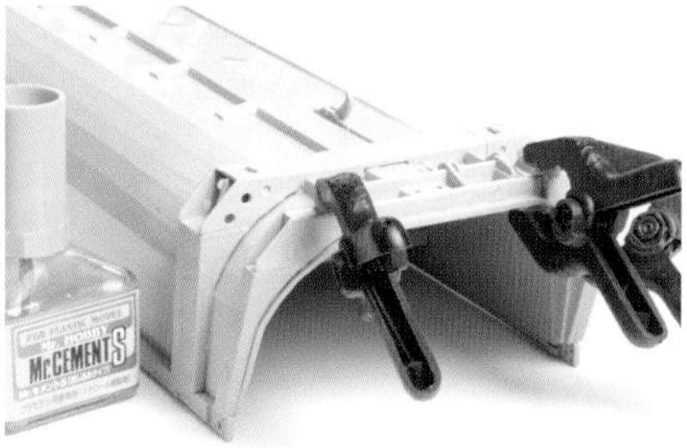

The external ribs also proved a challenge as they didn't conform to the dumper body's profile, and there was a lack of positive locating guides to aid alignment. Spring clamps were essential to affect secure bonds, but there were some large gaps to fill.

Perfect Plastic Putty was pumped into the gaps with a syringe and pinpoint applicator. The putty was applied in several stages, allowing each layer to cure before continuing.

With a damp swab, the putty can be shaped, or the excess cleaned away, before it dries; thus the amount of sanding required later is drastically reduced.

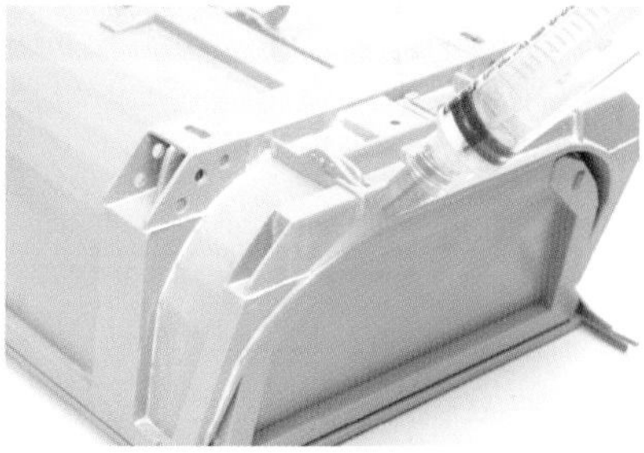

When all the filling and sanding was complete, the body was cleaned thoroughly. More Perfect Plastic Putty was decanted into a syringe, and raised welding seams were piped along the bracket joints.

After a coat of grey primer, the surface was rubbed down again until it was perfectly smooth. Tamiya's TS-44 Blue was applied in a series of individual coats until a consistent finish was achieved.

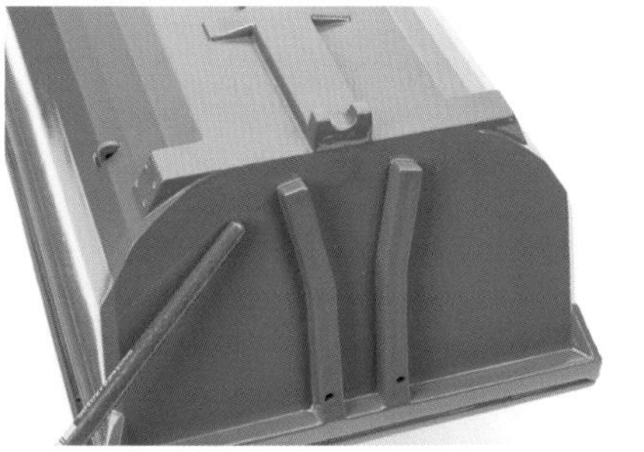

Due to over-eagerness, I managed to create a small amount of puddling at one end. If this happens, there's nothing to do other than allow the model to dry out for a few days.

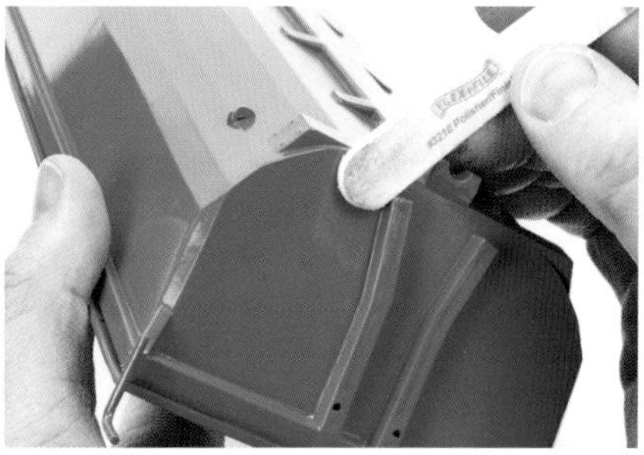

The puddling was levelled with abrasive pads, working through the grades until the surface was flat and smooth. A little soapy water helped to lubricate the abrasives and prevent clogging. Luckily I didn't have to apply more blue paint as the primer didn't show through, so just a clear gloss coat was needed to even out the finish.

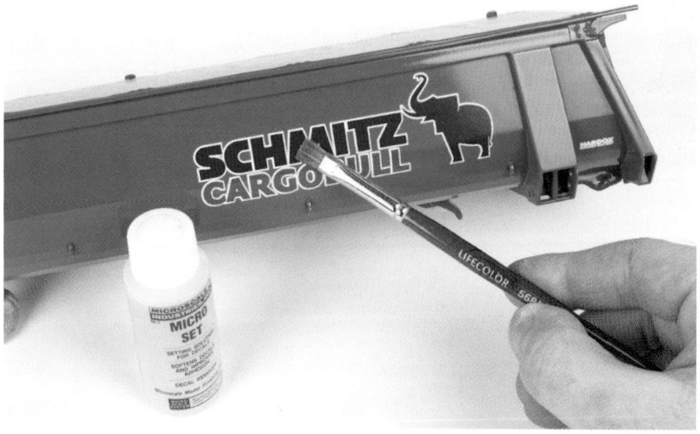

The clear gloss also provided the perfect base for the large waterslide decals. With logos of this size, the surface really does need to be super smooth as any imperfections will be magnified by the carrier film. The decals had a satin sheen, but another subsequent coat of clear gloss not only sealed them in place, but also rendered the carrier film invisible and provided a unifying shine to the bodywork as a whole. Finally, a coat of semi-gloss clear reduced the shine slightly for a more pleasing finish.

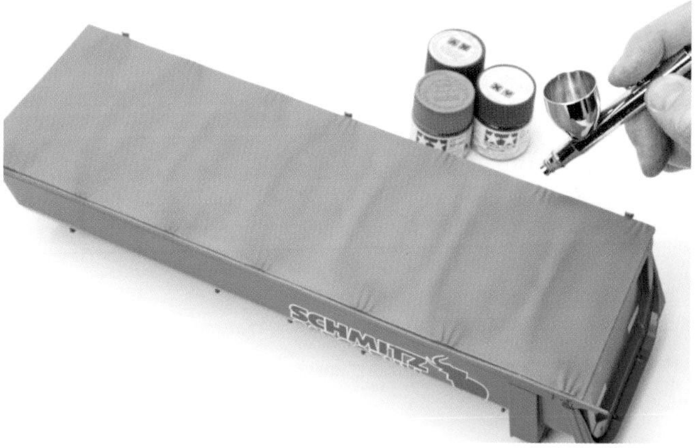

The canvas cover was the last element to be painted, using an airbrush to build up layers of Tamiya paints. A few similar shades were employed, targeting the darker tones into the moulded creases and depressions, while the lighter shades were misted over the peaks. The end results were very convincing. By carefully aiming the airbrush, it wasn't necessary to mask the sides, although this confidence comes from years of practice!

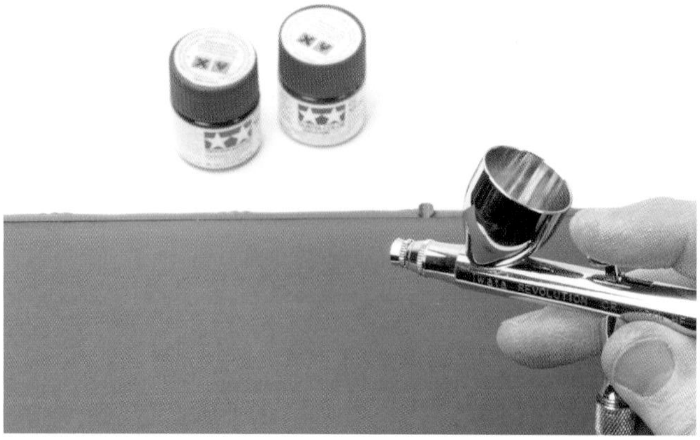

To treat the edges of the cover and the long retracting pole, a scrap of mounting card was used as a mask, held in place with my spare hand. As long as the edge of the card is cut cleanly in a straight line and the airbrush sprays across the joint (rather than being pointed directly at it), the demarcation of the colours will be nice and sharp.

affected the fit of the external ribs/tipping brackets, and the only way I could see to fix it was to fit internal braces. With the worst of the bowing at the upper edges, the braces would be difficult to bury beneath a stone load, so the bucket's cover would have to be installed after all.

My problems didn't end there, alas, as the external ribs still didn't fit very well, resulting in large gaps and a need for plenty of filler. It took a few sessions of filling and abrading until I was happy with the bonds, although the use of Deluxe Materials' Perfect Plastic Putty meant that the filler could be manipulated with water before it dried, thus reducing the amount of sanding involved. Finally, after thoroughly cleaning up the bucket, more Perfect Plastic Putty was piped through a syringe to mimic the distinctive weld seams on the ribs – which did feel like, literally, putting the icing on the cake.

Priming and painting followed, using aerosols. For this a protective mask was worn, even though an extraction booth was in use. Large items inevitably require large amounts of paint, especially when a deep, lustrous finish is planned, so there's bound to be a great deal of overspray and harmful vapours lingering in the air. The Tamiya topcoat

Attaching the tipping bucket to the chassis is simple, with two brackets securing it at the rear pivot point and the hydraulic hoist slotted into place at the front.

paint produced a lovely finish, but a little puddling occurred at the front end, due to an excessive amount of paint being applied. Nothing could be done about it until the paint was fully cured, so it was put aside for forty-eight hours to harden.

Successive grades of abrasive pads rubbed back the puddled paint to a flat, smooth surface, helped with warm soapy water. Luckily I'd already built up a few coats of colour by that point, so there was enough material to withstand the abrading without revealing the grey primer beneath. Once the bucket had been cleaned and dried, the finish was restored with a few coats of clear gloss, and it was soon ready for the decals.

The last job before final assembly was to paint the canvas top. A selection of blue-grey shades was employed, their use tailored in response to the profiles moulded into the plastic covering. It didn't take long to create some lifelike highlights and shading effects, and with careful aiming of the airbrush and a scrap of mounting card as a movable mask, there was no need to use tape to protect the bucket's paintwork.

The finished trailer sits well with the Actros tractor unit, and the combination doesn't take up as much space as I'd initially expected, thanks to the compact nature of the dumper. I've been surprised by my own restraint, as normally I'd be keen to give such a vehicle a dusty, weathered finish. That said, the shiny paintwork adds a touch of class and complements the tractor unit's showroom finish nicely, suggesting that the rig might be heading to a trade exhibition...!

WHAT TO BUILD NEXT?

Showcasing a trailer seems a fitting way to complete this collection of truck modelling projects. I hope that readers have found plenty of inspiration, and have enjoyed the journey as much as I have. Building each of these kits has taught me many valuable lessons in terms of practical techniques and problem solving, as well as a few things about the history of the prototypes themselves. Some kits presented a range of challenges and frustrations, but they all proved to be highly rewarding in the end. With some kits built over months – and even years – patience and perseverance were virtues that I had to work hard to maintain.

Universally, these kits offer fantastic value, and with a seemingly endless supply of trucks across the scales, I don't think I'll ever run out of potential new projects. Indeed, I'm already running out of room to store the ever-growing collection of unbuilt kits that I've been stockpiling for rainy days in the future, but I think I know which trucks I'll build next. There's the Italeri Volvo F16 I mentioned in Chapter 9, but I also want to finish yet another Mercedes-Benz truck: a Revell 1:25-scale 1628 tractor unit that I began converting into a rigid flatbed, as well as a few Soviet-era utility vehicles in 1:35 scale.

In fact, the more I think about it, the more the list grows. Will we ever build all the kits that we long to, in one lifetime? I doubt it, but that's one of the things that makes this such a compelling hobby.

The tipping dumper trailer is a good match for the Mercedes-Benz Actros MP3.

The combination of the vibrant colour scheme, stylish profile and the added interest of the tipping feature, makes for a very attractive trailer.

USEFUL CONTACTS

4D Model Shop Ltd
The Arches
120 Leman Street
London E1 8EU
Tel. 020 7264 1288
www.modelshop.co.uk
Modelling supplies, tools and equipment, including figures and scenic accessories in various scales.

The Airbrush Company
79 Marlborough Road
Lancing Business Park
West Sussex
BN15 8UF
Tel. 01903 767800
www.airbrushes.com
Airbrushes and equipment, modelling tools, paints and pigments (including Alclad II, Lifecolor, Wilder and Darkstar).

Airfix
www.airfix.com
Plastic kit manufacturer.

Albion Alloys/Albion Hobbies
518 Wallisdown Road
Bournemouth
BH11 8PT
Tel. 01202 511232
www.albionalloys.com
Metal and plastic strip, sheet and section, abrasives, paints, adhesives.

Atlantis Models
435 Brook Avenue
Unit 16 Deer Park
NY 11729
USA
www.atlantis-models.com
Plastic kit manufacturer. Range includes a few ex-Revell kits in 1:48 scale.

Automobilia
Unterkrumbach 48
D-91241 Kirchensittenbach
Germany
www.automobilia.de
Etched vehicle detailing parts for 1:87 and 1:43 scales.

Czech Truck Model
Karla Michala 53
156 00 Praha 5
Czech Republic
www.czechtruckmodel.com
Extensive range of 1:24-scale US and European truck detailing and conversion kits.

Deluxe Materials
Unit 13
Cufaude Business Park
Cufaude Lane
Bramley
RG26 5DL
Tel. 01256 883944
www.deluxematerials.co.uk
Modelling adhesives and aids.

Expo Tools
Unit 6
The Salterns
Tenby
SA70 7NJ
Tel. 01834 845150
www.expotools.com
Tools, airbrushes, paints, adhesives and modelling materials.

Fox Transfers
Unit 5
Priory Business Park
Wistow Road
Kibworth
Leicestershire
LE17 4AD
Tel. 0116 319 4950
www.fox-transfers.co.uk
Waterslide decals, paints and finishing materials.

ICM
www.icm.com.ua
Plastic kit manufacturer.

Italeri
www.italeri.com
Plastic kit manufacturer.

Jadar Hobby Shop
www.jadarhobby.pl
Source for kits and detailing parts for 1:35-scale kits.

Kit Form Services
7 Horbling Lane
Stickney
Boston
Lincs
PE22 8DG
Tel. 01205 480766
www.kitformservices.com
Superb range of 1:24-scale truck detailing and conversion kits.

Knightwing International
Malham Works
33 Almondbury Bank
Huddersfield
HD5 8HE
Tel. 01484 537191
www.knightwing.co.uk
Plastic truck kits in 1:76 scale.

Langley Models
166 Three Bridges Road
Crawley
West Sussex
RH10 1LE
www.langleymodels.co.uk
Etched and cast-metal truck kits and detailing parts in 1:76 and 1:43 scale.

PH Designs
www.phd-design-etchings.co.uk
Custom design and etching service.

Revell (USA)
www.revell.com
Revell (Europe)
www.revell.de
Plastic kit manufacturer.

RP Toolz
www.rptoolz.com
Modelling tools, including photo-etch bending tools and punch/die sets.

Scalemates
www.scalemates.com
Useful database of plastic kits and modeller galleries.

Scale Model Shop
Tel. 01422 405040
www.scalemodelshop.co.uk
Modelling tools, paints, glues and a huge range of kits.

The Small Shop
www.thesmallshop.com
Modelling tools.

Tamiya
www.tamiya.com
Plastic kit manufacturer.

Ten Commandments Models
20 Struan Drive
Inverkeithing
Fife
KY11 1AR
Tel. 01383 410032
www.tencommandmentsmodels.co.uk
Truck detailing packs and loads for 1:76 scale.

Wonderland Models
97, 101 & 103 Lothian Road
Edinburgh
Scotland
EH3 9AN
Tel. 0131 229 6428
www.wonderlandmodels.com
Model kits, paints, adhesives, tools and accessories.

York Modelmaking
Unit 13
The Bull Centre
Stockton-on-the-Forest
York
YO32 9LE
Tel. 01904 400358
Custom design and laser-cutting service, modelling aids.

GEORGE DENT ONLINE
www.georgedentmodelmaker.blogspot.com
www.instagram.com/dentmodelmaker

INDEX